Nine Ms and a Mother Like No Other

iUniverse, Inc.
New York Bloomington

Nine Ms and a Mother Like No Other

Our Journey from Messed to Blessed

iUniverse books may be ordered through booksellers or by contacting:

iUniverse
1663 Liberty Drive
Bloomington, IN 47403
www.iuniverse.com
1-800-Authors (1-800-288-4677)

ISBN: 978-1-4401-5508-6 (pbk)
ISBN: 978-1-4401-5510-9 (cloth)
ISBN: 978-1-4401-5509-3 (ebk)

Printed in the United States of America

iUniverse rev. date: 7/10/2009

Nine Ms and a Mother Like No Other

Our Journey from Messed to Blessed

A memoir by

MARTIAL BEDNAR

Author's note: This is a true story. Details are factual and accurate to the very best of my research and/or recollection. Please note that the names of most non-family members mentioned in this story have been changed out of respect for their privacy, or permission has been granted for their use.

Dedicated with love to all the Ms,
my mother like no other,
and all who have blessed my life so abundantly—
especially Barb and Alex.

Preface

Every family has a story to tell, and mine is no exception. No, we Bednars aren't Kennedy famous, and we're certainly not Rockefeller rich. We don't sing like the Osmonds, dance like the Jacksons, or even star in our own reality TV show like the Osbournes once did. In fact, our talents have never won any of us an Oscar, a Pulitzer, a Nobel Peace Prize, or, heck, even a Rotary Club award, and our scandals—thank God—have never caused the paparazzi to hide in the bushes and pounce as soon as we step out the front door.

Look closely at my family today and you'd be hard pressed to believe for a New York minute that behind our starched collars, shiny Nissans, and manicured lawns we could have any story worth telling at all. That's why most people will find it hard to believe that the story they're about to read could possibly be true—especially if they've come to know me or anyone in my family in more recent (what I'll call the more "normal") years. But truth, they say, is stranger than fiction, and the journey you're about to embark on down Bednar Boulevard is proof of that.

So what *is* so noteworthy about this family of mine? I assure you, it's not just the novelty that we could literally be our own baseball team—yes, there are nine of us kids—or that our names all begin with the letter "M." But that adds a nice layer of icing to the cake, I must say. Can there really be smoldering secrets, over-the-top escapades, or salacious storylines about the path to adulthood that molded common, everyday people: school teachers, business folk, a PR guy, and, heck, even a priest? (Surely, not enough to possibly warrant writing a whole book, right?) Can a buttoned-down family as seemingly all-American as the Cleavers or the Brady's—a close-knit clan who, as adults, actually look forward to family get-togethers, frequently call each other just to say hi, and even attend weekly Mass by their own choosing (well, most of the time)—have anything other than a bunch of warm fuzzies to share?

Ironically, it's precisely because we now do share "warm fuzzies" with each other, and the fact that we are a "normal"—as normal as any person or family can be, I guess—well-adjusted, self-assured, pretty likeable, relatively successful, and fairly sane bunch of siblings that the Bednar story is one well worth telling. Indeed, our chirpy little attitudes, successes, and lives (as traditional, suburban, and mundane as they now appear on the outside), were molded out of an absurd assortment of bizarre, against-the-odds, and downright unbelievable circumstances that few individuals or families could—or do—survive.

Yet miraculously, the Bednars not only survived.

We thrived.

PART I

Mom • Marriage • Mayhem

Chapter 1

It took guts to do what she did—and if nothing else, Aunt Sade had plenty of guts.

Although her cheating husband and most of her conniving siblings had robbed her of her happiness, her self respect, and her peace of mind, they could not strip away the gutsiness that she displayed so tragically at 9:48 a.m. on Thursday morning, July 18, 1946—just two days after her sixty-second birthday.

She appeared out of nowhere and stood between the tracks at the South Washington Street crossing. A deeply religious woman, she bowed her head as if praying.

Moments later—which to her may have felt like an eternity— the powerful eastbound passenger train collided with the frail, desperate woman who stood calmly in its path. The one hundred-ton killer catapulted her fragile, ninety-pound frame from the crossing and slammed it against a mail pouch standard some hundred and ten feet away. The locomotive simply roared on; its engineer, whose window faced away from the tragedy, knew nothing of the incident until he arrived at his next stop some fifteen miles away.

The people of the tiny western New York town of Randolph, busy with their days' errands and enjoying a sunny morning in their typically serene village, were horrified by what they had just witnessed. The unusual and disheveled woman from "the home," once again dressed in black from head to toe despite the hot July sun, had walked to the post office that day, like she had done so many times before, to drop yet another letter in the mailbox. She attracted no more attention or pity than usual, I imagine, as she made her way out of the building, walked just a few blocks, passed the local Catholic church—where it would not be uncommon for her to pay a visit— and ultimately made her way alongside the tracks.

As the swift-moving train made its way through the town, she knew the time had arrived. With the roar of the engine growing

1

louder and closer, she ignored the shouts of a handful of petrified spectators. Her heart must have been racing and her body drenched in sweat. Yet she stood firm and did not waver.

Did she, for one fleeting moment, I wonder, regret her decision?

Death, of course, was instant. But the impact of that horrifying day would live on for many years to come.

Just, I am sure, as Aunt Sade had planned.

* * *

Chapter 2

It all began under a tree—her life, that is.

That's right, my mom entered this world under a towering maple tree on South 13th Street in the "nice-to-grow-up-in" community of Olean, New York—an obscure but intriguing little community nestled among the enchanted hills of the southwestern corner of the Empire State. (My mom would kill me if I told you the year, but it's interesting to note that the Great Crash of '29 occurred just a couple months after she was born.) The tree, which was just minding its own business that first hot August day, was situated perfectly between the cracked sidewalk just a few feet in front of the simple white house that my mom's parents rented and the curb of that now historic (in my family's history, anyway) street. I'm not superstitious, but there is something rather peculiar about the fact that if this one-of-a-kind wonder had to be born on a street—instead of in a hospital, like most of us—it, of course, had to be 13th Street. Anyway, that bizarre and zany entrance into this great world of ours surely was an indication of things to come.

I guess that means that with my mom's life, my family's life—our life story—had its humble beginnings under that tree all those years ago. And as you'll come to learn, both her life and our story have been far sudsier than any episode of *The Young and the Restless*—my Gramma's favorite soap (and, if the truth be known, the rest of the family's as well). In all honesty, my mom—or Peg, as most who know her either lovingly or irreverently refer to her—has loved harder, laughed louder, shed more tears, received more glory, and climbed more mountains than Nikki Newman, Katherine Chancellor, or, heck, even Erika Kane could ever dream. She's the epitome of life at its very best and its very worst, all rolled into one lively package. Her tenacious spirit is often an inspiration, and at times a frustration. After meeting her for the first time—at a party, which she's usually the life of—a friend of mine summed it up in a nutshell: "Man. Your mom is a trip!"

Oh, yes ... a trip indeed.

But no matter how you slice it, this remarkable woman—who, yes, usually votes for herself for president of the United States of America—is the heart of my family's soul, and the glue that held us together in the worst of times.

As far as I know, no one actually planned for Peg to be born under that lucky tree on 13th Street. But I'm told that her mother, one very pregnant Josephine Richardson—an equally spunky, delightful character in and of herself—was painfully awaiting a ride from her doctor's office to the Olean General Hospital, some two miles away, as her water broke. But nature had no intention of waiting for a ride that August first, and thus created this most unique "grand entrance" into this world for this most unique "grande dame." This true episode is proof beyond a doubt that what goes around truly comes around, since today this lady I proudly call Mom has spent a good portion of her life bumming rides and being late! When Josephine did get to the hospital shortly after the harrowing episode, she somehow managed to present her newborn proudly at the desk before both were whisked away to be examined by the medical staff.

Amazingly, both mother and child survived the bizarre episode without too much wear and tear. As a matter of fact, the trauma of giving birth to her second child and first-born daughter, Margaret Anna Richardson, didn't faze Josephine a bit. She just kept on having more kids. Five more, in fact.

Which just goes to show that you really do have to be a little nuts to be a mother.

Chapter 3

My mom and dad were two people who never should have been married, but fate got in the way.

She was the spoiled princess who believed that life should be one big fairy tale, and he had all the makings of a dashing prince—or so she thought. When they met, she was in many ways Olean's version of a movie star: a wealthy glamour gal who turned heads with her stunning looks, vivacious personality, fun-loving ways, and black Pontiac convertible. As runner-up for "Ms. Bonaventure" at her collegiate alma mater (the actual title went in jest to a returning adult student), she was definitely the catch on the newly coed campus. Enter my dad: a tall, dark, and handsome basketball player who clearly knew all the moves, both on the court and off.

I'm sure they made a stunning couple.

Their courtship, from what Mom tells me, was short but intense. She was still on the rebound from a difficult break-up with the love of her life, and my dad—in basketball and in life—apparently knew how to rip a great rebound and slam dunk the game-winning score. They were definitely part of the "in" crowd, and apparently met at a party following one of his big games. They shared many of the same friends, and in less than a year from their first date in September of 1951, he proposed to her as they sat in her black Pontiac convertible parked on campus—near the statue of the Blessed Mother, of all things—just around Valentine's Day, 1952.

"I can't live without you," she says he told her, promising a life of happily-ever-afters.

And like any twenty-two-year-old girl who spends years dreaming of that magical moment, she believed him.

So after a whirlwind engagement lasting only four months, and just days after becoming a college grad, my mom became a gorgeous June bride in a lovely ceremony at the "Cathedral of the Southern Tier"—St. Mary's Roman Catholic Church in Olean. Everything about the ceremony apparently was as beautiful as the blushing bride, and it appeared as if the young lovers were on their way to their storybook life together. The wedding was followed by an elegant and festive reception with all the trimmings at the Castle, Olean's finest restaurant of the day. The fairy-tale celebration—complete with the custom bridal gown from Morrie Hämburger in New York and the champagne-flowing reception—was made possible for the most part by Peggy's over-flowing bank account. (More on that to come.) Mom's money also funded the romantic honeymoon in Niagara Falls, during which she claims she spent most of her time crying. (Yeah, right, like I believe that!)

At the time of my parents' marriage, my dad still had another year of college to complete, but that didn't seem to matter to the young lovers. They moved into their first home, a small and simple upstairs apartment on Virginia Street in Olean with high hopes and big dreams, with the rent, of course, paid by my mother's seemingly bottomless bank account. By the time my dad began his senior year, his bride was already expecting their first child. And just days after my dad became a college grad the following May, his wife gave birth (not on a street curb, thank heavens!) to a beautiful baby girl. And thus began my parents' seemingly non-stop seventeen-year span of pregnancies, kids, and more kids, resulting in nine little Bednars—and a whole lot more than either of them could have ever envisioned at that time.

Heaven only knows why, when naming their kids, they got so carried away with the whole "M thing". It started innocently enough, I suppose, with the pretty name Michele for their delicate firstborn, followed by their first son Michael (born just fifteen months after Michele). Then along came Mark, and I imagine this is where the "M thing" really started to catch on. By the time their next child came along in 1958, Mitchell seemed just right.

They should have stopped there—with the Ms and the kids—but they didn't. So along came Margaret (later to become the one and only Maggie), named after and born on the birthday of my Great Gramma Parmeter. When child number six, another son, arrived in July 1963, my mom's sister had recently named her newborn Matthew, so they considered the name Malacai (quite biblical, huh?). Thank God for his sake that the nurse who had by then helped deliver several Bednar kids (I'm sure she felt like part of the family by this point!) protested and suggested something equally unusual but definitely more charismatic: Merrick. So Merrick it was. The "M"-athon continued when baby number seven appeared less than two years after Merrick. The name Mollie seemed perfect for the petite and adorable little dolly.

After seven kids, most sane people would seriously question my parents' mental state (and seriously wonder how they ever found time to have sex!) because just one year and five days after Mollie's birth, child number eight—that would be me—entered the clan. Eight was enough long before the '70s TV show! Of course, I win the prize for the most bizarre "M" name, and to this day I'm still not sure how I ended up with Martial—unusual spelling and all—although my Mom told me she found it somewhere in a book of saints. I'm the least militant person you could ever meet, but I have to admit the name beats Mortimer or Malchezadek, about the only remaining unused male "M" names by the time I showed up. Oh, well, I've told myself that if I ever make in Hollywood, I'll never have to use a stage name.

Speaking of Hollywood, my desire to have my name in lights must have been nurtured at birth; after all, I was the fifteen thousandth baby to be born in Olean's St. Francis Hospital. Although unnamed when the *Times Herald* photographer came to take my picture with mother, father, and some hospital nun named Sr. Therese, I figure I used a good ten of my fifteen minutes of fame right then and there through the picture that promoted my "celebrity" birth throughout my hometown. Truth be known, I actually may have been the fifteen thousand and first baby born at the hospital. My mother thinks there was an unwed mother who was in labor at the same time and delivered before her. But in 1966, a Catholic hospital certainly didn't promote that!

After reading about the big event in the paper, one of my mother's bridge club partners summed up my birth the best, I think.

"I see the Bednars just had their fifteen thousandth baby," she announced sarcastically.

As a result of my famed entry into the world, my parents received lots of free diapers, clothes, and toys from several Olean merchants. Ahh ... the sweet rewards of fame.

Just when it looked like the Bednar baby boom was finally over, along came baby number nine, Maura, four years my junior. Although my mother, now forty years old, was thrilled about her newest bundle of joy, born the ninth day of 1970, the older kids were less than enthusiastic at the time.

"I'd rather have a dog than another baby!" moaned the seventeen-year-old Michele, who had had more than her share of babysitting and diaper-changing in her short life (and who secretly and desperately yearned for a collie named, of all things, Lassie).

"Are we going to keep this baby ... forever?!" I, the till-then baby of the family, reportedly asked when the adorable baby made her first appearance at home. The answer, incidentally, was yes. And for so many reasons, we're all grateful for that.

Fortunately, all of us Bednar babies were born healthy and strong, despite the fact that my mother smoked her filtered Kools and downed her share of extra dry Manhattans at her bridge club get-togethers during her pregnancies. From Mark on, however, we all did require blood exchanges at birth due to my mother's Rh factor, which, I understand, was considered pretty serious at that time.

Anyway, you'd think that a couple with enough chemistry

between them to create nine kids would have a picture-perfect marriage reserved solely for Disney ads. Not so in my parents case. In fact, you could argue that the only good that came from their twenty-some years of marriage were all the M and Ms they produced.

Even their early years of marriage, I'm told, were far from perfect. Of course, I wasn't there to observe those years, so all I know is what I've been told and what I've pieced together in some forty years of life. My parents opted to stay in Olean after my dad graduated from college. "There's never going to be a shortage of kids," the born salesman convinced my eager-to-please mother, who herself was well on her way to a baby boom of her own. So with his new bachelor's degree, and with aid from my mom's checkbook, my entrepreneurial father dove head-first into opening a children's store in uptown Olean. Not long into it, it went bust. I'm not sure if it was from lack of customers, or from lack of commitment on my dad's part. He apparently had a knack for that … and not just in his business dealings.

To tell you the truth, I'm not exactly sure when my dad started cheating on my mom (and I'm not sure I really want to know). But long before I arrived on the scene, my mother knew he was seeing other women. It seems so bizarre to me in this day and age that she didn't just cut her losses and leave him when she first found out, but life was obviously very different then. She'd confront him, they'd fight and argue, but ultimately kiss, make up—and end up pregnant again. Sadly, it was a vicious circle that neither of them seemed to have the guts to break, so along came more kids, a good dozen more years of that routine, and God (and my dad) only knows how many women. As the years went by, my parents played the game of the happy family for a while, complete with social outings, bridge clubs, weekly Mass, and Sunday evening trips to the Tastee Freeze. But eventually the money became scarcer, the fights became fiercer, the affairs became more obvious, my mother became more afraid to let go, and my dad became more cold-hearted toward her.

Of course, I'm positive that my mother didn't always make life easy for my dad; even she'd have to admit that she can be demanding, opinionated, stubborn, and self-centered. Of course, she can also be charming, funny, and loving. But I am certain that she was faithful to her marriage, and I know for a fact that she put her children's needs and wants above her own.

My older brothers and sisters, I'm sure, have a much clearer picture of what life was really like when both my parents were around. My dad was obviously much more actively involved in their lives than he was in us younger kids'. A natural athlete, he taught Mike, Mark, and Mitch how to shoot hoops, play golf, and, for all I know, drive. My mom, who ran a very tight ship, taught everyone how to pick up after themselves. From an early age, in fact, everyone had household duties, chores, and responsibilities—from folding the mountains of laundry to sweeping the kitchen floor every night after dinner. In many ways, it was like being in boot camp with Mom as the general, but with a small army of kids trashing the house everyday, I don't know how else anyone could maintain any order. Of course, in those early years, it was the mild-mannered and demure Michele who really paid the price—especially with three wild and rowdy brothers. As a teenager, she even went through the kitchen wall while trying to referee a brawl between her brothers Mike and Mark!

By the time I was old enough to notice, my dad was hardly ever around—away on another "business trip, " I guess. So my memories of him and his involvement in my early years of life are virtually non-existent. I do remember him doling out my dollar allowance every Sunday for a while when I was around five or six (which I would immediately spend on candy at Leo's Grocery Store), and him picking me up after my last day of kindergarten and buying me a bag of suckers. Sadly, that about sums up the extent of our father-son relationship.

Nonetheless, as a little kid, my early childhood seemed, to me at least, perfectly normal: I remember doing normal things like playing with my brothers and sisters and going grocery shopping with my sister Michele, who got stuck with the enormous task of shopping for the entire family, but who always had a soft spot for me and treated me to a yellow smiley-faced cookie from Leo's. Shortly after Maura was born, we moved from Gramma Jo's house on Henley Street in Olean into a big, newly built raised ranch with stately pillars on Upland Terrace in the ritzy section of nearby Allegany. In fact, Merrick and I thought we were the luckiest kids in the world when we moved into that house because we got bunk beds, complete with Charlie Brown sheets, for the room that we shared. Of course, being the younger brother, I always got stuck with the bottom bunk. That house, I'm sure, holds far worse memories for my parents and older siblings who witnessed the horror of a marriage blowing up like a bomb.

In fact, by the time the Carpenters ruled the airwaves by proclaiming "We've Only Just Begun," it definitely was all but over for my parents—and for any sense of normalcy for my family. My dad's hurtful remarks, his frequent "business trips," his shunning of responsibilities as a father, and his lipstick-stained collars that spurred loud, awful midnight fights that scared us kids trying to sleep away the fright, were too much. All that—coupled with the stress of raising nine kids all under the age of twenty, a hefty mortgage payment in a new house, and a recent miscarriage—put my forty-two-year-old mother—who once believed she had it all—over the edge.

Not unlike her dear Aunt Sade a quarter-century before, Peg literally fell apart: physically, mentally, and emotionally.

Chapter 4

Of all the colorful characters in my family's history (and trust me, there are many!), Aunt Sade would definitely win the prize as the most *colorful. Although I never even knew her, she had more hues than a Jamaican sunset, and her shadings were matched equally by her complexity. A worldly but eccentric woman, she lived life intensely, passionately, and nervously. In many ways, this fascinating lady molded and shaped my mother's life—and consequently, my family's history—like an artist molds clay. That's why the more I learn of this intriguing character, the more I wish I could have known the real thing.*

If you trace the lineage of my family and want to get technical about it, Aunt Sade is really my great-great aunt. She was my grandmother's mother's sister (if you follow that) or to put it more simply, my mom's great aunt. Who cares, you ask? Well, while most people really could care less about who their great-great aunts were (much less write about them), you can't fully appreciate the Bednar story without appreciating and learning a bit about Aunt Sade. She is a legend of sorts in my family.

Sarah McDivitt Messer—Sade for short—was a fascinating woman with a flair for the dramatic: part Bette Davis, part Joan Crawford, you might say. The product of a large family herself (she was one of twelve siblings, I believe), Aunt Sade was tall and slender with peppered hair that she wore pulled back tightly from her face. She dressed mysteriously (almost always in black), smoked nervously, and always wore a fancy corset. A resident of Bolivar, New York, "the land of deer and derrick," she and her husband, John Messer, were the well-to-do "first couple" of Olean's prosperous Messer Oil. They lived quite regally, relatively speaking, in the heydays of the Roaring Twenties, and enjoyed many luxuries of life thanks to the oil boom in the early part of the century. From the outside, they seemed to have it all: wealth, success, social standing, a good marriage; indeed, they were the envy of many. But one thing they did not have—and I'm not exactly sure why—was a child, a special little one to care for, dote on, and love to death. So they took an unusually strong liking to her niece Josephine's first-born daughter, Peggy.

My mom.

From the time Peggy was just a toddler, Uncle John and Aunt Sade treated the little girl as if she were their own. With the blessing of her mother (my Gramma Jo, to whom Sade was close)—and for some mysterious reason that to this day no one can fully explain— they took her in under their roof, became her legal guardians, treated her to a well-to-do upbringing that her siblings certainly never shared, and spoiled her with lavish gifts that few children in the years of the Great Depression enjoyed. She became their little Shirley Temple—quite literally, in fact. They even bought her an authentic Shirley Temple doll (which would be worth a fortune today) and a classic Shirley Temple polka-dotted, ruffled dress. On occasion, Uncle John would show Peggy off to his business associates and have her sing "The Good Ship Lollipop" for entertainment. And there was more. For Peggy's seventh birthday, Uncle John dedicated his large and fancy cabin, high atop the green hills of rustic Bolivar (thus the name "Hilltop") to his little cherub in what would be any little girl's fantasy birthday party, complete with a live band and servants in tuxedos. They even bought her a pony, Tony, which she never really liked or learned to ride. Day in and day out, however, Peggy lived a privileged childhood that only a few lucky kids ever know. Certainly her siblings didn't know it.

When it came time for school, the public school, naturally, was not good enough for the prized and precocious Peggy. So Aunt Sade enrolled her in St. Elizabeth's, a private boarding school for well-to-do girls, from kindergarten through eighth grade. The nuns ruled St. Elizabeth's with an iron fist, which probably explains my mother's hatred of strict policies and tough discipline.

As a school girl, Peggy was a cute, bubbly, effervescent little thing with a zest for life, a flair for the dramatics, and a yearning to be loved. Her outgoing nature and love of fun won her many friends, but could also get her into trouble. She never cared much for her studies—which didn't sit well with the nuns of St. Elizabeth's—but she had a big heart and even bigger dreams. Still, Peggy's wide-eyed and gregarious exterior concealed a lonely interior full of insecurity and self-doubt.

With each passing year, Peggy grew to loathe St. Elizabeth's more and more. Aside from her weekly piano lessons, which she eventually grew to like, the only other thing she anxiously awaited during her years there were her weekly visits from Aunt Sade.

Dear Aunt Sade would swoop up in her gray Packard and take her little princess shopping, out to lunch, to the movies at the Haven Theater, or on some wonderful adventure that made going back to that dreary convent even more miserable. "Please take me home," Peggy always pleaded, but Aunt Sade assured her it was for the best.

"It's important for you to get a good education, dear."

As the years went by and Peggy neared the end of her tenure at St. Elizabeth's, she was blossoming into an attractive and intelligent young lady who took notice that her dear Aunt Sade was not the same woman she once was.

And clearly, she wasn't.

But there was good reason: John, her beloved husband of many years—the one true love of her life—was cheating on her. And like every wife always does, Aunt Sade finally figured it out. To add insult to injury, the handsome, charming, and wealthy Uncle John was snaking around with a woman Aunt Sade knew and had even entertained in her own home on several occasions.

So when push came to shove, Uncle John decided that he had had more than enough of good old Aunt Sade, and like she was a used Packard, decided it was time to trade her in for a newer, younger, and sexier model. It was that simple, at least for him. Oh, feigning that he wanted to make it easier for her (which, of course, would make it easier for him and his lover), he assured Aunt Sade that despite a divorce, she would be well cared for. She would want for nothing.

How altruistic.

I can only begin to imagine the hurt and humiliation, the anguish and despair any woman feels when she's being dumped forever by the one she loves. But the pain of being dumped in 1941—by the person who literally was your life—had to be even more excruciating than when it happens today.

It could easily push someone over the edge.

Chapter 5

All hell officially broke loose when I was in second grade. Walking home from Little Bona's, the Catholic elementary school we attended in the early years, one sunny fall day with Merrick, Mollie, and our childhood best friend and neighbor, Mike Marra, we were alarmed and frightened, when, from a distance, we saw an ambulance parked in our driveway with its lights flashing. We raced as fast as we could to the house, only to discover the EMTs whisking our mother away on a stretcher while the neighbors gawked at all the commotion.

Thankfully, as a second grader, I was far too young to understand all that was unfolding in front of my eyes. My mother, we were told, had been vomiting blood, and needed to go to the hospital. I believe it was my Gramma Jo and her sister, Aunt Faye, who had come to visit and check in on my mother, only to find her passed out on the floor of the den where she would sit in the dark for days on end wadded up on the corner of the couch. Indeed she had been vomiting blood—apparently the result of the numerous sleeping pills she had swallowed earlier that day.

Sadly, my devastated and desperate mother had slowly but surely been suffering a complete breakdown … and either intentionally or unintentionally nearly took her own life that sunny fall day.

Thank God someone got to her in time and, in a panic, placed the call to 911.

To tell you the truth, I really don't know how it all unfolded from there, but with a mother who was hospitalized for severe depression, a dad who was rarely around, and only one responsible young adult—my sister Michele—in the house trying to supervise a small army of kids (including a couple wild high school brothers who liked to party, play sports, and whale on each other), someone in the neighborhood wisely contacted the authorities. And that's when the fun really began.

At first, we younger kids—Merrick, Mollie, Maura, and I—went to Gramma Jo, who kept a strict eye on us until Mom was discharged from the hospital and joined us there. Margaret, who was in sixth or seventh grade, ended up temporarily at her best friend's house (whose mom was a dear friend of my mom's). Mitch, Mark, and Mike stayed at Upland Terrace a bit longer—until the neighbors or their teachers or someone who gave a damn got so fed up with their wild antics that they finally contacted child protective services. They ultimately ended up going to live with a family who had cared for other needy kids in Olean.

At age twenty or so, oldest child Michele, the lone "adult" of the bunch—who was in the midst of pursuing her bachelor's degree in education at Bona's—was left to deal with this horrific mess. Alone—but blessed with good judgment, an undying sense of loyalty, a strong faith, and a kind heart—Michele found good friends whom she had met while working diligently in the bakery at Leo's Grocery Store. They became her primary source of sanity, strength, and shelter as she literally witnessed her family fall apart at the seams.

No wonder she ended up with an ulcer in her early twenties.

No wonder she never married and had kids.

No wonder that, to this day, we call her a saint.

Chapter 6

After escaping (I mean graduating) from St. Elizabeth's with the eighth grade "General Excellence" medal—and after learning of the demise of Aunt Sade and Uncle John's marriage from some acquaintance at a Christmas party—a saddened Peggy moved back in with her own mother and, by now, six siblings in a crowded and run-down rented house in Cuba, a sleepy little town not far from Olean. At times, I imagine she felt like an outsider in her own family, having spent eight years in boarding school and being raised in a totally different, more refined, and more disciplined world than her siblings. As a young girl, however, Peggy chummed around from time to time with her older brother, Jack, a good-natured jokester who was just two years her senior. The two of them shared good friends, old movies, and great times as kids—many of them courtesy of Aunt Sade and Uncle John. Peg's five other siblings were all younger, and as kids, she wasn't particularly close to any of them other than her sister Patricia (Pat), two years her junior. Then came Paula, Carlton (who earned the lifelong nickname "Jeep" as a young boy), Robert Ashley (who, God bless him, was given the nickname "Moe,"—which sadly stayed with him throughout his life), and finally, Mary Frances (who eventually became "Mimi" and "Mame.")

The Richardsons of Setchel Hill in Cuba were a far cry from a Norman Rockwell painting. In fact, several years ago, my little niece Tricia, all of six or seven at the time, saw an old black-and-white picture of the family standing on their porch in Cuba and matter-of-factly asked my mom—for real—"Is that the Addams Family?!" Amazingly, her observation was not far off the mark! Their mother, Josephine, was a loving, dedicated, and anything-but-stereotypical mother—a working mother to boot, which was highly unusual back then. She definitely drank, smoked, and swore more than most mothers. But despite being a bit rough around the edges, she had a heart of gold and labored hard both as a licensed nurse and as a parent to raise a decent family despite a part-time husband and father who provided little assistance or support.

I never even knew their dad, my grandfather, Robert Lyle Richardson—R.L.—so I hate to say anything bad about the guy. I'll begin, then, by telling you all the good things I've ever heard about him:

He was a talented musician.

That's it.

That's about the only good thing I've ever heard of Grandpa R.L.—although in all seriousness, I'm sure people who knew him personally were aware of many more qualities and talents. But whether or not R.L. could give Nat King Cole a run for his money, this was one music man who apparently hit more than a few sour notes in his role as husband and father.

R.L. was a handsome man who enjoyed his whiskey and women. His work for the telephone company in the 1930s and forties took him to faraway places like Saudi Arabia, where it's likely that he spent an inebriated Arabian night or two doing things a married man with seven children back home should never do. Oh, he would return from time to time. And when he did, he was usually drunk—and frighteningly violent. He often threatened that he was going to throw that "damn piano" that my mother played out the window. Then one horrible night in a drunken rage, he screamed, "I'm gonna kill you!" to a teen-aged Peggy, who had witnessed him throw her tiny mother down a flight of stairs. Petrified and in tears, Peggy fled their humble house and raced down Setchel Hill in her bare feet—running for her life in the freezing cold wearing nothing but a nightgown. After seeking help for her battered mother and terrified younger siblings at a neighbor's house, Peggy sought help for her aching and bleeding feet, embedded with tiny pieces of broken glass she picked up along the way.

When the sheriff arrived, my mom literally had her dad arrested and thrown in jail. Of course, he wasn't there for long. But when he

*got out, R.L. left Cuba for good ... and his wife and kids never heard
from him again.*

*Not long before that, near the start of the Great War, Aunt
Sade—who was enduring a painful war of a different kind in her
own world—believed a change would do her good and decided to
uproot the life she knew in Bolivar and move to the bustling city of
Olean some twenty-five miles away. After living in and out of apart-
ments for a couple of years—and after receiving the final divorce
settlement from her former husband—Aunt Sade found and rented
a big old white house on tree-lined West Henley Street with big rooms
and a small yard. For companionship during a very difficult time,
Aunt Sade asked her confidante Josephine—who clearly was enduring her own share of husband woes—if she and her kids would like
to move from Cuba into the big empty place in Olean. Josephine
willingly obliged.*

*And so, innocently enough, on March 4, 1944, my family's "love
affair" with the house at 512 West Henley Street began. Of course,
no one had any idea of the role that house—which would come to be
known simply as "512"—would come to play in the lives of so many
over the next fifty years.*

*My mom was a young teenager when her family moved from
Cuba to Olean. By now she was blossoming into a gorgeous and gregarious young flirt with beautiful auburn hair, porcelain skin, and
a knockout figure. She also had a real zest for life, but not necessarily
for school. She willingly transferred from the high school in Cuba to
good ol' Olean High, but she didn't really like it that much. Oh, she
made lots of friends and was courted often by the boys, but it was that
studying and homework stuff that didn't fit well with her fun-loving
and sometimes mischievous ways. Like her homework, she found her
home life anything but exciting—with all those younger siblings to
tend to, a working mother who expected her to help out, and a nervous and depressed aunt who wasn't quite herself anymore—so she'd
escape by hanging out and smoking with her girlfriends, dreaming of*

becoming an actress or a concert pianist, and wishing for a prince to come and sweep her away.

Unfortunately, the move to 512 didn't do much to help poor Aunt Sade. Despite the commotion in a house full of kids, she spent most of her time alone and withdrawn in a dark upstairs bedroom, smoking like a fiend and nervously tapping her fingers on her head. I'm sure the kids must have found it eerie. Even Peggy and Josephine had a hard time communicating with her.

So, a full eighteen months after moving to 512, even as the Nazis were seemingly taking over the world, a deep and painful depression—sealed by the marriage of Uncle John to that "other woman"—was taking over Aunt Sade. The once attractive and stylish woman had now become a disheveled, detached, and frail old lady. In fact, so deep was her despair and depression that the sixty-one-year-old decided—clearly with some serious coaxing from "concerned" relatives and friends—that the time had come to do something drastic about it.

Chapter 7

Ever since I can remember, I've always hated winter. Looking back, it's probably somehow related to a vivid, blinding January 1974 snowstorm that ultimately landed me, along with Merrick and Mollie, in a foster home for the second half of second grade and all of third.

I told you before: All hell broke loose when I was in second grade.

Let me explain: After my mom's breakdown and my dad's decision to ditch his family and move in with another woman, we four youngest kids moved in with Gramma Jo at 512. We stayed there through the fall of '73 and into the holidays. In fact, I distinctly recall Christmas that year: A "real" Santa Claus, with presents in tow, paid us a surprise visit in broad daylight a day or so before Christmas, courtesy of some well-intentioned friends who knew my mom and her kids had suddenly become charity cases.

Because Mom was barely functioning—she had probably dropped twenty to thirty pounds or more, rarely ate, and barely communicated—Gramma Jo watched us, fed us, and made sure we were up in plenty of time to walk two blocks to catch the city bus to Allegany for school. Of course, at that time, Gramma was a tough, no-nonsense, my-way-or-the-highway type of lady. She had a gruff tone that would scare the hell out of any sensitive seven-year-old like me. It wasn't until her golden years that she mellowed and I came to realize what a gem—and a savior—she was to us.

Anyway, one day in early January, I did something that really ticked Gramma off. In all honesty, to this day I don't even recall what it was: I may have mouthed off to her, talked back to her, or lied to her about something or other. Regardless, it started a huge argument between Gramma and my mom, with Gramma saying she wanted "that kid" (me!) out of her house. So mom rounded the four of us up, grabbed our coats, hats, and a few belongings, and—because she had no car—called a cab. Thirty minutes later we were stomping off the porch, in tears and a huff, and loading ourselves into the backseat of a dumpy taxi.

With nowhere to go, and basically no money to go on, Mom had the cabbie drive us to Aunt Faye's and Uncle Kenny's in Eldred. Aunt Faye, in her late sixties then, was Gramma's older sister and dearest friend, but in many ways her exact opposite: always pleasant, soft spoken, well dressed, impeccably manicured, and much younger-looking than she really was. A polished Grace Kelly to Gramma's no-holds-bar Bette Davis, you might say. At that time, Aunt Faye drove a sporty, two-door silver and black Buick Riviera that perfectly matched her weekly-styled gray hair, and she usually slipped us a buck or two whenever she'd pay a visit. She worked hard her whole life, and retired in the sixties as the first female postmaster of Eldred. Simply put, she was a woman ahead of her time—and everyone's favorite aunt.

Her husband, Uncle Kenny, was a former pilot. He was a handsome, good, and honest man with a gruff exterior but a kind heart. An electrician by trade, he, too, worked hard his whole life (he never really retired!), staying lean and fit as a fiddle well into his nineties. He had very little patience for nonsense, and the only vice (if you call it that!) that I'm aware of was his sweet tooth—which he'd satisfy each evening at 7:30 p.m. with ice cream, cookies, or some other good tasting treat. A committed husband and father, he provided a wonderful home for his wife and their delightful daughter, Suzanne.

Together, Aunt Faye and Uncle Kenny have always held a revered and legendary place in my family's history. The most "normal" of all of our crazy relatives, they were the least prone to controversy or problems, and the calm in the center of every storm. Ultimately married for sixty-five years, they remain a shining example of all that is good and decent in this world—and a true blessing to all who know and love them. Of course, that probably explains why they were the ones Mom always turned to first for guidance, advice, wisdom—or the cash to bail her out of some of life's sticky messes.

So we arrived at Aunt Faye's and Uncle Kenny's pleasant home at 15 First Street in Eldred this particularly snowy January day. After feeding us, listening to our woes, and treating us to their customary evening treat, they tucked us in for the night and reassured us that all would be fine.

The next morning, Aunt Faye awoke Merrick, Mollie, and me at the crack of dawn and fed us a good breakfast. After donning our uniforms like the good Catholic school kids we were, we piled into Uncle Kenny's green Jeep for the ride to school at Little Bona's. Of course, like some sort of awful omen, it was snowing like crazy that black-as-coffee morning, turning what should have been a thirty-minute ride into a nail-biting ninety-minute one. Uncle Kenny's Jeep, locked into four-wheel drive, crept along, determined to get us to school safely despite the horrific Western New York whiteouts. I'm convinced that it was that vivid and terrifying journey that turned me into a white-knuckled traveler in the snow at the ripe old age of seven.

Through the grace of God, Merrick, Mollie, and I made it to sixth, third, and second grades, respectively, that fateful day—and Uncle Kenny eventually made it back to Eldred. But the snow just kept on piling up outside the window, and school was going to be let out early because of the blizzard-like conditions. Panic-stricken, my mom, still back at Aunt Faye's with Maura, called her friend and former neighbor—who also happened to be Merrick's godmother—Betty, who lived in a beautiful house in our old neighborhood in Allegany, asking if she'd be kind enough to pick us up from school that day. She lived a mere mile or so from Little Bona's. I remember Betty—Mrs. Thomas—coming to Mrs. Martine's second-grade classroom that day, telling me that we'd be staying at her house because of the storm.

Great! I thought. Snowbound at the Thomases. Their house was like a mansion to us—or better yet, an arcade—with, among other things, pool and ping-pong tables, a jukebox, and a soda bar in the finished basement. For three snowbound kids, it was a lot of fun horsing around in that basement while listening to forty-fives of "Seasons in the Sun" and "Alone Again, Naturally."

Interestingly, that overnight stay ultimately turned into another, and another, and another. And even when the weather finally broke a few days later, we found ourselves staying at the Thomases for several weeks—heck, it may have even been a couple months. We'd talk periodically to Mom on the phone, but because she had no car, she remained in Eldred with Maura, at least initially.

The Thomases took good care of us, but something felt weird. Then one day after school, Mrs. Thomas told us that two guests were coming over that evening to visit. "They're very anxious to meet you," she told us. "So be on your very best behavior." Being relatively good kids, we obliged.

A few days later—it now had to be early spring—we raced back from school on a Friday, all excited because our pal Mike Marra had asked us to spend the night at his house. He lived just down the block, had great toys, and was a lot of fun.

"I'm afraid you can't this weekend," Mrs. Thomas informed us.

"Why not?" we asked, disappointed.

"Do you remember that nice couple whom you met earlier this week? Well, they were so impressed by you—and particularly by Merrick's polite handshake—that they want you to come and spend the weekend with them to get to know them better."

Mollie and I were furious at Merrick for getting us into this, but we ended up having to forego Mike's cool toys and spent the weekend with the Thomases' "friends." A week or so later, through the "help" of Catholic Charities, the three of us were moving in with these total strangers—the Carters.

Life at the Carters really wasn't bad—if you could overlook the bigger picture that we had suddenly become foster children.

Three kids without a home.

Catholic Charities caseloads.

Dr. and Mrs. Carter were good, decent people—a tad uptight, I might add—but caring and compassionate nonetheless. They had no children of their own, and I presume at that time they must have been in their early forties. (Of course, when you're seven or eight, that's ancient.) He was a professor of some sort at Bona's, and she didn't work. They had a modest ranch home with several acres on the West Five Mile in Allegany—or, as I'd call it today, the boondocks. Their home, like their personalities, was organized, tidy, and without frills. They had a little black mutt named Jonti, who for some strange reason I nicknamed Jonti Arnold. (I was a strange kid.) The Carters were, in a sense, ideal foster parents—but that in itself is an oxymoron. They lived by their schedule (or as Dr. Carter called it, "sheshule") and followed the foster parent "rule book" (if there ever were such a thing) like the Bible: eat your vegetables; no roughhousing; no obscene TV or loud music; brush twice a day; floss regularly. Homework, chores, then play; five dollars' weekly allowance every Friday, with half going into your newly formed savings account; fast food only twice a month; in bed by eight (Martial), eight-thirty (Mollie), and nine (Merrick); only boys age twelve or older may learn to use the riding lawnmower; etc., etc., etc. To their credit, they took great pride in their role and did everything "right." They also did a lot to entertain us, to make it seem like our lives were normal—build a tree house in the woods, plant a garden, take us swimming each Sunday (that's how I learned), on quarterly shopping sprees, or on vacations to Ohio and Michigan. Although not Catholic themselves, they saw to it that we got to Mass each Sunday, and that Mollie and I made our respective First Communions on time with our classmates. (I still have the children's Bible they gave me as a gift!) Heck, they even saw to it that we got cool toys for our birthday or for the Christmas we spent with them at their parents in Ohio. I loved Big Jims, Mollie loved the Sunshine Family, and even back then Merrick was into sporting goods and electronics.

Yes … we actually spent a Christmas in Ohio with a foster family.

The Carters really did do a great job caring for us and providing a safe, albeit sterile, haven for us three pseudo-orphans. But despite the bizarre sense of normalcy we had at the Carters—we were always on time for school, earned straight A's, rode sensible bikes with reflective flags, planted a garden, learned to play croquet, and even had rain ponchos—we were the most abnormal kids in the world, or so it seemed. In fact, now that I'm a parent myself, it's incredibly hard to look at the year and a half spent there in a positive light. I'd cry at the drop of a hat, especially if I had the chance to see Michele or my older brothers (who now also were scattered around Olean in foster homes or living with friends), if—God forbid—I'd hear "When Will I See You Again?" on the radio of the Carters' sensible cars (a purple AMC Pacer and a red Volkswagen station wagon), or especially if we'd get a call or a visit from Mom, who eventually had returned to Gramma Jo's with Maura while trying to get better, seek full custody during an official divorce process, and prove to the courts and her soon-to-be ex-husband that she was not an unfit mother.

No doubt, had we stayed at Carters any longer, the three of us would have definitely become the biggest geeks on the planet. For I've learned along the way that a little dysfunction is not a bad thing; it builds character and definitely breeds "function."

Chapter 8

Does admitting yourself to a mental institution prove you're weak or strong?

Can enduring electric shock therapy heal a broken heart?

Aunt Sade, whose life, like the world at large at that time, had endured simply too much pain and suffering, decided to find answers to those difficult questions by doing both.

She had nothing to lose, or so she figured.

And so, the one-time free spirit checked herself into the state mental hospital in Gowanda, New York, some sixty miles northwest of Olean.

Not once.

Not twice.

But, at the urging of many of her "concerned" relatives, three different times between 1943 and 1946.

I can't fully imagine just how horrific and frightening that must have been, especially to a woman of her age at that time. I envision the experience not unlike some terrible scene from a Frankenstein movie, yet it was all very real. How do you ever really survive an experience like that? But Aunt Sade obviously wanted to get better, and somehow believed that this could be a way to overcome the unbearable grief, the unspeakable depression, and the unending loss she had felt since her John left her. That also must have been why she agreed to the electric shock therapy—a new, albeit barbaric, way of treating depression at that time, I guess.

Initially, Sade had periodic visits from some of her brothers, sisters, and other relatives. Peggy, all of sixteen at the time, visited her on occasion with her mother, her uncle, and her grandmother, and was sickened and saddened by what she saw. Aunt Sade seemed to be getting worse instead of better.

"Pray for me," the faith-filled Aunt Sade would beg her dear niece.

As Sade's periodic yet voluntary admissions became more frequent and lasted longer, the visits from her brothers and sisters, many of whom had lived off or benefited from her generosity through the years, became fewer and fewer. They were too busy, it seems, plotting her demise: All of them except one (Gramma Parmeter) wanted Sade committed to the mental institution for good. They eventually petitioned the court to have her declared a nuisance to the State of New York.

And in the late spring of '46, those mean-spirited siblings got their wish.

Chapter 9

Growing up Bednar, I've come to learn that something good almost always comes out of something bad. It's just never easy to see that, at least initially.

But what good could possibly come out of a four-year-old being broadsided by a car?

When that four-year-old is your youngest daughter, maternal instincts automatically kick in. Suddenly, you forget the troubles that weigh you down and do whatever it takes to help your helpless little child.

So in many ways, it was Maura's brush with death at age four that ultimately helped my mother reclaim her own life.

It was just two days before Halloween 1974. We had been living at the Carters since the spring, and Mom and Maura, still with nowhere else to be, remained at Gramma Jo's. The rest of the family was still scattered around Olean. Maura was an adorable four-year-old—a cute little thing with dark hair, a sweet smile, and big ears. But she was too young to play unsupervised in the neighborhood, and definitely too young to be crossing a modestly busy Henley Street by herself. Yet there she was, across the street on the front porch of our good neighbors the Smiths, who also had nine kids in their family. Earlier in the day, Aunt Faye had brought a bag of Tootsie Pops to the house for trick-or-treaters, and for Maura's sweet-tooth that began at an early age. A candy-loving kid, Maura decided that she would share them with her friends that crisp fall day. "I'll be right back," the impetuous preschooler told them as she bolted down the porch stairs and headed for the street.

The neighbors next door to the Smiths happened to be moving, and an eighteen-wheel Mayflower moving van had been parked on Henley Street all day. As Maura darted across the street in search of her suckers to share, the driver of the car—a gentleman probably in his mid-forties—had absolutely no way of seeing the little girl before it was too late.

Inside 512, an immediate terror seized my mom and Gramma when they heard the horrific skidding of tires followed by frightening screams. Looking out the big front picture window, they saw Maura lying in the street with people quickly huddling around her. My mom raced out the front door in hysterics— "Dear God, dear God, dear God!"—to her baby in the middle of Henley Street. When Mom reached her, Maura was in tears and in shock, with both bones of her lower left leg protruding from under her skin.

"My sucker!" the four-year-old wailed hysterically, oblivious to her much bigger problems.

A neighbor who had witnessed the whole thing immediately called an ambulance, which fortunately only had to come from five blocks away. Within minutes of the accident, Maura and my mother were whisked to St. Francis Hospital's emergency room.

Our little sister was in surgery by the time Merrick, Mollie, and I learned about the accident from Mrs. Carter. We had just walked in the door from school, and she had a very serious look on her face. I thought I was in trouble for one reason or another.

After hearing the news, I bawled my eyes out—worried primarily about one thing, which is a big deal when you're a third grader: "Will Maura still be able to go trick-or-treating with us?"

Needless to say, Maura wasn't able to go trick-or-treating with us that year, but we made sure we got lots of extra candy for her! And while the accident certainly was a terrifying scare for the entire family, things could have been a lot worse. The surgery went quite well, and Maura spent just a week or so in the hospital. All the while, my mother kept round-the-clock vigil with her adorable little daughter with the broken tibia and fibula and a full cast on her leg. She shared meals with her, watched game shows, and slept in the chair in her hospital room so she would not be alone. She calmed her five-year-old fears (especially of a mean and crotchety old nurse) and wiped her five-year-old tears. She encouraged her, supported her, and laughed with her. Most importantly, she never left her side. It was, just like Helen Reddy sang at the time, the two of them against the world, and the start of a unique bond between mother and daughter that would continue to grow in the years to come. And that special medicine worked extremely well, because Maura desperately needed the love—and Mom desperately loved being needed.

Indeed, it was just what the doctor ordered, for both of them.

Chapter 10

"Mom, you've got to do something," a tearful Peggy pleaded on the telephone. "You've got to get Aunt Sade out of that place. It's just horrible."

From her cottage in Chautauqua, the famed institution where Aunt Sade paid to send her to summer school so she could accelerate her credits to finish high school early, Peggy called her mother back in Olean late Sunday afternoon, July 14, 1946. She had just been dropped off by her friend's father, who had driven them back to Chautauqua from a weekend in Olean. En route, the good man was kind enough to stop in the small town of Randolph so Peggy could pay a quick visit to Aunt Sade, who was now living in some sort of outpatient home there—"family care," as it was called.

"It was awful, Mom. Aunt Sade lives upstairs, and it was hot and filthy. There were chickens running around inside and out, and Aunt Sade just sat there," a panicky Peggy explained. "She looked terrible. She asked me to play the piano for her, which I did, but I couldn't for long because Marilyn and her dad were waiting in the driveway. So I gave Aunt Sade a kiss and told her I loved her. She told me that I was all she had to live for."

"I'm scared, Mom. Can't you do something?" Peggy begged tearfully. "I'm so worried. I'm really scared ... "

Josephine tried her long-distance best to calm her distraught daughter and alleviate her fears, but she was scared, too.

Very, very scared.

Chapter 11

The Lord definitely acts in strange ways, considering Maura's accident was just the kick in the pants Mom needed to get her life back on track. It forced her to stop wallowing in the years of grief and despair that had nearly destroyed her and put forth some positive energy to jump-start her life. Hell, she had just turned forty-five years old by the time of Maura's accident; she had nine kids to live for—and half of them weren't even in high school yet. She had people to see, places to go, and tons of trouble to cause.

Oh yeah, a comeback of Tina Turner proportions was in order.

But unlike her dear Aunt Sade a generation before, Peg was up to the challenge. Somehow, somewhere, she found the guts and the gumption it was going to take to overcome the complete breakdown she had suffered. If for nothing else, you've got to admire her for that. And just like it was for the ultra-cool Tina a decade later, love was going to have a lot to do with it.

In December of '74, Mom decided that the first step toward getting her life—and her family—back together was to get the hell out of Olean. She had filed for divorce and full custody of her kids and knew it would be a while for the divorce to be finalized. The thought of facing another cold, long, depressing winter in Olean was hardly appealing, so she decided to head to sunny Florida. A one-time mentor there, whom Mom had idolized some thirty years prior, agreed to let her try to stage her comeback.

Since Merrick, Mollie, and I were all being "reasonably cared for" at the Carters, Mom took Maura (now in a walking cast), Margaret, and Mike with her down to the Florida shortly before Christmas that year (the Christmas we spent in Ohio!). Mitch, Mark, and Michele each were still fending for themselves through friends or foster homes in Olean. She'd come back, she assured us, when she had a house and a job. So she rented a car with the measly profits made on the sale of the house in Allegany—coordinated by Michele—and, after a tearful goodbye, headed off to the Sunshine State.

Little did she know that her days there were going to be anything but sunny.

Knowing that my mom is not an easy houseguest, and probably never was, it doesn't surprise me that it wasn't long at all before she somehow wore out her welcome in the Sunshine State. Not having been there, I have no idea what really transpired, but I do know that somehow it involved the increasing and never-ending hostility between my two parents. And within a few weeks of arriving, Mom, her kids, and her problems were no longer welcome in southern Florida. I guess that's the point where my brother Mike, now twenty, decided that he could make it on his own and opted to plant his own roots—and sew more than a few wild oats—in the South.

Maura, who had turned all of five shortly after arriving in Florida, became the eye of the storm that erupted that February. Apparently my dad, now in the middle of an increasingly hostile divorce from my mom, had tried to convince Peg's long-lost mentor that his estranged wife was not a suitable parent. Well, apparently her one-time ally must have agreed, because I can't imagine why else she would have ever put a sweet five-year-old on, first, a helicopter, and then a plane that flew her alone back to western New York, where my dad could take her in at the home of his lady friend.

Nowadays we refer to the whole incident as Maura's kidnapping.

Well, that's all it took for a shocked, distraught, and furious Peg to once and for all figure out exactly what she had to do with her life: get back on her own two feet, finalize her divorce, and fight to get her kids back with her where they belonged. So she loaded Margaret in her rental car, drove as far north as Columbia, South Carolina, and convinced and entrusted Jack

Anderson—the younger brother of her former love-of-her-life from twenty-some years earlier who now lived there—to watch the only child in her care at the moment for a few months so she could get her act together. For the time had come for the down-on-her-luck lady to summon her "magic powers" deep within and somehow transform herself into the invincible Wonder Woman that lay hidden deep inside. And while she lacked the funky costume, magic lasso, and invisible plane, my mom miraculously discovered the inner strength, strong will, and heroic guts that she'd need to guide her through the fight of her life.

Chapter 12

News of Aunt Sade's death spread faster than the locomotive that seized her life that heartbreaking Thursday morning in 1946. Her dear sister Margaret—my Great-Gramma Parmeter—answered a phone call early that Thursday afternoon in her Eldred home, excused herself politely from the room where she was watching her two granddaughters Pat and Paula, and sobbed at the landing of the stairs in disbelief. Uncle John, who apparently learned the news within hours on Union Street in Olean as he exited his offices at Messer Oil, collapsed to his knees and wept bitterly. Was it my fault? *I'm sure he wondered after learning that his distraught ex-wife had killed herself by calmly standing in front of a train.*

As the news continued to spread like wildfire on that hot July day, my then sixteen-year-old mother was enjoying a carefree summer day sunning herself with her girlfriends on a dock at nearby Chautauqua, where she was spending the summer trying to pass her geometry Regents. She was quite perplexed to peer out from her sunglasses and see her mother and her mother's brother, Uncle Mark, walking briskly toward her early that afternoon. Something's wrong, *she thought.* Something's terribly wrong.

Josephine and Uncle Mark not only had the grim task of telling Sade's beloved niece—who was virtually like a daughter to her—what her dearest aunt had done to herself just a few hours before. They also had the horrific task of identifying Sade's mutilated body at the morgue, just an hour before arriving at the lake. Her body—the parts of it that remained—was so undistinguishable from the trauma of the accident that they had to rely on her trademark corset to positively identify the victim as Sarah Messer. Aunt Sade.

"No, no, no … Aunt Saaaaaade!" an in shock and in tears Peggy screamed as her mother held her tightly.

As was customary back then, Aunt Sade was waked at home, in this case, under the big front picture window of the house at 512, the last real home she knew. In January of that very year, she had given Josephine two thousand dollars to use as a down payment to buy it. Numerous mourners, including many of the seemingly heartless relatives who had driven her to the point of no return, came to pay final respects to a closed casket containing what remained of the once full of life Sade.

Following the surreal wake, where no one really spoke of the tragic circumstances of Aunt Sade's death, there was a funeral Mass held at St. Mary's in Olean, with burial at nearby St. Bonaventure Cemetery. Sade, obviously a woman keenly in tune with and not afraid of death, had purchased her own plot shortly after her divorce—as well as plots for her siblings, before they turned on her—and had even had her deceased parents' bodies exhumed and relocated to that picturesque burial spot. Then, one day on a shopping trip to Buffalo with Peggy, Aunt Sade personally selected a McDivitt Family headstone—a tall, pink stone depicting St. Therese, "the little flower," to whom she was deeply devoted. Peggy was a bit baffled and spooked by her aunt's unusual purchase, but was too polite to say anything about it.

Although it was the last thing she wanted to do, a grief-stricken and heartsick Peggy ultimately returned to summer school in Chautauqua shortly after those worst days of her young life. Upon returning to her Victorian cottage on the grounds of the institute for the wealthy, there was a letter awaiting her. She recognized the handwriting immediately and tore it open.

"Dear Peggy," it read. "Please pray for me every day. I have nothing to live for anymore. I love you forever. Aunt Sade."

And out of the envelope—postmarked July 18, 1946, the very day Aunt Sade walked to the post office and then to her death—fell an exquisite set of rosary beads, made of fourteen karat gold and engraved with the name 'Sally Messer.'

My mother wept uncontrollably.

Chapter 13

I am woman, hear me roar.

If I didn't know better, I'd swear that Helen Reddy's anthem for sisterhood in the '70s was written specifically as the soundtrack to my mom's miraculous metamorphosis that culminated in early 1975. I really don't know what she did—or, to tell you the truth, how the hell she did it—but somehow, with her nine kids in foster homes, with all the chips stacked again her, while holed up in the dumpy Motel DeSoto in Bradford, Pennsylvania, Peggy managed to get her groove back. Gone was Peg the poor, suffering, pitiful victim. Here to stay was Peg the afraid-of-nothing fighter, who was sick and tired of being, in her words, "conned and dumped on." She was woman, hear her roar! And just like a lion (she was a Leo, after all), Peg came roaring back with a vengeance—proof yet again of the immense power of adversity.

Of course I don't know all the details, but within a few weeks of her return north from South Carolina, and, I'm sure, after more than a few heated arguments with my dad, Peg first managed to get "my Maura," as she referred to her, out of the home of her ex, and back with her where she belonged. I believe it occurred with some sound advice from a lawyer friend, some assistance from Mitch, and some intervention from the local police. You can imagine how overjoyed both mother and daughter were to be together again. After all they had been through, they had become like counterparts in crime—indeed, each other's best friend, despite their forty-year age difference. Is it any wonder that they adopted Helen Reddy's other '70s hit as "their song"— *"You and Me Against the World"*?

Next, in March of 1975, Peg received her "emancipation proclamation": Her divorce finally became legal. And although the nuts and bolts of it (for example, the lack of alimony) would come back to haunt her for years to come, the knowledge of knowing that she was free definitely provided her with the fresh start she needed to reclaim her life.

Of course, along with those divorce papers and the freedom they offered came a healthy dose of gumption. Peg exercised it that March day by picking up Merrick, Mollie, and me from school—unbeknownst to us, without notifying the Carters or Catholic Charities (which was a big no-no)—and took us, along with our baby sister whom we hadn't seen in months, to the Bradford Burger King to celebrate her new life and the fact that we all soon would be together again. Mom was awarded custody in the divorce decree, but by court order, I guess, we kids had to remain in foster care until Peg could provide a "suitable home" for her minor children. Still, a burger, fries, and chocolate shake never tasted so good!

By dusk, Mom drove us back from Bradford to the Carters' house, where the Catholic Charities caseworker—an older man who spent more years than anyone probably should in the heart-breaking child welfare system—was waiting in his car in the stone driveway. Obviously, the Carters had notified him of what had happened.

I'm guessing that an emphatic, "Oh shit!" was the automatic phrase out of Mom's mouth as she pulled in the driveway behind the car waiting there. "Wait here," she instructed us, slamming the door to the rental car while getting out to face the visibly agitated caseworker. It was obvious that the exchange was anything but pleasant.

Within a minute or two, with tempers flaring and emotions running wild, eleven-year-old Merrick bolted out of the car to assist his mom, who was even more steamed than the caseworker.

"Merrick, please stay out of this …" the caseworker tried to advise calmly under his thinly masked anger with my mother.

"Leave her alone, you son of a bitch!!" Merrick screamed at him in tears, coming to Mom's defense.

Watching the good-natured, mild-mannered kid completely lose his cool, and seeing the rest of us kids now hysterical in tears, put an immediate end to the discussion between the law-abiding caseworker and my rule-breaking mother. After chastising Merrick for swearing and making him apologize to the caseworker, Mom, with Maura in tow, crying, "I want my kids!" headed back to their cheap motel room in Bradford, promising that we'd all be together again soon. The caseworker then made certain to get us safely in the house, where Dr. and Mrs. Carter—who had witnessed the whole sad scene out their front picture window—awaited.

From that point on, Mom was required to schedule limited times to see us, and Dr. Carter would always remind her how upsetting her visits were to us kids.

Ironically, it wasn't long after that incident that we learned that the Carters would be moving back to Ohio when the school year ended in a couple of months. As for Merrick, Mollie, and me, we would be moved … somewhere.

Chapter 14

God bless Aunt Sade. She may have been desperate and ill, but she certainly was smart enough to ensure that, in the end, she was in control. I can only imagine the shock and humiliation her greedy siblings (with the exception of her sister, my Great-Gramma Parmeter)—you know, the same people who had her committed and declared a nuisance to the State of New York—must have been when they assembled for the reading of her will, shortly after her death.

There they were, assembled in the law offices of Hornberg, Andrews, and Wade at the Bank of New York Building in Olean, supposedly mourning their loss, but dying, I'm sure, to hear how and when their sister's sizeable estate would be divided among them. I'm sure they were mighty miffed that Josephine had been asked to attend the meeting, too.

I can see it now: Aunt Sade's lawyer enters the room, politely expresses his sympathy, sits at the head of the large mahogany table, and finally opens a simple file marked "Messer, Sarah." He exudes a lawyerly confidence, but must be a nervous wreck beneath the surface.

With the tension in the air mounting, he slowly puts on his horn-rimmed glasses, clears his throat, and begins to read:

"The last will and testament of Sarah McDivitt Messer."

The silence, I'm sure, is deadening, and a nervous energy fills the air. "I, Sarah Messer, of the city of Olean, in the county of Cattaraugus, and State of New York, being of sound mind and memory, do make, publish, and declare this my last will and testament, in manner following that is to say:

FIRST: I direct that all my just debts and funeral expenses be paid.

SECOND: I give and bequeath all of the property that I am possessed of at the time of my death, both real and personal of whatsoever kind, and wheresoever situate, to The Exchange National Bank, Olean, New York, and Josephine Richardson of Cuba, New York, in trust nevertheless, for the following uses and purposes:

1.   *To pay the net income therefrom in convenient installments to my niece, Margaret Richardson, of Cuba, New York, until she attains the age of twenty-one years, at which time she shall then be paid over the principal of this trust fund.*

2.   *The trustees in making payments of income to my said niece may make such payments to others for her use and benefit for her maintenance, comfort, general welfare, and education, and at their discretion the trustees may make such payments, or some of them, direct to my said niece after she has attained the age of eighteen years, and her receipt, therefore, even though she is a minor, shall be sufficient voucher for the trustees.*

3.   *In the event that my said niece failed to survive me or surviving me dies before attaining the age of twenty-one years before the time for distribution of principal herein provided, the then trust fund shall be paid over to Josephine Richardson, the mother of my said niece.*

Lastly, I hereby appoint the Exchange National Bank of Olean, New York, and Josephine Richardson, Cuba, New York, executors and trustees of this, my last will and testament, hereby revoking all former wills by me made.

In witness thereof, I have hereunto subscribed my name the 13th day of January, 1943.

Sarah Messer

It is as if a bomb explodes in the office. The stunned siblings simply lose it.

"This is ludicrous!! She was insane!" I envision one screaming.

Another simply storms out of the office in a huff.

"Absurd!!" another shouts. "She can't give everything she had to that spoiled little brat!"

And I'm sure from her place in heaven (where she is, I pray), Aunt Sade was laughing hysterically at the pandemonium that was erupting.

Chapter 15

After finally passing that crazy geometry (her least favorite subject!) at Chautauqua, and finally earning all the credits she needed to complete high school a year early, Peggy headed for "home" at 512 at the close of that horrible summer of '46. As the bus dropped her off on the corner of Fifth Street in Olean, just a block away from the place where Aunt Sade had been laid out just a month before, she made her way slowly down the street with her bags in tow. Then, abruptly, she stopped and turned around. "There's no way I'm going back there," she decided, making, for what may have been the first time in her young life, her own decision. And, boy, did it feel good. The suddenly empowered and independent Peggy lugged those bags uptown to the bus station, dug through her purse for all the change she could find, and boarded the next bus out of Olean. Her great escape took her a mere fifteen miles away—but to Peggy it felt like a million—from the heartache and pain, and landed her in the little Pennsylvania borough of Eldred. Peggy figured she could stay a while with her dear Gramma Parmeter, whom she adored and had visited frequently with Aunt Sade when life was "normal."

"Maybe … just maybe … this is where I belong," she thought. And she was right. Gramma, who herself was still grieving the loss of her sister and distraught over her other siblings' legal actions, was thrilled to see her beautiful granddaughter on her doorstep.

Gramma Parmeter was good for Peggy at a time when life wasn't. In addition to sharing the same name, the two had always shared a special bond that only grew deeper because of their shared loss. Of course, if Aunt Sade was espresso, Gramma Parmeter was decaf: soft-spoken, easygoing, a lot less complicated. But Peggy loved her just the same. She found Gramma's modest Main Street home, like her heart, a warm, welcoming, and wonderful place, tender and full of love. Its big front porch was like arms that stretched out and embraced Peggy tightly when she arrived, providing much-needed comfort and security to the grieving teen who would soon be center stage in an ugly court battle. For you can be damn sure that most of Aunt Sade's living siblings were going to do everything in their power to make sure that "that spoiled little sixteen-year-old princess" was not going to inherit their share of an estate initially estimated in 1946 to be worth about seventy-five thousand dollars. In reality, it was worth more like two hundred and fifty thousand dollars— an astronomical figure at that time. After all, what could a mere teenager do with AT&T stock, Messer Oil stock, U.S. savings bonds, thousands in cash, diamond rings, genuine pearls, beautiful china, sterling silver, expensive furniture—heck, even a baby grand piano and a Stradivarius violin?

Within days of the reading of the will, the conniving siblings found their own lawyers, strategized with them, and, just four months after Aunt Sade's death—on November 20, 1946—officially filed all the papers needed to legally contest their sister's will. Their reason? Simple: She was nuts. When Sade prepared her last will and testament in January 1943, she clearly was not of sound mind. She was just months away from going to Gowanda for the first time, for God's sake. She was probably unduly influenced by Josephine. Or Peggy. Or both. It didn't matter—in a "normal" state of mind, they would try to convince a judge and jury, no woman, let alone their own sister, would have given everything she owned to a teenager.

And so, before the grass could even begin to grow on Aunt Sade's grave, the court battles began in New York State Supreme Court, Cattaraugus County.

Heartsick and confused, Peggy—who turned seventeen that August first and was now more or less living at Gramma Parmeter's— followed her mom's and the lawyers' advice to let them be the ones to defend Aunt Sade's wishes in court. This was more than fine with Peggy, who found herself thrust into a major legal drama and quickly becoming a frequent headline in the local and regional news. She surely wasn't up to spending her senior year of high school in court listening to relative after relative trash and belittle her beloved Aunt Sade. And trash they did:

"She was irrational," said one sister in a deposition.

"She was out of her mind," proclaimed another in the same deposition, later sealing the deal by bluntly and simply stating the following: "I don't think she was in her right mind when she made out the will." Of course, this was the same sister who, in a letter admitted as evidence to the court, had written to Sade while she was in Gowanda and told her, "I would be sure I was completely over those bad nerves before I left there," and never once visited. And while she claimed under oath that Sade was "fond" of Peggy, she also said Sade "claimed to be fond of all the other nieces and nephews, too."

"Did you ever hear her say she was fond of the others?" asked the lawyer for the proponents.

"She said they were worth a million dollars, the twins," she replied, referring to her own grandchildren.

Aaah … the things people will do in the name of greed.

Chapter 16

But what a difference a year makes.

It was now the summer of '47. Nearly a year had passed since Aunt Sade's death when word came that the court battles were over. And guess what? Despite all the legal battles, and despite all her siblings trying to convince the court that Aunt Sade was out of her mind when she gave her entire estate to her grand-niece, a jury in Little Valley, New York—on the morning of June 10—deliberated for little more than one hour and decided shortly before noon that she wasn't.

Margaret Anna Richardson was going to be a very wealthy young woman.

Of course, since Peggy was still a minor, there were several stipulations set forth: The bank and the lawyers would establish, oversee, and manage a trust fund. They apparently took quite a chunk of the money for doing so, too, and made certain that all legal fees were "appropriately" covered. As the will said, Peggy's mother would be responsible for the fund until her daughter turned twenty-one. At that point, the funds would be turned over to Peggy completely. They could petition the court for money for educational purposes only.

And so on, and so on, and so on.

Peggy didn't really care about all the stipulations. Although nothing could ever make up for the tragic death of her dear aunt and the trauma of the prior year, time—and now inheriting a small fortune—certainly helped ease the pain. Money may not have bought Aunt Sade happiness, but Peggy was confident that it would her.

And it was starting to look that way, when, in addition to all that money, something even sweeter came Peggy's way that summer: a dashing young man of her dreams to play the leading role in her unfolding nightmare-turned-fairy-tale.

His name was Bobby Anderson. And the way Mom tells it, Bobby was the Romeo to her Juliet—two star-crossed lovers destined to be together. The two definitely shared something magical that happens only once in a lifetime. Even today, more than fifty years after their great romance began, I see the sparkle reignite in my mom's eyes and the joy warm her heart whenever she recalls memories of the love of her life. Yes ... if ever there were a picture-perfect romance, it must have been the love affair between Peggy Richardson and Bobby Anderson that began in the summer of '47.

No wonder my mom says those were the best days of her life.

Peggy first met Bobby through her sister Pat, who was dating his younger brother. "Bobby Anderson wants to meet you," Pat told Peggy one sunny afternoon at Gramma Parmeter's. "He's waiting outside. Come say hi."

So Peggy casually strolled out the front door and met the handsome twenty-year-old sitting in a white Pontiac convertible parked by the curb. Her heart skipped a beat from the moment she saw his ruddy face, sandy, wavy hair, and dazzling smile.

A few days later, they spotted each other at a summer dance at the Pavilion at Cuba Lake. Although they had come with other dates, Bobby couldn't resist. Under the stars—as if the setting and script were straight out of Hollywood—he asked, "May I have this dance, Miss Richardson?"

"Of course," she answered.

At that moment, she knew he was as hooked as she was.

A week or so passed, but, quite surprisingly, no further word from Bobby. Maybe he didn't like her after all, Peggy thought. But a day or so later, while taking her younger cousin Suzanne on a Ferris wheel ride at the Eldred summer carnival, she spotted her prince again in that white Pontiac. The giddy schoolgirl in her—decked out in a cute skirt, top, and sandals—called out and waved to him from high atop the ride, and Bobby eagerly worked his way through the crowd to get to the princess on the king of rides.

As the Ferris wheel stopped, Peggy decided she was going to take matters into her own hands. Enough of this playing coy.

"Hi, Bobby!"

"Hi."

"Hey ... I'm a member of the Adelphia sorority," said the young coquette. *"We're having a dance next weekend, and the girls are supposed to invite the boys. I was wondering if you'd like to go with me ..."*

"I'll have to let you know ..." he said almost bashfully, before strolling away with his buddies who had now caught up with him.

"OK ..." said Peggy, a little put off and trying to hide her disappointment.

The next day, the phone rang at Gramma Parmeter's. It wasn't Bobby; it was his mother, Florence. Peggy was a little confused.

"Peggy, dear," said the warm voice on the other line. *"Bobby wanted me to phone you to let you know that he can't make the dance next week ..."*

Peggy's heart sunk.

"... but," Florence continued, *"he was wondering if you'd like to go out with him this Thursday, and come over and meet the family. Can he pick you up at seven o'clock?"*

Instantly, Peggy's spirit soared: *Mission accomplished.*

And so their great romance began. Unlike all of the other guys that Peggy had dated before—and for a seventeen-year-old, I think there had already been quite a few!—Bobby was different. He was a hard-working oil man, but a first-rate gentleman who treated his cherie *like a lady. He had a great sense of humor, which complemented her fun-loving ways perfectly. They laughed a lot, joked a lot, played a lot—and probably fooled around a lot. (But there are some things that I just don't want to know!) They went to movies, played cards with friends, hung out at Cuba Lake, and even spent holidays together at the Anderson home in rural Pennsylvania. They danced—oh, could they dance!—and he even taught her to drive a stick shift over Barnum Hill. Best of all, Bobby didn't really care about his gal's money. He didn't need to. His family had money of their own from their oil business. For nearly four years, the perfect* couple shared everything from ice cream cones to big dreams of a life together. They were the envy of all who knew them.

Indeed, Peggy had found her Prince Charming.

During those years, Peggy—trying to be true to Aunt Sade's wishes for her to obtain an education—decided reluctantly that she would enroll in college, even though it would mean being separated from Bobby. Quite proficient on the piano after all those years at St. Elizabeth's, and with Bobby's encouragement, she decided that a Catholic girls' school with a music program might make sense. So after graduating from Olean High School, she began her college career at Nazareth College in Kalamazoo, Michigan, simply because she heard that it had a good music program. It didn't take long for her to realize that she hated it, primarily because she was so far away from Bobby. She lasted one semester and never returned to Michigan.

Motivated by the fact that she could be the first person in her family to obtain a college degree, Peggy then transferred to another Nazareth College—this time, the all-girls school in Rochester, New York. It was a lot closer to Bobby, and if he didn't come and visit on the weekends, she'd spend the entire week figuring out if she'd take the train, ride the bus, or bum a ride back home. She seemed to like this Nazareth a little better—although, ruled by nuns, it still felt like another St. Elizabeth's to her. So after a semester there, she had had enough of that.

It was now 1950, and St. Bonaventure, Olean's hometown college, had just started admitting women as "dayhops." Perfect, Peggy thought. She'd enroll there, live at Gramma Parmeter's, and be close to Bobby all the time. By now, after all, the only degree that really mattered to her was her "MRS" degree.

Indeed, she longed to become Mrs. Bobby Anderson.

As one of the first few co-eds on a formerly all-male campus—and a real head-turner with a shiny new black Pontiac convertible, at that, thanks to her inheritance—the guys were attracted to Peggy like bees to honey. And while she was deeply committed to Bobby, I'm sure she didn't mind the attention—or the frequent requests for dates—she received from all the college guys. Oh, yes ... I'm sure it was a fun fall semester.

As Christmas approached that year and her romance with Bobby continued, Peggy was absolutely certain that Santa would be bringing her the only thing on her wish list: a sparkling diamond engagement ring. But like a kid on Christmas morning who gets coal in her stocking, I doubt the dramatic debutante did much to hide her disappointment on Christmas Day when, instead of that shiny new diamond, she opened a shiny new ... camera. Bobby, I'm sure, thought she'd be thrilled, but I'm certain it was no Kodak moment.

The impetuous Peggy's disappointment and temper got the best of her, which she readily admits in hindsight. "I'll show him!" she decided. "There are lots of guys out there who would love the chance to be married to me!"

And while that may have not actually been the case, there certainly were enough guys interested in getting to know the alluring heiress a whole lot better. In fact, several had been hitting on her throughout the previous semester. So when she returned to school after Christmas break and one eventually asked if she'd like to go to the NIT basketball tournament at Madison Square Garden with him—the Bonnies had quite a basketball team then—she decided the jealousy tactic would really make a point with Bobby.

And did it ever.

In a huff, Peggy told Bobby that she was going to let some handsome dude drive her car—with her in it—to New York. And despite the big time she likely had in the Big Apple with some insignificant fling, guilt set in. But by the time she returned to Olean, it was too late: She had lost the one true love of her life. Deeply hurt, Bobby broke it off with Peggy—permanently—and never truly forgave her. He felt totally betrayed.

And so, out of jealousy, or anger, or stupidity, or pride—or whatever—a promising life of "what should be" became a regret-filled life of "what could have been" for the two young lovers. Both went their separate ways, "for the best," so they decided. Less than a year later, Bobby married another woman.

A devastated and brokenhearted Peggy just kept searching for the answer to her dreams.

She found my father instead.

Chapter 17

The best part about being a child is that you never really know the difference between life when it's perfectly fine—or when it's spinning completely out of control. (Thank God for that! That's for adults to worry about. When you're a kid, life is just one big roll-with-it.) So thanks to the innocence of youth, it never even crossed my mind that my brother, my sister, and I were being kidnapped by our mother for summer vacation 1975.

While visiting Gramma Jo at 512 just days after school let out for the summer, Mom told Merrick (our faithful leader even then), soon to be twelve; Mollie, ten; and me, all of nine—three minors who were not officially under her custody yet, but who were soon to be "dispersed" to other foster homes since the Carters were about to move back to Ohio—that when we were outside playing with the neighbors and heard the ringing of the bell attached to Gramma's porch, we should hop on our bikes and ride two blocks to Olean's Oak Hill Park. Don't tell anyone, she advised. Then, around four o'clock, a cab would arrive with her and Maura (of whom she did have custody, at least I think she did) in it. Hop in and don't look back.

So at the signal, the three of us rode to Oak Hill, ditched our bikes in the bushes (naively believing they'd be there when we returned!), and catapulted down the stone steps leading to Fifth Street where our mother and baby sister showed up as planned in some dumpy cab. Mom's first goal: Get the hell out of New York State before the cops or the social workers found her. So down Fifth and several other back streets of Olean the cabbie took us, over the South Union Street bridge. Up the hill we sputtered, making an eventual left at the top of the hill onto Barnum Road, heading toward the Pennsylvania state line. The cabbie dropped us off at an old junkyard just this side of Eldred. There, our chariot awaited: a 1959 Ford Galaxie—a black-and-white roadster with fins that belonged on a whale, a manual transmission on the steering column, and a knack for burning oil. My mom had schemed with my good ol' cousin to plan the grand escape. But take it from me: If you're planning to kidnap your kids, make sure your getaway car is a little less conspicuous.

At any rate, with the wind at her back, four kids in her backseat, and a few bucks in her purse from pawning most of her earthly possessions, my mother was taking us on the ride of our lives.

And the adventures were just beginning.

Chapter 18

No one—including my mother—really had any idea where we were going, which made getting there a lot harder. So we just kept driving. South. Like birds for the winter, except it was hot. Very hot. And the Galaxie had no air conditioning. We traveled the bumpy back roads of Pennsylvania like a bunch of vagabonds, all the while belting out the Captain and Tennille's "Love Will Keep Us Together" and other appropriately titled Top Forty songs like "Games People Play," and "Someone Saved My Life Tonight"—which poured continuously out of the car's vertical AM radio. Our collective love of music and knack of knowing all the words to seemingly all pop songs of the '70s were nurtured on joy rides such as these, since Mom couldn't travel anywhere without music blasting. Along the way, we'd stop at a roadside Tastee Freeze for a greasy burger and side of fries. By dusk that first evening, my mom somehow managed to find her way to "God's Country"—Coudersport, Potter County, Pennsylvania—when we found out that, on top of the stalling problem that plagued my cousin's car, the jitney also had only one headlight.

"Hey, lady!" some dude on the street called out to the hard-to-miss woman in the funky car. "Turn on your lights!"

Mom pulled the switch.

"Both of them!" he commanded.

It was going to be a long ride.

Thankfully, the power of the Holy Spirit guided us throughout God's country and beyond that summer, because Lord knows my mother could barely read a map. Merrick, on the other hand, became quite adept at it. Although I was too young to have a real sense of time or to even begin to understand what was happening, I recall vividly, albeit not perfectly, many of the bizarre experiences of the longest summer of my life:

With no real place to go, and no real money to go on, my

good-intentioned but desperate mother—a woman with the savvy of a good con artist—finagled her way into getting rooms at cheap motels around northwestern Pennsylvania: the Canoe Place Inn, the Potato City Inn, and the like. She bounced a few checks along the way, but with the real intention of someday paying everyone back when she got her alimony. We'd stay for the night, take a shower, and grab whatever we could scrounge up to eat. Sometimes, Mollie and I would hide in the car when Mom checked in so that it would look like there were only two kids instead of four. One awful time, the nasty motel clerk actually came out and checked out the car—only to find us crouched down on the floor. Needless to say, we didn't stay there. Then we'd pack up each morning and cut out without checking out, but always with the hotel key in hand. Mom said she'd mail it back someday with the payment. I can only imagine what a bunch of scrounges we must have looked like—especially if we'd pay a surprise visit to some unsuspecting relative or acquaintance of Mom's.

Obviously, it didn't take long for that routine to grow old, so Mom discovered a "vacation home" for us: an obscure hunting cabin/motel in the thriving metropolis of Roulette, Pennsylvania, population: 200, that we could rent by the week. Since Roulette is hardly the vacation capital of the universe, the rates must have been pretty good. Actually, the old love of Mom's life—a now divorced Bobby Anderson—lived nearby, and with nowhere else to turn, Mom figured she at least had a friend there. But as it turned out, the Bobby she knew and loved twenty-five years earlier was no more—his life had become a mess, too—so he could offer her nothing more than encouragement to go on for the sake of her kids.

It seemed like we stayed in Roulette forever, but two weeks is a long time when you're a couple months shy of fourth grade. It was sort of like an adventure from my favorite childhood book at the time, *The Boxcar Children*. We bought groceries at the local

market, ate lots of peanut butter and jelly, occasionally cooked
burgers on the outdoor grill, rinsed our clothes in the sink and
hung them over the railing to dry, and even took my cousin's
jalopy to the drive-in movie one hot summer night for entertainment. But that was the night Maura got over a hundred mos-
quito bites and Mom lost her makeup bag that concealed her
only money, so it was time to figure out where to go next.

I'm not exactly sure how we actually avoided being tracked
down by the authorities that summer—especially since I think
Mom missed some important court date, so a bench warrant had
been issued for her arrest in New York State. She did contact
Mitch and Michele by phone—they were still living with friends
in Olean—to let them know that we were together and safe, and,
I assume, to see if they had any money to spare.

With cash running low and the Galaxie on its last leg, my
mom decided to hock one of the few treasures that remained
from Aunt Sade—several hundred shares of AT&T stock—for
a few hundred bucks. It was just enough to put the first month's
payment and security deposit down on a rental car—a 1975 green
Ford Granada—from the one car dealer in Roulette, gas up, tune
in the radio to "Rock the Boat" and "For Once in My Life" and
hit the road. This time, though, we actually had a destination in
mind: Columbia, South Carolina, to pick up Margaret at Jack
Anderson's.

I still can't quite figure out how my mother actually navigated
her way there—no doubt we took the long way—but a week or
so and plenty of arguments later we Northern vagabonds passed
South of the Border and arrived in South Carolina, with probably just a dime to spare for a phone call. I'm quite sure that my
mom, always full of surprises, didn't call my sister or Jack until
we were lost in some bad part of downtown Columbia. Being
nine, I remember how excited I was, though: This was the first
time I had ever stepped foot in the downtown area of a city big-

ger than Olean—not to mention the first time I had ever seen a palm tree!

Despite their initial surprise at learning we were just a few miles away, Margaret and Jack seemed genuinely delighted to see us when they came to "rescue" us from some downtown parking lot. We were so excited to see Margaret again—make that "Maggie," as those laid-back southerners decided to recast her uptight name—since it had been more than six months since we had all seen each other. After the initial hugs, formal introductions to Mr. Anderson, and a quick explanation of what we were doing there, the good-hearted and hospitable Jack invited this motley crew back to his house—although to us, it was more like a mansion.

Jack Anderson obviously was a successful man. A prominent architect with a lovely wife and three kids of his own, he lived in a spectacular self-designed contemporary home on a manmade lake in a ritzy part of state capital. I'm quite positive that our arrival there must have been like the Beverly Hillbillies invading the Royal Palace. I recall the home's four-car garage with an upstairs guest apartment, an in-ground swimming pool and huge yard, and a spectacular indoor balcony that overlooked the main living room. For six months or so, Maggie had indeed been living the high life. We enjoyed it for a week or so, as we ate, drank, and were oh-so-merry to our hearts content. Jack and his family entertained us kids, reminisced with my mom, and—most importantly—tried to help her figure out what to do next.

But like all good vacations, our visit to fantasyland ended much too quickly. Inspired by some wise advice from Jack to make a new home for her kids and, I'm sure, aided by a generous wad of his cash to make our exit possible, my mom piled Maggie and the rest of us back into the green Granada one sunny July morning. With the sun in our eyes, we reluctantly left palm tree-lined Lakeshore Boulevard and embarked on our next reality-ridden road trip on the highways and byways of life.

Chapter 19

Five kids and one adult in a car made for four is not what I call traveling in style. But despite occasional wrong turns here and there and being crammed in the car as tightly as elephants in an elevator, we had a lot of laughs on our journey north. We were silly kids who liked to laugh, and were simply happy to have Margaret—I mean, Maggie—with us again. Screaming "Chew the hot dog!" (to the tune of "Do the Hustle") out the window as semis drove by somehow seemed funny at the time. I'm sure everyone who passed us thought we were a bunch of losers!

It clearly was Jack Anderson's advice that led my mom to head back to her roots in Pennsylvania to start a new life with her five youngest kids. I'm sure it wasn't his advice, however, to have the car overheat along the way—and then to have Maggie go to the door of the nearest farmhouse to ask for a bucket of water to put in the radiator. But that's what happened. Thank God Merrick, who always loved cars, figured out how to open the hood! From there, we somehow managed to putt along ever so slowly to the nearest town—Shippensburg, Pennsylvania, I recall—one Sunday, and ended up spending several days in a Motel 6 or other fine establishment while the car was being worked on. Maura, still five but going on twenty-five, had a few classic answers to the basic questions asked of her by most adults who would see the adorable but scroungy preschooler.

"Where's your daddy, little girl?" the serviceman asked.

"He's on a business trip," she'd lie, while raiding the station's vending machine in search of a fix of candy.

Or, "Where's your daddy, little girl?" the hotel clerk or house-keeper would ask.

"He left us," the precocious preschooler would answer matter-of-factly without batting an eye.

That's not funny, but that's what she'd say—among other, even more inappropriate, ditties!

After Shippensburg's finest finally fixed the major leak in the rental car's radiator, we all piled in again and Mom drove as far as Erie (make that, "dreary Erie," as she would refer to it), where she remembered she had an old boyfriend whom she had heard now owned a pizza shop. She figured she'd look him up, if for nothing else than a free meal. Hey, by this time, she was most likely running low on cash.

As usual, the traffic and construction was its typical mess along Interstate 90 through Erie—plus it was getting dark as the summer nights were getting shorter, and Mom hated driving at night—so the good lady exited at Parade Street, where a Ramada Inn beckoned directly off the exit. When she checked us in for a night or two, though, I don't even think she imagined the place would become our home for the remainder of the summer. But it did.

Actually, it could have been a whole lot worse. Sure, we all crammed into one modest room with two double beds and a rollaway, but there was cable TV, maid service, a decent pool, a simple coffee shop, and a family arcade area with a few pinball machines. After spending the day at the pool listening to "Silly Love Songs" play over and over on the radio, we'd hang there at night (with Maggie as our chaperone) with the other "vacationers," and learn from a few of the mischievous kids we met how to rack up free games on one of the machines using a bent hanger. Good thing, too, since it was rare that any of us actually ever had a quarter.

Mom usually spent her days on the phone or traipsing off on impromptu visits to lawyers' offices, child support services, church rectories, old acquaintances—anyone she could think of—just trying desperately to find someone who could help make my dad cough up some cash to put a roof over our head and some food on the table. When she got nowhere, she'd get ticked off and call my dad—usually at wherever it was he was working at that time—to beg for money, and he'd simply slam down the receiver on her. But since he was living just an hour or so away from our "command central" in Erie, Mom piled us in the car one afternoon and drove us by his girlfriend's house. Then she stopped at the nearest pay phone and had Maggie dial him up, thinking he couldn't refuse his own daughter's urgent plea for help.

"I don't have a red cent!" he finally barked at Maggie.

"Then what about a green one?" replied the teenaged smart aleck before slamming the receiver down and storming back to the car in tears.

After two or three weeks at the Ramada, Mom's well of cash was definitely running dry. Not knowing what to do next, I think she probably placed a call to our guardian angel, dear Aunt Faye, who agreed to wire her several hundred dollars. Not knowing where to go next (and knowing that the beginning of school was just week or so away by now), our enterprising mother piled us all in the car yet again and headed about ninety miles away to the small town of Emporium, Pennsylvania—ironically, not far from where our all our journeys that summer began in "God's Country." I think she had met someone in Erie who told her that he had some affordable rental property there.

And sure enough, he did.

It was a big old white house on a corner lot just a few blocks from the town center. As I recall, it had big rooms with high ceilings and lots of windows, and a curved staircase leading up to three good-sized bedrooms. It wasn't in total disrepair, but it definitely was in need of a fresh coat of paint and some new carpeting. Don't ask me how, but my smooth-talking mother talked the guy into renting it to her on a month-to-month basis. Bummer thing is that the first month's rent took up most of her remaining cash.

Of course, we didn't have any furniture, but that was beside the point. We slept on makeshift beds made out of blankets we had amassed on our journeys that summer.

We didn't have much money for food, either, but we didn't starve. Mom convinced the local milkman to deliver milk and ice cream once a week on credit and bill her at the end of the month. (Wasn't that nice of him?! There are definitely advantages to small town living!) She also must have had a little cash left over for an occasional trip to the grocery store to buy whatever was on sale. Onions for thirty-nine cents a pound? I was amazed, but fried onions tasted pretty darn good the night Mom whipped them up in the electric frying pan that was left in the kitchen—and that doubled as our stove.

We didn't even have any toilet paper! That was perhaps the biggest tragedy of all. But one day Merrick—of all people— "snuck" a roll out of the bathroom at the local car dealer. My mother was appalled (and probably made him go to confession for taking it), but I'm sure the rest of us were grateful.

OK, so it wasn't the Ritz, but with a "home" and an actual address now, Mom went ahead and registered us for school, which was set to begin right around Labor Day. But because she feared (by this time, most likely incorrectly) that the authorities, social workers, or good old dad were all out to get her (and us) in their effort to separate us for good, my gutsy mother actually enrolled us in school under different names. (Now as an adult, I still cannot believe she did this!)

Yup, Maura started kindergarten in Emporium, Pennsylvania, as "Mandy." Barry Manilow's song by the same title was popular at the time, and Maura loved to sing it. I started fourth grade as "M.J." Mollie started fifth grade as "Mollie Jo." (Original, huh?) Merrick started seventh grade as "Mac." And Maggie started ninth grade using her newly adopted "Carolina name."

Oh … and our last name?

Anderson.

… And that's how we spent our summer vacation 1975.

It didn't seem that unusual to me back then, but it's very clear to me now that we crammed a lifetime of extreme living into two of the longest months of my short life.

Chapter 20

God bless Aunt Faye and Uncle Kenny. If it weren't for them coming to our rescue once again, we young gypsies might have literally become tramps and thieves.

Clearly, it was only a matter of time before the Emporium roof caved in (both literally and figuratively!). Fortunately, we only had been in school a week or so when it became clear that there was no way my mom could pull off our new life there. So when she was picked up by the cops and thrown in the town jail for "renting" that Ford Granada too long without making a payment, who do you think she called?

As quickly as possible, our dear great aunt was putting up the money to bust my good-intentioned but desperate mom out of her night or two in the slammer, while our stern but compassionate Uncle Kenny loaded us kids and our few belongings in his Jeep and drove us to salvation in the humble borough of Eldred.

Initially, Mom and the five of us kids lived with Aunt Faye and Uncle Kenny for a short while. But when you're in your sixties and retired, the last thing you want (or need)—no matter how wonderful and kind you are—is a houseful of great nieces and nephews everywhere you turn. Plus, Peg was determined to make a home for us—and where better, she finally decided, than the tiny borough where she had spent some of the happiest years of her life? (Nothing like living in the past!) Of course, with no job, no money, no alimony, no child support, and nowhere else to turn, Peg reluctantly opted for a little help from the State of Pennsylvania. So one early fall day, she finally put aside her pride, wrapped her head in a scarf, no doubt donned her cat-eyed sunglasses, and bummed a ride from Aunt Faye to the McKean County Department of Social Services. With five kids to feed and barely a penny in her purse, the one-time heiress filed the paperwork and officially became the reluctant reliefer. I'm sure it was this experience that forever sealed her hatred of bureaucracy. But, hey, thank God for programs like this when truly needed and used appropriately.

So with her piddly little welfare check, which she vowed she would rely on only temporarily, Peg was eventually able to rent an old house—literally, a little gray shack by the tracks—on the way out of town. It was tidy and clean, and freshly painted on the inside, with a long dirt driveway and a small side yard that led to the landlord's much nicer home. With a few mismatched furnishings from Aunt Faye's and Gramma Jo's, we set up house. It wasn't fancy by any stretch of the imagination, but at least it was a roof over our heads and a place to finally call home.

My fondest—or shall I say, most vivid—memories about living in Eldred? Hmmm ... there are so many it's hard to choose. Maybe it was living without TV and phone service for the better part of our nearly two years there. No, it wasn't for any altruistic or educational reason: Both were simply turned off for lack of payment. Heck, Peg could barely pay the rent on her pittance; a TV and phone were major luxuries! As you can imagine, there was nothing more embarrassing than having a friend find out that we were phoneless—let alone TV-less!

Speaking of embarrassment, I can't possibly recall our life in Eldred without recalling the White Ghost—the name we gave our family car. I use the term "car" loosely. The White Ghost was hardly what you'd call your typical family automobile. Mom bought the rusty, white, two-door, late-sixties-model Chevy Impala for a dollar from her good pal Joyce not long after we moved to Eldred. Trust me: That's about all it was worth! Its pale blue, hole-ridden, plastic interior was a sight to behold—as was my mom driving it. I still can picture her disguising herself with her scarf and sunglasses, motoring around in this beat-up whoopie (usually with the pint-size Maura commandeering the front seat from her elder siblings!) while frequently grinding the manual gearshift on the steering column. Every time we stopped to get gas, we also had the gas man add a quart of oil since the bomb of a car burnt more oil than a Pennsylvania refinery. We were all quite mortified to be seen in the White Ghost—especially after we painted it with Gramma Jo's leftover antique white house paint to cover the rust spots—but at least it got us where we needed to go some of the time, anyway. Maggie even learned to drive in this heap, no small feat in and of itself. The car was on its last leg even before my mom bought it, but when it slid down the driveway on a glare of ice one winter's eve and ended up in a ditch across the road, we knew its days were numbered. That incident unfortunately happened the winter *after* it conked out on the day of Maura's First Communion, causing my mom, Gramma Jo, and the little tike in the white dress and veil to miss the entire service while the rest of us were at St. Raphael's. Don't even ask why Mom decided to get Maura's white sandals in Olean the morning of her First Communion!

Of course, Christmas in Eldred ranks right up there as one of those never to be forgotten as well. We did have a tree—a spare artificial one from Aunt Faye, as I recall—but didn't have much to put on it, or under it. So Mom had the ingenious idea of wrapping up her empty Virginia Slims packages (she switched temporarily from Marlboros because they were more ladylike) in gold wrapping paper to make it look like there were some presents from Santa. Fortunately, Aunt Faye and Michele pulled through with presents for each of us. That was also the year Mom hauled me with her to pay a surprise Christmas Eve visit to my dad, who lived about two hours away, to see if we could guilt him into paying his back child support. She navigated—if you can believe it—the White Ghost through yet another horrible snowstorm only to find out that Dad wouldn't (or supposedly couldn't) do anything to help.

Merry Christmas!

New Year's Eve 1975 was a memorable one, too. Not because it was full of sentiment or anything like that. It's just because

Mom had Merrick and me walk to the Eldred VFW, a good mile from where we lived, in another wicked snowstorm with a note and a couple of bucks in hand to buy her a pack of cigarettes. No wonder I don't like winter! Obviously, her nicotine addiction was at an all-time high.

But I think the all-time winner in the "Eldred vivid memory" department is an even shorter journey that Merrick and I embarked on: a short walk next door to the landlord's house early one bitterly cold winter (of course!) morning, each lugging the biggest kettle we could find from our kitchen cupboard.

"Hi," the two somewhat loveable urchins said when the landlord's daughter answered the doorbell at 6:30 a.m.

"Do you think we could borrow some water? Our pipes are frozen and we don't have any …"

Indeed, living in Eldred was no picnic, but it certainly was a great feast in character-building. And character, Mom would remind us, is built more by trials than by triumphs.

Chapter 21

And then there was that whole thing known as school.

Even now I cringe when I think about my life from fourth to seventh grade, which is how you track your life when you're a kid, you know. Elementary school, junior high, and high school—some of the pivotal years that Mollie, Merrick, Maggie, and I spanned during our time in Eldred—are challenging enough on their own, don't you think? But trying to endure them, much less excel in them, was no easy task given our bizarre family life and financial plight at the time.

Anyway, Maggie was starting ninth grade when we landed in Eldred, so Mom enrolled her in the regional middle/high school, Otto-Eldred, in nearby Duke Center. After months of independence in South Carolina that had expanded her horizons considerably, Maggie spent one day at Otto-Eldred and vowed she would never return. Of course, getting attacked by a bunch of girls in gym class is not exactly the kindest way to welcome someone to her new school. So she managed to get herself enrolled in the Catholic high school in Bradford some seventeen miles away, finagled a way to work off her tuition, and bummed a daily ride with the parish priest from Eldred who taught there. Independence, ingenuity, and spunk: Maggie wrote the book on these qualities, and the first chapter no doubt started in Eldred. Heck, her "professional life" started in Eldred, too, at age fifteen, as the cutest and perkiest cashier at Jim's Shopwise, the local grocery store. That's where she was asked out on her first date by "the cute guy with the cool 'Starsky and Hutch' car," Alan Copeland, who, by the way, eventually became her husband and father of her three fine children!

Merrick—also known as Mac, his Emporium pseudonym that temporarily stuck during our time in Eldred—managed to somehow last at Otto-Eldred through seventh and eighth grade.

In fact, he even seemed to enjoy it, making friends and developing a keen interest in sports. Looking back, Merrick's adaptability was evident even back then.

Mollie also fared pretty well. Mom was able to enroll her in fifth grade at the local elementary school, where she made some nice friends, learned from some nice teachers, and generally excelled in school. It was in Eldred where she discovered her real passion: sports. Although cute as a little dolly, Mollie the tomboy became the pitcher on the boys' softball team, which played in the field across the street from the school.

As my luck would have it, there was no room in Eldred's two fourth grade classrooms for latecomers like me that school year. So I had the "privilege" of riding the high school bus to and from rinky-dink ol' Rixford, some ten miles away, for fourth grade. What a hell year that was. If the bus ride with all those older and rowdy high schoolers didn't kill me (it did land me a punch in the nose intended for someone else one day) the girls in gym class with hockey sticks would. My mom always insists on telling the embarrassing story of how they all ganged up on me once and tried beating me up. The truth of the matter was that the smart girls in the class were threatened by the new "smart kid" on the block—yes, that would be me—who outperformed them and was tested for the gifted and talented program. Of course, I did make my stage debut at Rixford as the lead in some Christmas play called *Reindeer on the Roof* (it was a public school—no story of Mary, Joseph, and a baby at Christmas, that's for sure!), so it wasn't all bad. I clearly had my mom, Maggie, Aunt Faye, and the rest of the audience in stitches during the actual performance, which was a long way from Broadway, but I think is where I first caught the bug for all things dramatic.

Somehow, I managed to survive the perils of fourth grade—barely—and was able to transfer to Eldred at the start of fifth grade. Eldred became my fourth school in two years. I actually stayed in one school that entire year, so it seemed like a pretty good year. I also once again landed the lead role in our class Christmas production—a spoof called *'Twas the Night After Christmas*—so in my mind the lights of the Great White Way were all but beckoning.

As was the norm by now, Maura's experience with any-thing—in this case, school—was far from typical. Confident that she simply had the world's brightest kid, Mom decided that her little darling didn't need kindergarten (it must have been those few days she spent in it in Emporium!) and enrolled the worldly five-year-old directly in first grade. And despite the fact that Mom would send Maura off to school in curlers hidden beneath a furry white hat (handed down from Aunt Faye's granddaugh-ter, Jennifer), the little tike excelled academically from the very beginning. I think it also helped that Maura had a crush on her first teacher—the young and energetic Mr. Jones—so she'd work extra hard to please him.

Our music education continued in Eldred as well—albeit Mom's version of music education. In addition to Top Forty radio, it included a few forty-fives that we'd play on an old record player (come on, who didn't love "Billy Don't Be A Hero"?) as well as Mom's rendition of the "Boogie Woogie"—some jazzy tune she would improvise nightly on our black upright piano, which Maggie bought at a garage sale with her earnings from Jim's Shopwise. Peg would usually perform this late night ritual after hanging out and downing a few too many at the Betty Blue Inn a mile or so away. Since Mom never was much of a sleeper—for years, she slept on the couch, for crying out loud!—she fig-ured a little music would make the night go faster, I guess. It may not have been Beethoven or Mozart, but Mom loved music and made sure we had an appreciation of it, too. Of course, I now wish I could have taken piano lessons!

In all honesty, don't ask me how we all ended up being straight-A students. Heck, it's a miracle we even made it through grade school—much less high school and eventually college (with high honors, thank you very much)—without ever failing, given the wacky existence we had during what most educators would consider pretty significant years. My Lord: From fourth to seventh grade alone I transferred schools—count 'em—eight times! (Not something I'm particularly proud of, by the way.) Sixth grade was a particularly "fun" year for me: I changed schools three times in six months! It's amazing I ever even made it to seventh grade.

With all of her kids in school, no real professional experience under her belt, and an ex-husband who clearly did not give a hoot, Mom decided that an advanced degree was her only ticket to somewhere. So she enrolled herself in a graduate program in business education at her alma mater, St. Bonaventure. She then eagerly applied for all the student loans she could to help tide her over, and began a new life as a non-traditional adult student. Peg was quite a hit with the younger grad students and a few (though not all) of her professors, and was quite a sight bombing around campus in the White Ghost—often with a bunch of kids in the back seat. But God love her: Although she was usually late for class and generally unprepared, she somehow managed to muddle her way through the thirty-plus credit hour program. She always tried to be creative in her methods classes, and usually tried to incorporate music into all her lesson plans. In fact, in one of her summer school classes near the end of her degree program, she had Maura do a pompom routine to "Le Freak," and made the two of us do some ridiculous disco dance to "Staying Alive" and other tunes from the soundtrack from *Saturday Night Fever*. Don't ask me what any of this had to do with business education; I'm quite certain my mom didn't know either.

Of course, the "book money" from Mom's student loans obviously didn't go very far. Desperate for cash, my mom saw a help wanted sign at the Eldred Tastee Freeze, which was just a mile or so from our shack by the tracks, our first spring there. She had met the owners before (Merrick had even picked up an odd job from them cutting their lawn), and figured the buck-eighty-five or so an hour she could earn scooping ice cream during the evenings might help make things a little better for us. So she applied for and got the job. But she soon learned that small town Tastee Freezes after baseball games can be busier than Grand Central Station at rush hour—and that the twenty bucks or so she'd earn after taxes certainly wasn't worth the aggravation. So her career at the Eldred Tastee Freeze lasted about as long as a soft-serve cone on a hot July day.

Meanwhile, my oldest siblings (Michele, Mike, Mark, and Mitch) missed out on most of our crazy Eldred adventures, which took place from the fall of '75 until the late spring of '77—but that may not have necessarily been a good thing. Although only in their late teens and early twenties at that time, they were off fending for themselves for the most part, and we'd only see them on occasion. Michele remained in Olean with friends, working at Leo's grocery store, pursuing her teaching degree at Bona's, and worrying about the horrific mess her family was in. Mike, who had landed in the South with Mom, remained there, floating from place to place—Florida, Georgia, the Carolinas, Texas— eventually hooking up with some free-spirited pothead buddies, picking up odd jobs, and partying way too much. At age twenty, Mark believed that marrying his high school sweetheart would be the answer to his dreams. Mom had a complete fit—a pattern that would ultimately continue each time one of her kids got engaged, and Mark eventually (and sadly) learned the hard way a few years into it that Mom was right. However, Mark and his then-fiancée did bring us our only family pet that we ever had growing up: a cute tiger kitten that we named Claire! And Mitch, who graduated from high school in June of '76, had earned a scholarship to play basketball at a small Pennsylvania college he had visited only once—on his way with buddies to spring break in Florida that year.

So who was "luckier"?

I'd say it's a toss-up.

Yet despite the trials and tribulations—and believe me, there were plenty more—of our time in Eldred, several very good things did emerge from our time there. We met some incredibly wonderful people, like my eventual brother-in-law Alan and the entire Slavin family, other relatives of my Aunt Faye and Uncle Kenny, who simply refused to judge a book by its cover and who came to make an enduring impact in our lives. We recognized the importance of always striving to do our best (in school, at least), even if there were plenty of reasons to fail. Perhaps unknowingly, we began to understand and appreciate during those plentiful times of going without that less can often be better than more. That absence really does make the heart grow fonder. And probably most importantly, by laughing a lot, crying a lot, relying on each other a lot, and never missing weekly Mass no matter what the circumstance, that family and faith are really what it's all about.

But lessons learned certainly don't pay the bills, and by the time the "Farrah Phenomenon" was in full swing and I finished fifth grade in June of '77, Mom simply couldn't keep up with the influx of bills or notices from bill collectors. The phone and TV had long been turned off, thereby causing me to miss the whole first season of *Charlie's Angels*, but with the water and electricity slated to be next, the time had come for us to pack up and pull out.

With nowhere else to turn, Mom "temporarily" went full circle back to the place where all of our adventures had started just a few years before. The one place that neither my mom nor us could ever really escape: 512 West Henley.

Chapter 22

The house at 512 West Henley Street was no Taj Mahal. But like its owner, Gramma Jo, it was one of a kind—a true original, with lots of character and lots of spunk.

From the outside, "5-12" (as everyone always referred to it) was just an old, ordinary, in-need-of-some-work, white house set back from tree-lined Henley Street. It had a recessed porch that usually had a faded American flag hanging from it, and a mailbox on the porch with the silver numbers 512 displayed proudly above it. There was even an old-fashioned bell to the left of the door that Gramma would ring when we were kids, indicating that it was time for dinner or time to come in (9 p.m.). Some of the house's white shingles were chipped, and the shrub underneath the big front picture window was almost always overgrown. There was a small but pleasant front yard and a welcoming sidewalk to the house, with enough cracks and spaces to let lots of green grass grow where it never should have. The part-grass, part-dirt driveway didn't do much to enhance its curb appeal.

When you entered the house, it usually reeked of smoke, thanks to Gramma Jo's Larks and Mom's Marlboros. In the entranceway hung coats galore, and even some of Gramma's everyday wear. The main hallway was always cluttered with purses, gloves, and other important junk, and always looked like it was in need of a good paint job. There were doors everywhere, which usually confused infrequent visitors who were never quite sure which doors to use and which doors were off limits. The main bathroom, directly off the hallway, was always cold—even in the summer. You quickly learned always to hook the old-fashioned latch.

If you made your way through the maze of doors correctly, you'd enter the huge, boy-is-there-a-lot-of-wasted-space-in-here kitchen, which boasted about as many cupboards as you'd find in, say, the kitchen of a studio apartment—explaining why the countertops were always cluttered with packages of bread, boxes of cereal, small appliances, a radio, and other trinkets that no one ever knew where to put. In the center of the room stood a round wooden table, usually covered with a less-than-beautiful plastic tablecloth that almost always clashed with the less than striking floral curtains. (I loved Gramma Jo dearly, but sophisticated interior designer she was not.) We'd gather around that table daily, except Sundays and holidays, for most meals. Of course, oftentimes those meals were accompanied by the obnoxious background music of the aging washer and dryer (almost always running from morning 'til night), which were in plain sight just inches away from the table. Near the end of its twenty-year life, the washer would literally clank and bounce around the floor if it was not held securely in place during the spin cycle, all the while leaving a huge puddle of water for those in stocking feet to step in. The brown double-door Frigidaire, purchased used, stood alone, majestically, and had a life of its own, thanks to a short in its electrical system that would—sporadically and without warning—shock the unlucky random soul in search of the Kool-Aid or the ketchup.

Coming from the kitchen, you'd enter the spacious dining room, which, relatively speaking, was the nicest room in the house. The table, hutch, and buffet were all Aunt Sade's at one time, and reflected her more refined style and taste. Over the years, however, the center leg of the table came closer and closer to falling off whenever you moved it to add one of its three leaves for Sunday or Christmas dinner. Directly over the center of the table hung a lovely antique chandelier, which Gramma decided to paint antique white in one of her paint-the-entire-house-the-same-color moods—walls, floors, and ceilings! I don't know which was worse: the pea green mood or the pastel pink mood. On the far wall underneath the four long windows was the five-foot-long, knee-high radiator, which warmed many a butt on a cold winter's day. Of course, after Gramma suffered a series of strokes in the late eighties, the hospital bed in which she slept added a great deal to the dining room's decor.

If you were lucky enough to navigate your way correctly through the 512 labyrinth, you'd eventually come full circle from the dining room, pass through a large archway and enter the, shall we say, eclectic living room. The first thing first-time visitors couldn't help but notice was the funeral-parlor-red carpeting, purchased when Gramma was in her red mood, but most were too polite to say anything about the red sea that stretched from wall to wall. The more you came and went, the less shocking it became. As for the furniture, it changed only once during the twenty or so years that I remember, and the arrangement of that furniture in the room where so much living took place never changed. Never to move, as if permanently stuck in super glue, were two mismatched couches, two coffee tables and three end tables (all spray painted gold—you guessed it, during Gramma's gold phase), and three of the world's most uncomfortable chairs, which we kids took the liberty of naming. "Armoff-buttonloose" was the gold high-backed rocker in the back of the room with the loose buttons and the right arm that would fall off on occasion, making unsuspecting visitors think that they must have broken it; the "Gooky Monster" was Gramma's grungy green garage sale special parked prominently near the paned front picture window, which allowed the dear senior citizen to gawk out at the action on Henley Street; and the most popular seat in the house was "Numb-Butt," so named because the butt of whoever sat in it to watch TV (which was a mere two feet away from the high-backed chair, but always controlled by Gramma) would eventually go numb, due to the lack of cushioning in the seat and the weird angle of the chair. From time to time, all three chairs and two couches were draped in a startling array of slip covers, which never stayed on correctly and therefore only worsened the look of the room they diligently tried to enhance. The room boasted an old, non-functioning (at least during my lifetime) brick fire-place with a grand mantel and a flat hearth, which, of course, were painted whatever color the walls happened to be. Finally, the two old-time four-foot tall radiators in two far corners of the room added their own special dimension—especially when draped with blue jeans, socks, and underwear. Until we had one, all the radiators in the house doubled as the dryer.

Suffice it to say, the living room, like the whole house, had lots of untapped potential.

Of course, if you thought the downstairs was a decorator's nightmare, the upstairs was even more frightening. The once lovely old staircase with the attractive wooden banister and intri-cate spindles, unfortunately, couldn't hide the years of abuse they had taken from umpteen kids sliding down the painted banister and poking their heads through the matching narrow spokes. After ascending its thirteen stairs, you'd wind up in another open hallway, to be greeted by an old dresser, a broken chair with three legs, or a wooden clothes rack covered with the day's laundry. The harsh overhead light—one of many that lit the upstairs—had no globe or cover, so the exposed bulb cast your shadow in all directions, as if you were an escapee from Alcatraz. If you were, you'd never get away anyhow, because the hallway floor creaked so loudly.

Like the downstairs, the upstairs had doors, doors, and more doors leading to a variety of rooms, each one with its own unique personality. Behind door number one, to your immediate right at the top of the stairs, was the upstairs bathroom, which by the rest of the house's standards, was pretty nice. It featured a big, old, deep tub that didn't work, so it doubled as a linen closet of sorts, for behind the plastic curtain you could usually find a case of toilet paper, some cleaning supplies, and the mop that Mom used to wipe the ceilings. Its other main attraction was the simple window above the toilet that, in nice weather, always remained open—thereby showcasing the beat-up screen with more holes than a golf course, stuffed each summer with white cotton balls to keep the pesky insects out. And out that window every winter, without fail, grew the most enormous icicle you've ever seen, due to the poorest (and probably dirtiest) gutter system a house could ever have. So each winter, also without fail, Gramma Jo would make Merrick or me take a hammer and a screwdriver (just about the only two tools in the house), lean out that window, and try to chisel it down—which was sort of like trying to chisel away the iceberg that sunk the Titanic. If we didn't, though, a January thaw would usually cause some periodic flooding in the bathroom, or worse yet, would totally destroy the neighbor's side fence, which it did once when it came crashing down. And let me tell you, Gramma was not too happy about that—and neither was the mean old neighbor, who thought someone at 512 drove a car into it!

The rest of the second floor was an interesting collection of five bedrooms, none of which ever had to worry about being featured in a *House Beautiful* photo spread. The two most interesting bedrooms were mine, which we aptly nicknamed The Dungeon, and Gramma Jo's, which in later years we referred to as The Honeymoon Suite. Both were appropriately titled.

The Dungeon earned its endearing name for being, hands-down, the darkest room in the house. Oh, it had two side by side windows, but all you could see from them were the side of the neighbor's gray house a mere eight feet away (which blocked the sun from ever entering) and the front of Teri Tilly's house across Fifth Street. The room did boast a fairly large closet, but it—like all the closets in this house of many doors—had no door, so your wardrobe was on display for all to see. Over the years we kids played "musical bedrooms" at 512 from time to time, but for the most part the dungeon was my room, so I tried to brighten it up with posters of Farrah Fawcett, *Charlie's Angels*, and Heather Thomas. (Was I in the midst of puberty or what?) The furnishings were far from fancy, but like any kid, I had a strange sense of pride in my room.

Interestingly, the dungeon was actually part of a suite of three rooms that at one point, long before I was born, was an upstairs apartment in 512. It was connected to Maura's room by—of all things—a kitchen, complete with an old-time sink, stove, and icebox, which in our years at 512 was used as the biggest junk room you'd ever seen. Chucked full of more stuff than you could buy at a ten garage sales, the kitchen also served as our ironing room; DJ booth, with an old record player to spin our forty-fives of "Le Freak" and "Boogie-Oogie-Oogie" over our Mr. Microphone; an in-a-jam-with-nowhere-to-sleep spare bedroom; and ultimately, as Maura's walk-in-closet. It was quite a sight to behold.

I think it's my sister-in-law Eileen who deserves credit for naming Gramma Jo's room the Honeymoon Suite. When we were kids, Gramma always kept her bedroom under lock and key. We all knew it was off limits, and rarely entered her ruffly, pink floral sanctuary that never changed in all the years that I knew it. But as she mellowed with age and suffered a series of strokes, Gramma graciously began unlocking her private palace and offering it to 512's most distinguished guests. After marrying Mitch and having the pleasure of her first "official" holiday at 512, Eileen and her hubby were commanded by Gramma to sleep there. Eileen, of course, politely accepted, but experienced the worst night of her life. She tossed and turned in the lumpy and crusty old mattress, nearly suffocated from the embedded smell of years of cigarette smoke that consumed the room like a layer of smog, and was totally spooked out by the creaky and creepy sounds of 512 after dark.

"Well, how'd you sleep, my dear?" Gramma Jo would always ask the VIP who was lucky enough to spend the longest night of her life in her special dwelling.

"Great!" said my always enthusiastic sister-in-law, and anyone else who had the privilege. After I got married, my wife and

I had the honor as well. Like Eileen, she had the same glorious experience.

Of course, Eileen was not the first person to be spooked at 512. The house always had a spooky aspect to it, and the older you (and it) got, the spookier it became. In my opinion, it all started with the third floor, which you could reach by climbing the narrow staircase right off Gramma's room. At the top of the stairs were two doors: The left one provided access to yet another three-room apartment/firetrap full of junk, and the right door opened to a dark and creepy attic with a few floorboards and some mysterious old trunks stuffed with God knows what. The house also was made spooky by the cobweb-filled dirt basement that you entered from the outside. We stored a hose and the one bike we kids all shared for years down there. When getting or storing the bike, you'd duck your head and dart in and out of there faster than a rabbit. My mom was convinced that Aunt Sade, who, remember, initially found and purchased the house in the 1940s and was laid out under the front picture window in the living room after her suicide, still roamed the house as a ghost. That crazy notion became a running joke, but maybe it had some truth to it.

Despite its occasional spookiness and plentiful physical imperfections, 512 had an appealing aura about it that made it much more attractive than you might imagine. Sure, it wasn't the White House, but it wasn't a dump, either—at least not in the traditional sense of the word. Despite the clutter, 512 was always neat and clean, the dishes always washed, the beds always made, the vacuum always run, the lawn always cut. Through our daily chores, we kids were expected to keep it that way, and we dutifully did—although, like any kids, we sometimes grumbled about having to do so.

Still, spending most of my youth in that house never really seemed like a much of a treat, especially when friends grew up in nicer homes, with parents who had a car or two in the driveway,

a little money in the bank, and no spare bathtub on the front
porch. Yes, we had one, for the better part of seventh grade.
Uncle Kenny installed a shower in the downstairs bathroom, and
Gramma didn't want to throw away the old tub! But looking
back, growing up in 512 was a blessing of sorts. Its distinctive
character gave it more warmth than houses ten times nicer, fancier, or more expensive. The house had more foot traffic than
Grand Central Station, and everyone—from the closest of family
friends to the most distant relatives and even the host of home
health aides who invaded the place daily in Gramma's last few
years of life—always felt welcome there. (For obvious reasons,
however, only the lucky few were allowed upstairs!) They could
always grab a simple snack, a peaceful snooze, a reinvigorating
shower, or some much-needed love and laughter. Gramma Jo
intended it that way. Her house truly was her castle, and she
was mighty proud of it. Her castle lived the trite little poem that
was written on a set of collectible teapot-shaped salt-and-pepper
shakers that sat on the shelf to the right of the kitchen sink for as
many years as I can remember. (No doubt purchased at a garage
sale!) After so many years of washing dishes at that sink, that little
poem is permanently etched in my mind—and I have no idea
who wrote it:

> *My house is small, no mansion for a millionaire*
> *but there is room for love,*
> *and there is room for friends,*
> *that's all I care.*
> *Guests, you are welcome, be at your ease*
> *Get up when you're ready, go to bed when you please ...*
> *You don't have to thank us, or laugh at our jokes*
> *Sit back and come often; you're one of the folks.*

By opening the oh-so-many doors of her humble house to
us and to countless other wanderers, whether happy-go-lucky or

down-on-their-luck, my outrageous and extraordinary grand-mother opened her heart to troubled souls—and set a wonderful, living, and loving example of the importance of helping others, finding happiness and taking pride in whatever you have, and laughing at yourself along the way. In her unorthodox ways, she provided a wacky but wonderful safe haven to us and to anyone who needed a place to hang their hat, whether for a nighttime or a lifetime.

The place known as 5-12 was much more than a house. It was the oddball but likeable member of the family who dressed funny and never uttered a single word. The one always taken for granted. The brunt of countless jokes. But the one always there when you need something. Just like that weird relative, that colorful character known to us as 5-12 was an integral part of our childhood. Its distinctive personality, etched so vividly in the minds of all who knew it, will never be forgotten—nor will the many memories that my family created there. Because for so many very critical years, that white house at 512 West Henley Street was the only security my family knew.

It certainly wasn't the Ritz, but it definitely was home.

Chapter 23

Don't ask me how, but my mom kept plugging along trying to earn all the credits she needed for that elusive master's degree even when we moved back to 512. So each morning through the summer of '77, she'd trek off to summer school, leaving a list of chores for us kids to do and Gramma Jo to keep us in line.

By the end of the summer, something quite remarkable happened: Some Catholic high school in Columbia, South Carolina, which my mom had learned about through the career office at Bona's, was looking for a typing teacher. The school actually called her for an interview, and ultimately was crazy enough to hire her without an in-person interview for the fall. They clearly must have been desperate for teachers, as Mom always said, and they more or less paid in holy cards, but Mom was bold enough to give it a try.

So once again, with a new school year looming, Mom loaded us in a car—this time a borrowed brown Buick LeSabre station wagon from her brother Jeep—and headed off to South Carolina. This time, however, things were a little different: Instead of running in desperation, we were heading toward a new life (or so Mom thought). But Maggie didn't join us on this little southern adventure. She was about to begin her junior year of high school, and was very happy and independent. She pleaded with my mom to let her stay with a friend and her family, and Peg ultimately agreed. Lucky for Maggie, as she missed out on round two of our Carolina capers.

In typical Bednar fashion, we arrived just days before the start of the school year. As luck would have it, Mom met some good folks at her new school who had a relatively cute but simple ranch home for rent, and they offered it to her. I think they even agreed to wait until Mom got paid for the first time for the rent! It was unfurnished, but by now that seemed liked no big deal to us. We somehow came up with a few cots and a TV and set up house.

Mom was able to enroll Merrick, who was about to begin ninth grade, in the Catholic high school where she'd be working. (Free tuition for children of faculty!) But there was no room in the private middle school for Mollie, who was about to begin seventh grade, and Mom had heard terrible things about the city middle schools. So she wait-listed her twelve-year-old daughter, and began bringing Mollie to work with her as the school year started. Not the typical way to start your new job, and certainly not the typical way to begin seventh grade. But Mollie sat quietly in Mom's classroom and quickly learned how to type!

Despite being temporarily truant, I dare say Mollie was far better off than Maura and me. Mom enrolled us in the local elementary school—I was beginning sixth grade, Maura third— but the two of us were absolutely petrified from day one. The bus picked us up right outside our house and drove us God- knows-where, for what seemed like forever, through downtown Columbia before dropping us off at school. The return trip home was by some other equally scary but seemingly longer route, and the two of us were convinced we'd never actually make it home alive. Now keep in mind, we weren't racist; we were ignorant. So it was frightening as hell for two young, naïve, white kids who had only attended schools in either rural New York or Pennsylvania, barely knew any black people personally, and knew absolutely nothing about city life, to be thrust into a large urban school in the South, where we were definitely in the minority. I liken it to throwing two baby cubs born and raised at the zoo into the huge forest and asking them to find their way around. So Maura and I would sit together on the bus, fret over recess, and cry when we separated for the day. But nothing bad ever happened to us, which, ironically, was not the case for me in rural Pennsylvania! I do remember doing terribly on my first spelling test, though—

not because I didn't know how to spell, just because I was an absolute wreck.

For the first week or so, we were all kind of proud and excited about the new life on which we were embarking. But as reality set in—the job was work, the pay stunk, school was awful, and there were lots of bugs!—the dream of that new life in South Carolina seemed more and more like a stinking nightmare.

Then, one night, we were awoken by Mom screaming at the top of her lungs and bolting out of her cot.

"Dear God in heaven!! A mouse!! It just ran across my leg!!"

We all freaked out and started screaming, and turned to Merrick—the man of the house—to check the whole house for the mouse ... or worse. He never found the rodent, but Mom's convinced that that episode was the beginning of what ultimately became a blood clot in her leg.

As if that wasn't enough ammunition for us to flee the state (and it was—we all HATE critters!), just a few nights later, Mom was awoken in the dark once again by something much spookier than a mouse: the bright light of a flashlight peering through the front curtainless picture window. Scared out of her wits, she crawled on her knees, woke us all, and huddled us together in the dark. As Merrick, our resident "Joe Mannix," peered out a different window to detect whatever he could, he saw a shadowy figure hop into a parked car near the end of the driveway and speed away like a bat out of hell.

Well, that did it.

As daylight approached and the Carolina sun rose, Mom had already made up her mind: We were so outta there. Convinced that it was either her nemesis Mr. Bednar sending someone to scare the heck out of us, a random burglar who knew that a single woman and four kids were living there alone, or possibly the seemingly nice landlords who grew creepier by the day, Mom took Merrick and Mollie to school with her that day and ordered Maura and me not to take the bus home. As luck would have it, we had a half day for some reason, so the two of us waited on the school steps for literally hours until Mom finally pulled up in the wagon around four o'clock to pick us up. We didn't realize until we got in the car that we were never going back to that place. And while we were relieved about that, Maura and I bawled our eyes out because we left our cool Mead Data-Center portfolios and favorite markers that Aunt Faye had bought us before we left Olean in our desks!

Bummer.

So back we headed: Back to Olean. Back to 512. Back to the life Mom was trying so desperately to escape. Thank God that Gramma Jo never turned her back on us, although I'm sure there were times when it would have been easy to do so.

For Mollie and me, it also meant back to Little Bona's after three years away. Maura joined us there, too, for third grade; Merrick entered ninth grade at Archbishop Walsh, the same high school our older siblings attended. But now we had reached the age when things were getting embarrassing: In and out of schools. Always late. Rarely picked up on time. Mom drove us, and timeliness was never one of her best attributes. In fact, more than once, Mollie, Maura, and I, after waiting hours after school for a ride from Mom, would walk the three and a half miles home from Little Bona's to 512. Needless to say, we'd seen better times.

One step forward and ten steps back.

That about summed up our lives in the fall of '77.

Chapter 24

I always wanted to tour the United States, but trekking around the country as a twelve-year-old in a 1970-something, beat-up brown Buick station wagon with a hundred and twenty thousand miles, a major muffler problem, and a tendency to overheat was not exactly how I envisioned it.

Yes, that aptly describes our chariot for our next "cut-out-of-town" escapade. Bummer that our windows to the world usually got stuck whenever we'd try to roll them down.

Once again, I wasn't exactly sure where we were going—or why. Mom was still in search of a new life. Law school beckoned this time, or so she thought. Heck, after battling the courts for alimony and child support and getting all but nowhere—and taking one business law course as a nontraditional college student—my mother, now pushing fifty, seriously, if only momentarily, wanted to be a lawyer!

Arming that woman with a career aspiration, a car, and a couple of bucks always meant trouble.

Anyway, it was the middle part of sixth grade—sometime in January '78, I recall, a week or two before my twelfth birthday—and our next road trip (probably the grandest of them all) started out as spontaneously as all the others. Mom had definitely tired of the wintry weather (and must have hocked something or other to come up with some quick cash). So one day after school she simply picked up Merrick (from Walsh), Mollie, Maura, and me (from Little Bona's) in the jam-packed wagon for, shall we say, a "mid-winter recess." But this time, instead of heading south, we were heading west. Toward the sunset.

The golden state of California was beckoning, apparently.

As usual, our road trip west was not the route the AAA would have recommended. In fact, the furthest west we got—at least that first snowy night—was a hotel in (where else?) Erie,

Pennsylvania, before we took a quick detour south the next week or so. I think that Mom decided that since we were out, we might as well stop by and surprise Mark and his new bride, who were living in a suburb of Atlanta at that time. After wearing out our welcome there in just a few days, and, no doubt, bumming some money from Mark, Mom figured we might as well "pop in" and visit Mike, who was now doing construction work somewhere in Houston. So from Atlanta we took a two or three day journey through the deep south, like a bunch of vagabonds, in a vehicle that should have never made it through the entire state of Alabama, across the marshlands and Gulf Coast of Mississippi, around the outskirts of the Big Easy, and all the way to Baton Rouge, Louisiana, before the radiator finally gave out, overheating like a pot of boiling water with the lid smothering it. I'm positive that it was pure sympathy at this pathetic sight—single mom, four upset kids, and a more or less burning car—that motivated the mechanics at the nearest Sunoco on a Sunday to jimmy-rig the radiator to get the car moving again.

To pass the zillion or so miles we seemed to be traveling, we kids did what most kids do when riding long distances: Listened to stories from Mom, belted out the Bee Gees on the radio, munched on junk food, played under backseat "tents" made out of Mollie's Strawberry Shortcake sleeping bag, cried every now and then—and fought like cats and dogs. Dear God, how on earth did we ever do this?

"Knock it off, or I'll pull this car over right now!" Mom would threaten while traveling on a busy highway.

Nightfall and rain had arrived by the time we hit the traffic—and construction—of sprawling Houston. That awful combination probably explains why Peg ended up driving down a coned-off portion of some superhighway. Thank God it was a Sunday evening, and traffic was light, by Houston standards, anyway. It's a miracle we weren't all killed then and there. But killed is exactly what someone had been the night before in the first hotel we stopped at, so Mom decided we'd upgrade to the nearest Holiday Inn.

"I wouldn't give you a nickel for the entire state of Texas," Mom proclaimed after only a few hours in the Lone Star State.

And while I doubt she gave Texas a fair shake, one thing was for sure: We definitely weren't in Olean anymore.

Chapter 25

"HO-LY SHHH-I-I-I-T!!"

Those had to have been the first two words out of my shocked twenty-something-seventies hippy brother Mike as he opened the door to the upstairs Houston apartment that he shared with a couple of other doobie-lovin' dudes. The last people he ever expected to see on his doorstep that early Monday morning in February '78 were his mother and younger brother Merrick—both of whom he hadn't seen in at least a year or more.

If nothing else, Mom was always full of surprises.

And where were Mollie, Maura, and I, you ask? Bolted in the hotel room where Mom demanded that we remain until she and Merrick returned from finding Mike's apartment.

"Michael!" said Mom, equally shocked—primarily by his new, free-spirited, look: long dark hair, mustache, and closely cropped beard. "You look like the Lord!"

Leave it to my mom to find a religious reference in the most secular of settings.

My brother Mike may have looked like the Lord, but he and his buddies certainly didn't live his holy lifestyle. Their bachelor pad—not prepared for an unexpected visit from any mom, let alone Peg—had all the fixings, as I recall: empty beer bottles galore, the stench of lingering smoke (not that I knew any better then, but I'm sure it was not just from cigarettes), a filthy kitchen, a huge stereo, and a few *Playboys* in the bathroom. As if that weren't enough, one of Mike's roommates had a disgusting pet snake, which he kept in a glass cage in his bedroom.

Needless to say, Mike and his roomies found Mom's visit, her self-invitation to stay for a few days (with four kids in tow), her perceived right to clean (and go through) everything, and her daily preaching on their morality about as pleasant as a visit from the warden.

Mike tried his best to keep his cool, entertain his younger siblings in between his construction job, and maintain his friendships with his buddies who had to have been all over him to get us the hell out of there. But none of us kids had any idea how strained things were in that tiny apartment for the few days we were there. It all boiled over one night at dinner—which Mom, naturally, took it upon herself to fix and serve.

Steely Dan's "Peg" came on the radio, which Mom had long ago tuned to her preferred station. Just as it was beginning and we were sitting down to eat in the small dining area, Mike abruptly turned it to his classic rock station.

"Lord, I like that song, Michael," Mom said. "Can you turn it back?"

Well, that did it. Mike snapped. And after a few choice words, a huge argument, and some money that Mike threw at Mom to get us on our way, we were back in the Buick wagon again, continuing our slow but steady journey from sea to shining sea.

Chapter 26

Who knew we had relatives in Albuquerque? No matter how distant, we paid them a brief visit, I think just to get out of the car after our seemingly never-ending trek across Texas, to put some more coolant in the radiator, and to ask directions to the nearest church. Skipping Mass, no matter what the circumstance, was simply not a choice. Our destination was now Phoenix, where my mom's brother, Uncle Jack, and his wife lived. Mom and Maura had flown out to Phoenix several years earlier when Mom was trying to get her life—and her family—back together. Maybe Phoenix is where we need to be, she thought.

By now, it was the first or second week of February and we had missed at least two or three weeks of school. "Lord, think of all you're learning …" Mom would rationalize. "Other kids just read about and study our country. You're seeing it firsthand." She had a point—sort of—although I think most educators would frown on using that overstuffed brown Buick as a classroom. But we did learn some useful things on our journeys, like U.S. geography, how to read a map, and of course, the names of all the state capitals. For fun, we'd quiz Maura on them! Along the way, we also learned all sorts of useless trivia:

"Lord, sometimes it gets so hot in Phoenix that you can fry an egg on the sidewalk," Mom told us. Hmmm … I think I could have survived not knowing this, but it must have made an impression on me if I can still remember it after all these years.

Anyway, by the time we got to Phoenix, I think we all felt like we had reached the Promised Land. Although I didn't know Uncle Jack and his wife Aunt Phyllis all that well at the time, he was a hoot, his house was cool and comfortable—and the car's muffler and tailpipe were on their last leg. Uncle Jack fed us, made us laugh, tried his darndest, I'm sure, to help Peg figure out her next step—and took the wagon to his trusted mechanic to get it properly checked before the next leg of our journey to wherever.

The mechanic took one look under that car.

"Is this car for real?!!" he asked, amazed that we had made it this far given the Buick's numerous woes.

Against his better judgment, but for a few hundred bucks that no doubt Uncle Jack covered, he did everything he could to get the Peg-mobile in working order again. And then, a day or two later, we were on our way again. We had come so close, Mom decided, that we weren't going to stop until we reached California. Law school still beckoned. The sun and the sea were calling out to us. Besides, Mom had learned from Uncle Jack that an old high school boyfriend of hers—who had gone on to become a pilot—lived near Los Angeles.

Maybe we'd surprise him, too.

Chapter 27

The California of my dreams—especially as a twelve-year-old—was a lot more exciting than the reality of my first visit there in 1978. Like most kids, I envisioned a fantasy trip to Hollywood, where we'd visit the back lot of a movie studio—or better yet, the set of *Charlie's Angels*—and run into Farrah Fawcett, Kate Jackson, and Jaclyn Smith, all of whom would demand that I'd be cast in an upcoming episode. We'd then explore all the sites—the Hollywood Walk of Fame, Rodeo Drive, and of course Disneyland—on a fun-filled family vacation.

But despite the bragging rights I earned as a kid to say, "Yeah, I've been to California before!" the truth of the matter is the phrase "fun-filled family vacation" is anything but the way I would describe the memories of my time there.

After our extended cross-country journey in the wonder wagon, reaching the California state line should have made us feel as proud as an injured runner who finally made it to the finish line of the Boston Marathon. But our arrival was less euphoric. We were greeted at the border of the Golden State by an endless line of traffic and the state police, who were stopping every vehicle, we soon learned, on the lookout for an escaped convict.

Lovely.

Of course, I think even the state trooper figured, upon querying Mom and taking one look in our pathetic jitney, that an escaped convict would be completely nuts to tangle himself up with our car and the crew of misfits inside it. Still, knowing there was a criminal on the loose didn't necessarily fill any of us with vacation giddiness.

But onward we went toward Los Angeles, thanks to Merrick's navigational skills. Of course, if we thought traffic in Houston was bad, it seemed like a walk in the park compared to the hellish highways we were now on as we neared the City of Angels. To calm her nerves, Mom puffed like a madwoman on her cigarettes, turned off the radio, and this time literally did pull off the hectic highway to scream at us for fighting and making her a nervous wreck. By now we were all in tears—wishing this was just a bad movie straight out of Hollywood.

I think by this time even Mom was thinking, *What the hell am I doing here?*

After regaining her composure, Mom merged back on the highway—nearly getting sideswiped, as I recall—and finally decided she would pull off at the nearest exit or rest-stop to check in with Maggie, who (lucky for her) was three thousand miles away back in Bradford. A loved one's voice and encouragement are indeed powerful weapons when you're at wits-end.

She couldn't reach Maggie, so from the pay phone somewhere in California, I'm quite certain Mom placed a call—collect, most likely—to Aunt Faye. She talked on the phone for quite a while, keeping an eye on us kids waiting in the car, and became visibly upset. We had no idea what was going on, but it was a pathetic, heartbreaking sight.

It was so heartbreaking because Mom's heart literally was breaking. It had now been a few days since we left Phoenix and Uncle Jack, and we hadn't even spoken to anyone from our "real life" in Olean since then. So Aunt Faye had to break the horrific news to Mom that her spunky thirty-nine-year-old sister with four kids, Mimi—who shared her love for Billy Joel's "Just the Way You Are," among other things—had died unexpectedly a few days before on February 15. She had been struggling with complications from an overactive thyroid for a few years now, and it had ultimately—and tragically—led to heart failure. Maggie, Mitch, and Michele had all attended the funeral, but had no way of reaching us.

We kids were devastated. *Mimi was so young, so full of life and good cheer.*

Peg was even more devastated. *I didn't even know my own sister died, and now I've missed her funeral.*

I can't even begin to know the guilt Mom must have felt.

Gramma Jo was the most devastated. *How does a parent ever cope with losing a child?*

We never did make it to L.A. Or track down Mom's old flame. Or check out that law school we headed west in search of. In fact, we hadn't even been in California for twenty-four hours when Mom finally figured out where she was supposed to be.

Back in Olean.

Chapter 28

If we had been thinking clearly, we would have never headed back east on a desolate highway that took us straight through California's Mojave Desert—especially given the brown Buick's track record. Heck, if we had been thinking clearly, we would have never been in California or in that car in the first place! But I think we dozed in the car at a rest stop that evening after finding out about Mimi and followed the sunrise, and the nearest route, into the desert the next morning.

It must have been a Sunday, because I vaguely remember Mom harping about how we needed to get to Mass. In light of her sister's death, I'm sure she felt the need to get to church. But did we really think we'd find a church in the middle of the desert? We soon discovered miles and miles of nothing. Just a flat highway, lots of sand, and an occasional cactus here and there. The setting somehow reminded me of a Road Runner cartoon. If only it had been.

So there we were—a single mom and four kids in a clunker of a car—out in the middle of nowhere. Of course Murphy's Law had to prevail. More than halfway through the desert—some thirty miles or so away from Needles, California, according to the last road sign we saw—the car once again overheated in a big way. The "check engine" light came on. Smoke came billowing out of the front end. Tears came streaming down all of our faces, including Mom's.

Merrick got out and opened the hood, which he had grown accustomed to doing long ago. Mom swore a bit at first, stopped crying, then told us not to worry—pretending to remain calm. Of course we were traveling with no water or engine coolant. So we'd just wait for someone—anyone—to drive by and help us. We'd wait. And wait. And wait. It was the desert, after all.

Some nine hours later—thankfully right before nightfall and

after lots of prayers —some kind souls finally stopped and offered to help this desperate and panicked clan. By now the engine had cooled; they had some extra coolant in their truck, which they poured in our radiator, and then followed us all the way to the small town of Needles on the California/Arizona border—where I think we spent the night in the lot of the rinky-dink service station, praying now that they'd be able to fix the car the next morning.

Needless to say, we didn't get to Mass that day. But there was a whole lot of praying going on. The fact that, not unlike Moses, we eventually got out of the desert safely proves that the good Lord definitely heard our prayers.

Chapter 29

After our stint in the desert, the rest of our long—and I mean long, as in a couple of weeks—journey home seemed pretty mundane by comparison. From Needles, we traveled to Flagstaff, Arizona, where we got the car serviced (again) for real. By now I'm quite certain Mom was nearly out of cash, so I assume she wrote a couple bum checks to get us on our merry way, again, with the intention of paying back all her debts when she eventually got her back child support. We continued east—it must have been on Route 40, as I look back now—to Albuquerque, where, for a change of scenery we decided to go north to Colorado Springs. I think Mom had known someone who had gone to the Air Force Academy there eons ago. We arrived there at night, because I distinctly remember staying—again, probably on one of Mom's bum checks—at a beautiful hotel directly across from Pikes Peak for a day or two. We didn't tour it, but we could see the snowcapped mountain from our hotel room. From there we headed north to Denver to pick up Route 70 that would take us across the heartland of America. (On the highway near Denver, I vividly remember seeing a big overhead road sign for Cheyenne; that's how I always remember that Cheyenne is the capital of Wyoming.) Our journey across Kansas seemed endless, but I think we did it in a day and ended up spending the night near Kansas City. By now, we were all so sick of riding in that car for so long—it had been at least five or six weeks by now, all told—that we knew exactly how Dorothy from *The Wizard of Oz* felt as she professed, "There's no place like home." Who can travel through Kansas as a kid and not be reminded of *The Wizard of Oz*?

From Kansas City our journey east continued, and the next place I distinctly remember was St. Louis, Missouri, where we passed by the great arch. "It's the gateway to the West," Mom told us, as if we were in social studies class. Of course, by now it had been weeks since any of us had been in a classroom, so Mom would impart whatever bit of education she could. Looking back, it would have been nice if we had actually left town with a camera—you know, like real tourists on vacation—to capture some of these otherwise touristy sites and destinations. But at that time, we felt more like convicts on the run than tourists on the go. It seemed we wanted to do anything we could to forget—not remember—these memories in the making.

From there it was into Illinois just briefly (boy, I wish we would have taken a detour to Chicago!) and onto Indianapolis. When we finally entered western Ohio, somehow it felt like we were almost home—despite the fact that we still had another day or so of travel ahead of us. I know we stayed at other places along the way, but they must not have made much of an impression on me as a suddenly worldly twelve-year-old.

Hard to believe that we made it that far without any additional car trouble, although I think the ol' Buick was being held together at this point with a few screws, some rubber bands, a wing, and a prayer. When we finally hit Pennsylvania, it's like the car sensed that it hadn't given us much grief in quite a while. We had exited off the highway into some podunk Pennsylvania town to find a McDonald's or other fine dining establishment. After driving over a railroad crossing, we heard a thunderous boom that scared us all half to death. As we looked behind us to see what the heck happened, we saw our tailpipe and muffler laying in the middle of the road.

"Lord!" Mom shouted in frustration. She pulled over, and ordered Merrick and me to go get it. But do you think we gave one second's thought to the fact that a fresh-from-the-bottom-of-the-running-car muffler and tailpipe are sizzling hot? We both burned our hands, but ultimately got the stupid parts into the back portion of the wagon—just behind the backseat, propped against all the junk we had piled up. Of course, the next big bump in the road brought it tumbling down over the junk—smack-dab on Maura's head. We laugh hysterically about it now, but believe me, Maura the eight-year-old cried hysterically back then about being clobbered by a muffler.

By now, we were all so desperate to get home that I think we just ventured along in the mufflerless Peg-mobile despite the obvious stares and occasional shouts we'd get from other drivers. Miraculously, the car somehow made it a few more hours to Olean. And when at long last—nearly a month and a half after leaving town—we pulled into the driveway of 512, the car was truly on death's door. But we all suddenly felt like we had been given a new lease on life.

Indeed, Olean—and 512—never looked so good.

Until we walked in the front door.

Chapter 30

There was no life in the living room of 512. Death and darkness had completely taken over by the time we returned from our cross-country escapades. And grief and despair were consuming Gramma Jo, who, when we first walked in the house, was sitting in her rocker with the curtains completely drawn—despite the bright, late-winter sun that was melting the snow outside— sobbing silently.

They say that losing a child is the hardest loss of all. Even when that child is thirty-nine years old.

"Mom, I'm here …" said a broken-up Peggy as she embraced her devastated seventy-one-year-old mother. "We're here …" she corrected herself as Merrick, Mollie, Maura, and I all gathered around to group hug our grieving Gramma whose world had changed in the worst possible way since we had last seen her.

I learned early on—most likely from my Gramma Jo and my mom, neither of whom ever shied away from displaying their emotions for all the world to see—that there's nothing quite like a good cry to soothe a broken heart. It's as if the tears are intended to wash away all the pain and hurt that's bottled up inside. In fact, I think we kids were experts in nothing else but crying by this point in our young lives. So that's what I remember about our return to 512 that March day. We cried. We cried and cried for what seemed like hours—it was probably just ten or fifteen minutes—caught up in a world of overwhelming emotions: sadness over the death of Mimi, relief to be home again, elation from being out of that godforsaken Buick.

I guess maybe this is when it first dawned on me, at least knowingly, that the power of love really is greater than the power of death. Because despite their differences through the years—and believe me, there were many—Peg *had* to be there for her mom in her hour of greatest need. And Gramma was genuinely happy to have all of us back in her big, empty home again. Naturally, it didn't take long for us to make it feel not so empty.

I certainly didn't realize back then, but I now know that there were all sorts of valuable life lessons revealed to us on that long journey home, and on our ridiculous trips across and around the country (which we now affectionately refer to as our family vacations). Indeed, in that burning bomb of a car and in very unconventional ways, we kids somehow did learn how to cope, how to trust, how to appreciate, how to forgive. We witnessed firsthand the kindness of strangers, the beauty of nature, the promise of a new day. We discovered that home really is where the heart is, and that when all is said and done, family is what it's all about. But perhaps most of all, we discovered, many years later, that there someday comes a time when you can look back on some of life's most horrific experiences and see the rainbow, instead of just the rain.

So maybe Mom was right, after all. (She usually was.) We did learn a lot on our "vacations" that we would never have learned in the classroom.

Chapter 31

Believe it or not, I think even Mom had officially grown weary of the traipsing-across-the-country thing after our last road trip. So in the spring of '78, we settled in to 512 once again, this time more or less for good. Plus, I think Peg finally accepted the fact that we really did need to be in school—especially after the principal (a stern nun) at St. Mary's, the school up the street from 512 where Mollie was lucky enough to be enrolled for the end of seventh grade, informed her that "your daughter has been truant" for most of the school year.

Merrick was able to return to Walsh after his "semester break" and resume a normal freshman year—after having to deal with the embarrassing "Where were you?!" questions from his classmates and teachers. But as Maura's and my luck would have it, there was no room for us at St. Mary's, so we had to finish out the school year at the public school located just a block away from 512. I absolutely hated it, but it wasn't necessarily the school's fault. Could it have possibly been that this was now my third school that year alone? Looking back, it's a miracle that I ever passed sixth grade. I am certain that's why to this day I don't understand probability. It had to have been taught in sixth grade!

Despite our school woes, life somehow started to become a bit more normal, by Bednar standards anyway. By the time the summer of '78 arrived—and *Grease* was the word—life was beginning to look about as sunny as Olivia Newton John's on-screen personality. Now, granted, Mom had no real job, no major source of income (other than a measly eighty-five dollars a week in child support that my dad was eventually ordered to pay, which he did only sporadically), and no car. Yes, the Buick wagon really did bite the dust once and for all. I think the junkyard only gave Mom and Jeep fifty bucks for the whole thing, which they split! In fact, for the most part, Peg thrived on mayhem and manhattans, extra dry, with a twist, but insisted that we kids "do as I say, not as I do." To help make ends meet, she decided that she could earn a few extra bucks as a substitute teacher, an occasional pianist, and a full-time pain-in-the-you-know-what to Family Court. Her newest gig? To battle Mr. Bednar, as she always referred to him, for increased child support and the alimony which she had been denied in her divorce.

In an odd sense, petitioning the court and hauling my dad in and out of it became Mom's life's work for the next several years. In the front bedroom of 512, she set up her office—a card table, and old typewriter, and scores of yellow legal pads with her chicken-scratched notes on them—and worked diligently while we were at school preparing petitions, writing motions, and researching other legal mumbo-jumbo. Then she'd traipse up to the post office and mail her work to God knows who (judges, lawyers, court examiners, assemblymen, I think even the governor!) before walking another block or so to the Olean House, her favorite watering hole—where she'd imbibe a bit too much with her Golden Girl friends. Of course, my dad unknowingly helped energize Mom's "legal career" by never giving in and fighting her tooth and nail on every motion served. Needless to say, their divorce was a far cry from amicable. And as the years progressed, neither of them mellowed.

Fortunately, at that pivotal time in our young lives, we were lucky to have a few guardian angels watching over us: Gramma Jo, who put a roof over our head, paid the utilities with her Social Security check, and laid the law down like the town sheriff (thanks, Gramma); Aunt Faye (with the silent but ever watchful eye of Uncle Kenny), who made sure we kids had essentials like groceries, winter boots, and an occasional five bucks spending cash; and Michele—now in her mid-twenties, living on her own in nearby Allegany, and working full-time as an elementary teacher—who made sure that we had "normal" things every now and then like homemade cookies, a present or two at Christmas, jelly beans at Easter, and a ride to those few places to which we couldn't walk, bum a ride, or take the one ten-speed bike that we ultimately all shared (purchased at Sears by Gramma).

The summer of '78 also brought Maggie "home" to 512 (from Bradford), where she then spent her senior year of high school at Walsh. She picked up a job working as an aide at a local nursing home—sparking an interest in a career initially as a nurse but eventually health care in general—and earning three bucks or so an hour that kept spending money in her (and her younger siblings') pockets. Merrick started his sophomore year of high school at Walsh that fall, while Mollie returned to St. Mary's for eighth grade. Maura and I began our tenure at St. Mary's for fourth and seventh grades, respectively. I think at that time, tuition was free for parishioners. That's how Mom could afford to send us to Catholic elementary school. In high school, you had to work to subsidize your tuition.

If it was second grade when all hell broke loose, it was definitely junior high when the pieces finally seemed to be glued back together. In fact, I now joke with my wife that she should have known me then—seventh and eighth grades were definitely my peak years! I think because I was the new kid on the block, I came across as cuter, cooler, smarter, friendlier, and more popular that I really was. The guys liked me. The girls *loved* me. The teachers loved me. I got good grades. I made friends. In fact, Mollie and I shared many of the same friends—including our lifelong neighbor and onetime childhood nemesis Teri Tilly, who came to the door of 512 one day in seventh grade and asked us if we'd like to come to her house and play Payday. Since then, there's never been a friend quite like Teri! Heck, I was even named the MVP of the JV basketball team in seventh grade. I was hot stuff! And in eighth grade, things only got better. I landed a good role in my first real play, *Oliver Twist*, thereby officially sealing my love of the theater. Bummer thing was, the show was cancelled for some reason before we ever even got the chance to stage it!

I also met this wonderful, newly ordained young priest—Fr. Lary—who inspired me tremendously. I even got my first job in eighth grade as an occasional busboy at Antonio's, an Italian restaurant owned by the parents of my best friend, Mike—thereby officially beginning my working life, my financial independence, and my understanding of the value of a hard-earned dollar. Was it any surprise that by the time eighth grade was over, I was the class valedictorian and had earned a partial scholarship to Walsh? Who would have ever thought?

Our lives continued on this relatively normal track for the next few years. Maggie crossed the official threshold of adulthood and headed off to Boston College (I remember all of us being so sad to see her go), so then it was back to the four of us (Merrick, Mollie, Maura, and me) at 512 with Mom and Gramma. Oh, sure, we experienced the inevitable ups and downs of being adolescents and teenagers. We bickered (mainly with Maura!). We'd argue with Mom. We were mischievous occasionally with our friends. But for the most part, we were turning out to be pretty decent and responsible kids. We got good grades (don't ask me how!), hung with the right crowd for the most part, even got involved. All of which was quite miraculous considering everything we were lacking: money, a car, and a father, among other things.

So by the time MTV was all the rage—which Gramma certainly wouldn't let us watch, so I would catch it at Mike's—it seemed like the worst for the Bednar family was definitely behind us and the best was yet to come.

But as it turned out, even though we thought we had seen it all, we hadn't seen nothin' yet.

PART II

Merrick • Miracles • Marrow

Chapter 32

Growing up, I never thought once about my brother Merrick being any more or less special than anyone else. None of us did. He was just my brother. With just a two and a half year age difference, we were the best of brothers and the best of friends, especially as little kids. Except maybe for the time that I, at the age of five or six, punched him and broke his glasses. He hated those glasses, so in reality I think I did him a huge favor. If anyone had told me thirty years ago that Merrick was more special than most people I'd ever encounter in my lifetime, I never would have believed it. Nor would I have ever believed that Merrick's life would unfold in the extraordinary way it did.

Merrick was an adorable but somewhat squirrely kid—of course, so was I—who was fascinated with Hot Wheels, electronics, baseball, *The Wild, Wild West*, and super heroes, especially Batman. Those passions eventually evolved into an adult fascination with cool cars, gadgets of all kinds, every sport imaginable, action and adventure movies, and even more Batman. He so loved Batman, in fact, that as a kid he would frequently don a blue towel and I a yellow one and as fast as you could say, "To the Bat Cave!" we'd be transformed into the youngest and happiest dynamic duo that ever walked Gotham City (or the city of Olean, for that matter). One Christmas before the family fell completely apart, Santa brought him the best gift ever: a kid-sized, riding Batmobile and a Bat-utility belt.

As we got a bit older, Merrick definitely assumed the responsible role of big brother to his three younger siblings. Sometimes, in the heat of silly childhood arguments, we'd tell him, "You're not my father!" but for the most part, he was. Wise beyond his years, even as a kid, he'd protect us (after all, he was the man of the house for years), stand up for us (like the time in the Carters' driveway when he told the social worker he was a son of a bitch), or take the heat for us—except maybe for the time when Gramma Jo accused Maura and me of eating all her Fig Newtons. Merrick sat there, silent.

"We didn't eat them, Gramma. We don't even like them, I swear."

"Well, they didn't just walk away!" she said angrily in her gruff, disciplinarian voice.

"We don't know what happened to them, really," we pleaded honestly.

Several years later, Merrick 'fessed up to eating the cookies. You better believe we never let him live that down!

On all those outrageous adventures across country, Merrick was our chief navigator, despite being a few years shy of the legal driving age. Like Chewbacca in *Star Wars,* he took his role of Mom's co-pilot quite seriously, and somehow managed to guide her through a galaxy of four-lane highways, busy city streets, or desolate country roads. Of course, there were inevitably a few goof-ups, like the time Mom entered that busy Houston highway at night headed in the wrong direction, the time she drove the wrong way down a one-way street in Atlanta, or the time we got on the West Virginia Turnpike and had to take it a good twenty miles before being able to turn around and head in the direction we should have gone in the first place. But no matter what the mishap, Merrick miraculously guided us around and across country, three times, and kept his desperate mother and the three young siblings traveling in the backseat as safe as possible.

As life became slightly more normal, people were always drawn to Merrick like a magnet—an appeal that only increased as he got older. He was everything you could ever wish for in a son, and rightfully a huge source of pride for my mother: smart as a whip, friendly and polite to all, responsible, hard-working, kind and sincere, yet fun-loving, popular, and handsome. Standing about five foot nine, with a slim build, he was the shortest of the five Bednar brothers. He wore his hair neatly parted on the side, had a warm smile, an infectious laugh, and sincere brown eyes that also revealed an occasional devilish side to those who knew him well. Definitely the type of guy that most concerned parents of teenage daughters would wish for their daughter's date to the prom. (And date he did, although never too seriously.) Of course, Merrick was the first to say he was far from perfect. But he never was trying to be. He was always just himself, which explains why everyone who knew him loved him and enjoyed being with him.

When we were kids playing Matchbox, Merrick always dreamed of driving a Cadillac (boring Mike Marra and me to death with the details of the custom interior!), owning a car dealership and/or a restaurant, and living the good life—the kind we certainly never knew as kids. As a high school student at Walsh, he was a member of the National Honor Society, a presence at nearly all Walsh sporting events, an all-around nice guy, and, ultimately, the president of his senior class. However, by the middle part of his senior year, his avocation toward all things worldly had evolved humbly into a calling to something higher: the priesthood.

There are varying accounts about how my mother reacted when Merrick told her that he was thinking about becoming a priest. Never short on drama, I think my mom overreacted as she usually did to unexpected bombs like this with a "Dear Lord in heaven!" For despite the priesthood being the ultimate career choice for the son of a Catholic mother, I think Peg was completely caught off guard—something that didn't happen very often. "I'm gonna be a priest whether you like it or not," he emphatically told her. Fortunately, after getting over the surprise of the out-of-left-field news, it didn't take long for Peg, and all of us, to realize that Merrick's calling was, in fact, very real. Plus, being the mother of a priest-in-the-making had a certain cachet to it!

Merrick's long path to the priesthood was proof beyond a

doubt that the Good Lord definitely acts in mysterious ways. Here was this intelligent, well-liked, handsome kid in high school—who loved sports, cars, and having fun—who was looking into a prestigious Ivy League school (Cornell) among other respected colleges, who, instead, felt called to attend the unglamorous, one-oversized-building, all-male campus of Wadhams Hall Seminary College, home to no more than maybe a hundred students, in the tiny, cold Upstate New York town of Ogdensburg (population, fifteen thousand and dwindling) on the St. Lawrence River. Hardly the choice that most eighteen-year-olds would make—in 1981 or today. Many thought he was making the wrong decision, yet Merrick's powerful instincts told him otherwise.

While we all hated to see him leave home, Merrick's first year at Wadhams Hall, I recall, was a good one overall, although like many kids away at college during their first year, Merrick experienced some doubts about his chosen course of study. However, he performed well academically and made some new friends that first year, so he decided—after much thought, consideration, and, I'm sure, prayer—to return for a second year.

Like many college students, Merrick seemed to hit his stride during his sophomore year. Things were going well academically, socially, and, obviously, spiritually. But when he returned home to 512 for Christmas vacation that year, he was feeling pretty lousy. Maybe it was the flu, we all thought. But a few months later, at Easter vacation 1983, the young seminarian definitely wasn't his usual self. He still didn't feel well, he said, and, as I recall, he didn't look too terrific either—gray, thinner than usual, and frail. Fatigued and without an appetite, Merrick, along with everyone else, thought he was just worn out and dealing with the stress of a challenging semester. Nothing some serious sleep and a few good Peg meals couldn't fix.

Upon his return to Wadhams Hall to finish the school year, Merrick's flu bug continued to worsen. His fatigue consumed him, his once vigorous appetite was non-existent, and he even began to notice that, oddly, his favorite Docksiders were getting too tight despite his small frame. Then, one early May morning, after literally dragging himself out of bed for class, Merrick couldn't even put his shoes on—his ankles and feet were so swollen. At that moment, he knew it was definitely something more than the flu. Concerned, but never the type to panic, he calmly asked one of his friends in the dorm if he could borrow his car. With no nurse in the school at that time, he thought, just to play it safe he'd pay a visit to the emergency room. So he waddled out to his buddy's orange Ford Pinto in some flip-flops—the only thing he could get on his suddenly fat feet—and drove himself to the Ogdensburg Hospital.

Fortunately, the ER in Ogdensburg was no Bellevue, so Merrick was seen quickly by the doctor on duty. After asking his patient a few questions, checking some of his vitals, and ordering some tests, the doctor could not believe what had just walked in the door:

A nineteen-year-old seminarian in complete heart failure.

Chapter 33

We call it Bednar luck.

But, believe me, it won't win you the lottery.

"Lord," my mom would always say. "If it weren't for bad luck, I'd have no luck at all."

So it figures that any sense of relative normalcy we had came to a screeching halt on, till then, perhaps the biggest day of my seventeen-year-old life: Friday, May 6, 1983, opening night of Walsh's annual spring musical, *Oklahoma!* I was all set to make my big debut as the tap-dancing, scene-stealing Will Parker in the high school gym. OK, it wasn't Broadway, but I was still pretty excited. That was the day we learned that Merrick was playing—for real—the role of a heart patient in serious condition in the intensive care unit at a hospital some six hours away.

Was it a heart attack? A heart problem? Who knows? It couldn't be. Merrick was only nineteen, two months away from twenty. *He'll be fine,* Mollie, Maura, Mom, and I collectively told ourselves, after initially falling apart upon hearing the news, and then spreading it by phone to the rest of the family. Mom—and, when he heard the news, my brother Mitch—was in touch with the rector of the seminary, who was now at Merrick's side and dealing with the doctors until someone could get there.

"Tell Martial to 'break a leg' tonight," Merrick told the priest, who relayed the message by phone. "Everything's going to be OK."

Just like the song says: "*Oklahoma, you're OK!*"

And it was—at least for the weekend. The show went on, I nailed my part each night, and I think I even received a standing ovation (most likely out of sympathy as the news about Merrick spread).

But, unlike a Rodgers and Hammerstein musical, Merrick's

problems weren't resolved in two hours—and they definitely weren't something worth singing about.

Chapter 34

"We're not exactly sure what's wrong with Merrick …"

"Merrick's situation is very unusual …"

"Merrick is very sick …"

So went the initial reports from the doctors in Ogdensberg who cared for Merrick those first few days in ICU. My brother had always been easy-going, but his newfound medical situation was anything but.

"We'd like to transfer him to Upstate Medical Center in Syracuse for more tests." That was about the only thing the doctors could agree on.

By this time, my brother Mitch was on the case—which was a good thing, because in May 1983 he was about the only one in the family who had the wherewithal to see a big huge forest looming beyond the trees. In times of crisis, logic, objectivity, and any sense of calmness went out the window when it came to my mom. I love her dearly, but those were never among her best traits. Maura, Mollie, and I were basically just kids who didn't even begin to understand the severity of the situation at hand. Not long before Merrick started feeling sick, Maggie and her longtime boyfriend Alan had become engaged and were about to be married at the end of the month, so they were a bit distracted to say the least. As for twenty-somethings Mark and Mike, their Southern lives were seemingly coming apart at the seams, and they had all they could do to deal with their own problems. And by now, my dad hadn't been involved in our lives, especially for us younger kids, in nearly ten years.

So Mitch—and, of course, the always reliable and concerned Michele—stepped up to the plate in a big way in a role typically reserved for parents.

Now there's a reason why, up to this point, you haven't heard a lot about my brother Mitch. Seven years my senior, that made him about fourteen when the family *really* fell apart—which is the exact time that I can begin recalling most of my childhood memories. Since Mitch was lucky enough to escape our bizarre around the country three times and back escapades in the mid seventies (of course, his life back in Olean was no picnic then, either), I felt like I barely knew him as a kid. Then, as I grew older, he had managed to put himself through college, so I only saw him occasionally. My mom used to always say, "Lord, it's like I had two families"—and in a way, with a seventeen-year span between her youngest and oldest child, and a nasty divorce in between, it was true. Mitch was definitely part of the "older family," as were Mark and Mike. Michele, and to an extent, Maggie, were the only siblings who bridged both.

Anyway, in May 1983, Mitch was a couple months shy of twenty-five and worlds away from his roots in Olean. He, too, was engaged—to his college sweetheart, Eileen—but he was also on the corporate fast-track at Eastman Kodak Company. In the few short years since his graduation from St. Bonaventure in 1980, Mitch had become a successful, self reliant, self-assured (some would say cocky) rising star of a businessman—in all seriousness, thanks to no one but himself. For despite—or most likely, because of—the chaos in his teen years, he was disciplined, hard working, self-directed, self-motivated, and a heck of an athlete to boot! Those traits, among others in Mitch, were ones that, ultimately, his younger siblings would eventually try to emulate. Yet, in all honesty, at that time Mom and us younger kids were often put off by Mitch. We sometimes perceived his "newfound wealth" (which was simply a consistent and hard-earned paycheck!) as something that placed him in the category of the "haves" while we were definitely still the "have-nots." His sales career at Kodak initially catapulted him from podunk Olean to bustling Boston, where he lived for a few years, and then on to other exciting destinations through his travels. And his businesslike demeanor and sometimes gruff exterior often masked his sense of humor, his deep concern for our plight, and his genuine heart of gold. Still, as a kid, Mitch always came across to me as a "do-you-have-your-homework-done?" father instead of a "give-'em-a-wedgy!" brother.

In sharp contrast to Mitch, there was Michele: the demure, diligent, soft-spoken school teacher who was about to turn thirty and finish her master's degree, and who was building a much simpler life in and around Olean. Like Mitch, Michele, too, could came across as strict to us younger kids, but her kind heart all but glowed, and like Mary Tyler Moore—to whom we often likened our oldest sister because of her appearance, her tall, slender build, and her seventies single-girl lifestyle—she could turn the world on with her smile. While we didn't see her each and every day growing up, Michele was much more of a presence in our daily lives.

So there they were: Mitch, the born leader and strategist with a bark and bite that commanded attention; and Michele, the always reliable, detail-oriented, behind-the-scenes first mate who could take orders and execute well. All of the sudden, more out of necessity than desire, they had become the captains of our ship, guiding this family, with some help and support from a few of Merrick's close priest friends, into the new, uncharted, and often choppy waters that lie ahead.

Smooth sailing it was not—especially for Merrick.

Chapter 35

"There is absolutely no medical reason I can tell you why your brother is alive."

That, according to Mitch years later, was the sobering way he was first greeted by the cardiologist at Upstate Medical Center who examined Merrick, who had by now appointed Mitch as the family go-to guy.

It was clear from the get-go that the doctors—and now Merrick and Mitch—knew that something was seriously wrong with Merrick's heart. The tests ruled out an actual heart attack—which was good news, we all thought—but the diagnosis was still not clear, at least to most of us in the family. It had something to do with an enlarged heart, but I, for one, didn't really understand it all. I never was big on biology!

When I first saw Rick—did I mention that I had started using a shortened version of Merrick's name sort of on a lark in high school, and it began to stick?—it seemed like medicine alone was going to fix whatever the heck his problem was. In fact, by the time I finally made it to the hospital to see him, he looked good, his spirits were up, and his swelling was down—thanks to lots of Lasix and other drugs, no doubt. It was a huge relief to see him again, especially after the panic we had all felt when we first learned about his visit to ICU several days before.

In the short term, the doctors treated Merrick's symptoms and focused on getting him well enough to be able to leave the hospital. So in addition to putting him on a bunch of medications, they recommended some basic lifestyle changes that all cardiac patients must follow—a low-salt diet, reduced stress, limited physical activity, and the like—and suggested that he follow up with his family doctor. Considering that we really didn't have one back in Olean—*did we even have any health insurance?*—that was easier said than done.

In light of all that had happened, I believe that Wadhams Hall had exempted Merrick from his finals that year—he was at the top of his class anyway—so he returned to Olean to relax and recharge for the summer of '83. With guidance from Mitch's close doctor friend and others, Merrick found and was seen by a cardiologist in Buffalo, who apparently maintained the status quo for a while. Not surprising, Rick was an excellent patient, and followed doctors' orders to a tee. Maybe this wasn't going to be as bad as we had all first imagined.

It wasn't exactly the summer vacation of a college student's dreams, yet from the get-go, Merrick adjusted to his new sedentary lifestyle as if it were no big deal. During the day, he spent most of his time reading and watching the *Young and the Restless* daily from 12:30 to 1:30. During the evenings, he played Stratomatic, a geeky baseball board game, with a couple of his baseball-obsessed buddies from his high school days. (Maura and I quit during the first "season.") Not exactly how most guys turning twenty would choose to spend their summer vacation, but it seemed OK in Merrick's case—since playing baseball for real, or getting a summer job, or climbing stairs for that matter, was out of the question. But looking back, I've got to believe that Merrick also spent more hours than anyone knows planning for—and praying about—whatever lay ahead.

Of course, Merrick's health scare was not my family's only big event of the summer of '83. Mom, at long last, had somehow managed to finish that elusive master's degree she had started seemingly a lifetime ago in Eldred. Mollie graduated from high school and was now college-bound, and Maura graduated from eighth grade and was Walsh-bound. Even Maggie was graduating—to motherhood—as she and her new husband announced that they were expecting. As for me, I had decided early in my junior year of high school to accelerate my courses; then, by taking a summer English course at Bona's, I'd have all the credits I'd need to graduate a year early. So that's what I did—much to the chagrin of the principal and guidance counselor at the time.

"Martial, I'm afraid you're shortchanging yourself," the kind but strict nun told me. "You say now that you're planning to go to college, but you probably won't …"

But in all honesty, I simply had had enough of high school in general—and Walsh in particular—after three years, and Mom backed me up, primarily because she couldn't stand it if anyone told her kids no.

It's not that I didn't have good times and good friends in my class, because I did. But my very best buddies (Mike Marra and MaryAnne McCormick) were graduating with Mollie—which bummed me out in a big way—and Mike, who bombed around in his mom's Chevy truck, had become my primary source of transportation. Plus, I had been working now for a year or so at McDonald's (I was the best drive-through guy you could ever imagine!) and Antonio's (even waiting tables on occasion), and convinced myself that I could sock away a small fortune for college. (Yeah, right—on three fifty an hour!) Digging deeper, though, I think the biggest reason why I wanted out early was because I had finally realized that everything about my life was so abnormal. I had no dad, no car, no money except what I earned, no phone on occasion, a grandma that ruled the roost, and only one parent … who definitely marched to the beat of her own drum and only sometimes paid the tuition …while most of my classmates and peers came from such seemingly normal families. I wasn't jealous, just insecure, I guess. In grade school, it was bearable. But in high school, at least to me in the early 1980s, there was nothing worse or more embarrassing than that. Ironically, had I been a lousy student who got bad grades and caused trouble, it probably would have been easier. I might have fit in better, at least in my mind. But instead, I had the curse of being an honor student, a class officer, and a pretty well liked guy. Oh, well … as Merrick would say: "What are you gonna do …?"

So I guess we grew up a lot during the summer of '83. By sharing some of life's ups and downs with a collective focus on Merrick, who, thank God didn't seem to get any worse by summer's end, we matured, both as individuals and as a family, in ways that I know we didn't realize at the time. Like we had always done, we simply dealt with whatever curveball life threw our way, and tried hard not to strike out.

Chapter 36

So there's also this thing we call "Bednar timing."

For the most part, it goes hand in hand with the aforementioned "Bednar luck."

It's kind of like Murphy's Law, Bednar style.

For instance, it's like finding out that Merrick was seriously sick on the opening night of *Oklahoma!* Or finding out that he's even sicker on Mitch and Eileen's wedding day: September 10, 1983.

At least it was at the reception.

Mitch and Eileen's wedding was the first normal wedding I remember. That's because Eileen was the first daughter to be married from a very nice, normal family—two happily-married parents and three younger sisters—so tradition and marriage in general actually had real meaning. Anyway, even before Merrick had became sick months before, Mitch had asked him to be one of his groomsmen. Trust me: That was about the only normal thing that our side of the family brought to the table at Mitch's wedding—but that's a whole other story!

Having just returned to Wadhams Hall after his low-key, no-crisis summer to begin his junior year a couple of weeks before the wedding, Merrick's normal "I'm OK" attitude made it seem like he was, in fact, OK. I think he bummed a ride from a classmate from Ogdensberg to Syracuse, Eileen's hometown, where we met up with him from Olean the day before the ceremony. And while he looked dapper in his tux the Saturday morning of the wedding (a whole lot dapper, I might add, than my mom's date who wore a brown leisure suit and white socks!), the photos of that day clearly show that his coloring definitely was off—even though we didn't notice right away.

To tell you the truth, the whole episode is kind of a blur to me. But by the time Merrick made it with the wedding party to the reception, he had to race into the men's room to puke his guts out. He was sweating, breathing hard, and feeling lousy—and he hadn't touched a bit of booze. Not wanting to totally disrupt his own wedding, Mitch-the-groom discreetly informed Mollie and his doctor friend who was there as a guest, and the two of them took Merrick to, you guessed it, the honeymoon suite to tend to him.

The next thing I knew, Merrick was back in the emergency room at Upstate Medical Center a few hours later—ironically, the exact same hospital he had been sent a few months before.

But this time it didn't take long for the doctors to figure out what the sick kid in the tux needed: a pacemaker for his heart, which was barely beating.

Chapter 37

So in September 1983—at the ripe old age of twenty—my brother became the proud owner of a new pacemaker, which, just days after Mitch's wedding, was implanted in Merrick's upper left chest to help regulate the erratic beating of his own heart. Now, it would seem like the whole thing should have been a very big deal, but once again somehow Merrick made it seem like it wasn't—at least to his mother, his brothers, and his sisters. In fact, from the very onset of his health issues only a few months before, Merrick—a twenty-year-old kid—had this uncanny, almost unbelievably calm and rational way of dealing with things that would freak most people out, thereby reducing the fears and worries of all of us who cared about him.

"Everything's going to be OK," he'd always reassure us oh-so-nonchalantly. And with a restricted diet, limited activity, and numerous medications, it seemed like it was.

At the time, I didn't think much of it.

Now I marvel at it.

So before long, Merrick was back at Wadhams Hall again, able to continue his junior year of college without missing a beat—literally—and, within limits, even becoming a bit more active. Of course, how mean was I? I used to tease him to "Call Cardio Care!"—some monitoring service for people with pacemakers—when, on breaks, he'd come home to 512 and get frustrated, flushed, or stressed out for any reason. We used to both crack up about it.

With Merrick seemingly on the mend, it was back to life as we knew it in Olean. In January '84, I turned eighteen and—like all eighteen-year-olds—believed full well that I knew it all. So during the yearlong sabbatical that I was enjoying from high school—now working in the men's department of AM&A's, a store in the Olean Center Mall, in addition to waiting tables every now and then at Antonio's—I had decided that I, with all of three or four Walsh theatrical productions under my belt, was going to be an actor. Watch out Hollywood, here I come! With absolutely no guidance whatsoever, I applied to colleges far and wide that had a theater major. I ultimately visited, auditioned at, and chose to attend a small liberal arts college that had a strong theater program—and a brand new theater, with which I fell in love the moment I saw it. The only problem, which I didn't pay a stitch of attention to until I got there in the fall of '84, was that it basically was located in the middle of a cornfield in rural Pennsylvania.

Not exactly the launching pad for many Academy Award winners—and not exactly my idea of a fun place to spend the next four years.

It was no coincidence that it was Merrick, who had now begun his final year at Wadhams Hall, who helped me realize, through phone calls and letters back and forth, that it was OK to transfer after one semester. "Who cares? If you don't like it, get out of there," he advised his little brother, who still seemed to turn to him in times of need.

So after just one semester—even though I landed an understudy role in the first collegiate role for which I auditioned (a real coup for a freshman, I learned)—I transferred to Nazareth College, a school my mom had wanted me to consider when I first applied to college, in January 1985. Peg didn't ever really want me to leave Olean—or her—but since she had attended Nazareth for that one semester in the forties, and because it was only two hours away in Rochester, it was on the "Mom-approved" list. Fortunately, my decision to attend "Naz" turned out to be a very good one. And thankfully, between scholarships, loans, and earnings, I was able to scrape up enough to pay the tuition and room and board.

But just as my life took a turn for the better, Merrick's took another turn for the worse: In February '85, he went back into heart failure and subsequently needed his pacemaker replaced, again at Upstate Medical, where he was now seemingly becoming a regular. "No big deal," he assured us all, and again, he made it look true. In fact, just a few months later, he stood proudly in his cap and gown delivering the commencement address at his graduation from Wadhams Hall. It was definitely a high moment for all of us, given the numerous lows Merrick had experienced health-wise since he entered Wadhams.

But it definitely *was* a bigger deal than my now officially seminary-bound brother let on.

Merrick was living on borrowed time.

And, unlike his heart, the clock was steadily ticking.

Chapter 38

Somehow, when life is plugging along and things for the most part are OK, we all go about our lives, believing that terrible things simply won't happen to us or someone we love. You know, things like horrible accidents ... awful crimes ... life-threatening illness. They happen to people you don't know. Distant people. People you only read about in the newspaper. People you pity on the evening news. Terrible things certainly aren't supposed to rain down on your twenty-two-year-old brother who's studying to be a priest.

But by the summer of '86, Merrick's downpour was just beginning.

I had just completed a great sophomore year of college at Nazareth and had returned home to Olean for a carefree, stress-free summer. Now twenty, I was waiting tables at Antonio's in the evening as my summer job, and overall things seemed pretty good to naïve and fun-loving me.

It was a sunny and warm morning, Memorial Day 1986. Merrick, who had just completed his first year of graduate studies in theology at Christ the King Seminary near Buffalo, despite going into heart failure again in January, was sitting on the porch of 512, his now frequently swollen ankles elevated, reading the *Times Herald* as I dashed out the door to the honk of Teri Tilly's blue AMC hatchback. Mollie, who was already in the car, and I were headed to Teri's parents' camp for a dip in the pool. Merrick stopped me on my way.

"Where you going?" he asked, uncharacteristically short.

"To Teri's camp, swimming," I replied.

"Well, I want you guys back by six o'clock," he commanded. "I want to have a meeting."

"A meeting? About what?" I asked, confused by his mysterious request and unusually serious nature.

"I'll tell you later," he said, firmly and slightly irritated. "Just be there. And make sure Mollie is here, too."

"Whatever ..." And off we went to enjoy the holiday, not giving much more thought to Merrick's request.

By the time six o'clock rolled around, everyone was assembled in the living room of 512 as Merrick had instructed each of us individually throughout the day: Mom, Maura, Mollie, Michele, Maggie and Alan—even Mitch and Eileen, who had, surprisingly, come down from Rochester for the day. They hardly ever just did that. Gramma Jo had spent the day at her daughter Paula's, which she would typically do on Sundays and holidays.

I remember I was seated in the middle of the green-striped couch, and Merrick was in arm-off-button-loose.

"There's really no easy way to tell you this ..." the calm and rational Merrick began.

"Oh, dear Lord ..." Mom instantly started to panic, without even knowing where he was going with this.

"Will you please just hear me out?" he snapped. Then he continued.

My twenty-two-year-old brother went on to calmly and rationally tell all of us for the first time—except Mitch and Michele, with whom he had met with just a few weeks prior to plan the rollout of this major news—that his most recent biopsy (a word with which we had become increasingly familiar) indicated that he was in immediate need of a heart transplant.

Did I hear that right?

A heart transplant?!

Yes. A heart transplant.

Chapter 39

We all thought Merrick "just" had an enlarged heart. Well, he did, he explained. But he also told us that he had been living the past three years with cardiomyopathy—a word I had never heard before then, I assure you—a degenerative heart disease for which there is no cure.

Except for a successful heart transplant.

Although we were just beginning to understand the life-and-death nature of Merrick's heart condition, he had been living the past three years knowing the seriousness of it. The cardiologist at Upstate, we later learned, first suspected it and mentioned it to Mitch, who, from the beginning, helped Merrick work through the choices he would ultimately have to face. Then it was confirmed by his cardiologist in Buffalo, who later referred him to the National Institutes of Health for a series of studies, which ultimately indicated that he could be an ideal candidate for a potential transplant.

In plain talk, my unbelievably under-control soon-to-be-twenty-three-year-old brother told his stunned and scared siblings and his emotional wreck of a mother that his enlarged heart simply was not, and had not been, functioning properly. He had learned just weeks ago that he now was in urgent need of a new heart in order to live, and, after consultations with his doctors, his close priest friends and spiritual advisers, and Mitch and Michele, he had made up his mind that he was going to go through this life-threatening surgery. He wanted to live, he assured us. There was no doubt about that.

Like a good doctor talking to his confused patients, Merrick explained as much as he could about the process he would have to endure, the success rates of heart transplants, and, at the recommendation of his doctors, that he would undergo his surgery in Pittsburgh—a four hour drive from Olean, but "one of the best transplant centers in the world." He acknowledged that he didn't begin to have all the answers to our questions—*What?! When? How? Why?*—but that he would know more once he went for his final evaluation in the week ahead. If all went well, he would be placed on a national donor list, and then wait for a good match. To help enlighten us, he even had a copy of a made-for-TV movie about a young guy who needed a heart transplant—I think it was called *Tuesday's Child*—starring Rob Lowe.

I dare say that most people facing this ordeal would be in hysterics and denial. Not Merrick. He simply reassured us that he was going to get through this, but that there were risks involved. He was placing his faith in God and the doctors. He needed us to do the same, and to give him our prayers and support.

Initially, I was too young and ignorant to fully comprehend that Merrick would be receiving the heart of someone who would die, most likely suddenly and tragically. I also was too naïve at that time to know that there were far more people in need of a heart than there were people willing to donate them.

All my family and I really knew is that we were in definite need of a miracle.

"Just keep the faith," Merrick assured us, "and everything will be OK."

Chapter 40

Over the next several weeks, while awaiting final confirmation from the doctors that he was indeed a suitable candidate for transplant—and from the social workers that Medicare and/or Medicaid would pay for it—Merrick failed rapidly: tiring after any kind of activity, barely eating a full meal, vomiting frequently, and severely bloating as if pregnant. It was now easy for everyone to clearly see that he was in heart failure, and desperately needed that new heart to come.

I think this is when prayer took on a new and urgent meaning to me and the rest of my family. *Please God, help Merrick. Please God, help us.*

As a seminarian, our brother, before taking seriously ill, had been placed in a summer residency at a large urban church in Buffalo—St. James—originally to help at the parish and learn about his future ministry. But given his unusual circumstances, he obviously couldn't do much but still was allowed to reside there—specifically because it was about fifteen minutes from the Buffalo airport. He had learned that when—no, make that *if*—he got a call that the hospital had received a donor heart, he'd only have about four hours before needing to be prepped for surgery in Pittsburgh. So staying in Olean, nearly two hours from the airport and a good four drive to Pittsburgh, was out of the question.

After spending most of the month of June at 512 with us and trying, as best as we all could, to plan the details of his transplant (we wisely started a journal to keep track of everything), Michele, Mom, and I drove Merrick to St. James on Sunday, June 29. We were greeted by a friendly priest, Fr. Bob, who showed us around the rectory and assured us that Merrick would be in good hands. Still, it was hard to leave him there.

By the time Merrick's twenty-third birthday rolled around

just sixteen days later on July 15, and we saw him again, our brother was weaker, more bloated, and more uncomfortable than ever. He also had had another heart biopsy and several other tests which showed that, on top of everything else, he had developed fluid in his lungs and around his hips, which made it very difficult to sit or lie comfortably, and that his liver was distended. Despite this, Merrick still somehow managed to have good spirits and remarkable control of his emotions.

In honor of his birthday, my Mom had brought her ailing son a heart-shaped helium-filled balloon—she always loved balloons—which he ended up tying around his bedpost. Fr. Bob predicted that by the time that balloon hit the ground, Merrick would get his new heart.

Oh, wouldn't that be great? While no one verbalized it, we all knew—most of all, Merrick—that we were running out of time.

A week later, on Wednesday, July 23, Maggie called Merrick at St. James to check in.

"I'm two weeks overdue," the poor guy said, likening himself with his huge protruding belly to a ready-to-pop pregnant woman. He was terribly uncomfortable, and the intense July heat and humidity that year only made things worse. Rarely one to complain, he simply couldn't hide how difficult it was to sit, stand, or sleep. Feeling terrible for him—while trying to juggle our own schedules of work and life—Maggie told Merrick and noted in the journal: "Plan road-trip on Saturday, 7-26."

By the time Merrick attempted to go to sleep two days later, on a muggy Friday evening, he noticed that his birthday balloon was nearly touching the ground.

Chapter 41

There's nothing quite like that ring of the phone that startles you out of a deep sleep. It scares the hell out of you and sets your heart racing from zero to sixty, literally, in a heartbeat. Calls like that stay with you forever.

Like the one that pierced the Saturday morning silence at 512 on July 26, 1986.

Despite the horrible night's sleep I had just had, thanks to the unbearable July humidity that summer, I shot up from bed, startled, but almost as if I knew the call was coming. I squinted at the digital alarm clock on the dresser: 6:42 a.m. I stumbled across the partially sunlit room to the phone, now beginning to ring a second time, and, trying to sound like I'd been awake for hours (why is it that everyone always does that?), cleared my throat and answered.

"Hello?" I said sheepishly.

"Is Merrick there?" asked the incredibly calm, friendly, and awake voice on the other end.

Confused, I began to stutter, "No … he … uh … is in Buffalo."

Before I could manage to spit out any more words, my mother interrupted on the downstairs extension. I did not hang up.

"Hello," she answered quickly, urgently.

The voice on the other end began again. "Hello, Mrs. Bednar? This is Dr. Getty from the University of Pittsburgh Medical Center. I'm calling to get in touch with Merrick. We've located a suitable donor heart for him."

I stood there, momentarily paralyzed—unable to speak, unable to actually believe what I had just heard. Then, like a bolt of lightning, Mollie burst into the room, knowing full well what was happening without me uttering a single word. We huddled around the phone, listening wholeheartedly to the conversation that continued between our mother and the doctor.

"... Yes, Mrs. Bednar, I realize that Merrick is in Buffalo," Dr. Getty, one of the best cardiothoracic surgeons in the country, continued. "But we prefer that his family contact him with the news and then have him get in touch with us immediately. I'll give you the number."

"Just ... uh ... let me get a piece of paper, doctor," my mother somehow managed to stutter in her frenzied state. I'm sure her heart was beating as fast as mine.

The doctor slowly gave the number of his private extension to my mother, gave it again, and repeated it a third time. Then he asked her to repeat what she had just written. It was a good thing, too, for she had copied it down incorrectly, as he had anticipated. By now, no doubt, this type of confusion was routine to him.

The July sun was already peeking through the curtains of the front room as I hung up the phone. My heart was racing, but I said nothing as I raced Mollie down the hallway of 512 to Maura's room.

"Maura," I blurted out as I burst open her bedroom door. "Rick's got a heart!"

Instantly, she popped up from underneath the covers in disbelief. "Really?"

As if it were Christmas morning, Mollie, Maura, and I bolted downstairs into the kitchen, where the pandemonium was just beginning. We dialed Rick's number at St. James, huddled around the phone, and told him the news collectively: "You've got a heart!" we said, with 90 percent enthusiasm and 10 percent fear. We all wanted to talk to him individually, to reassure him, to tell him we loved him, but the clock was ticking, so we did so briefly, and then said a quick group "Our Father." In typical Bednar fashion, we got all choked up, and I could tell Rick was, too. I knew that his tears, like ours, were primarily tears of joy, but I'd be lying if I said there were no tears of fear mixed in.

Despite the early morning chaos, we tried hard to remain calm. There was a great deal to be done in a short amount of time—people to notify, plans to put into motion, as we had discussed—and until that moment, we thought we had everything under control. But despite our best-laid plans, we soon discovered that there's no such thing as a dress rehearsal for your brother's heart transplant. Still, we managed to overcome the immediate hysteria and did what we were supposed to do: alert the troops. In spite of the seriousness of the moment, it was downright funny to experience everyone's initial 7 a.m. over-the-telephone reactions:

The first person we called, of course, was Michele. And in typical, matter-of-fact, and soft-spoken fashion, she simply said, "OK, I'll be right up." And true to form, she arrived to pick up Mom some thirty minutes later—with muffins in hand. She was already up and had been baking them to take to Merrick's that day.

Merrick was to call Mitch and his priest friend/mentor/ spiritual adviser at the time, Fr. Paul. They were the two who would accompany Merrick on the chartered flight from Buffalo to Pittsburgh. We now laugh at what Mitch—for lack of a better term, our transplant captain—did after finding out and kicking into high gear: Since he lived in Rochester at the time, some seventy miles away from Merrick, he ordered Michele to call the New York State Police at 7 a.m. to tell them that their brother was having a heart transplant, that both he and she would be speeding, and they needed an escort. Probably thinking this was some sort of prank call, the dispatcher told Michele, "Ma'am, the speed limit is there for your safety." (So much for the police escort!)

Getting ahold of Maggie and Alan proved to be an unexpected challenge. We tried and tried and tried, and yet for some reason they were not answering their phone. So I think Mom had the brilliant idea of calling the Bradford police to explain the situation and have an officer go to their house to pound on the door, which—amazingly—they did. It turned out that Maggie and Alan, who had just had a brand new waterbed delivered the day before but had had a dreadful night's sleep on it (or whatever!), had finally fallen sound asleep not long before morning broke and simply never heard the phone ring. They were startled in a big way from their deep sleep by the loud rapping on their front door. I suspect that it was Alan who got up, in nothing but his boxer shorts, to find a cop at his front door delivering the amazing news. Only in this family!

Now obviously, Gramma Jo had woken up at 512 during all the commotion and had come downstairs to see what was happening. At seventy-nine years old, she was simply overwhelmed and overcome by it all and sat down at the kitchen table sobbing silently, shoulders shaking almost as if she were laughing. We kids did our best to comfort her and calm her down. But we knew she'd have to go to Paula's house for the day as the stress was simply too much for the dear woman—who absolutely adored Merrick—to handle.

The only other people we called right away were Aunt Faye and Uncle Kenny, as Mitch was going to take care of contacting Mike and Mark. As I've said before, our dear great-aunt and uncle have always been the calm in every Bednar family storm, and today was no exception. Aunt Faye, still driving and sharp as a tack at eighty-one, said she'd be over from Eldred after she and "Kenneth" attended morning Mass. "How's Jo?" she inquired.

I still marvel at how my mother was holding it together throughout all of this. Considering that her son who had just turned twenty-three years old eleven days ago was about to undergo heart transplant surgery in four hours, Peg was a rock. The lady is something else, I've got to admit. For while I have always been mystified by the fact that she would completely lose it when some minor "bad" thing—like Maura getting her ear pierced for the second time!—or some wonderful thing that she didn't like—like any of her kids getting engaged!—would happen, during times of *genuine* crisis like this, nothing could topple this wonder woman. So, smoking like a fiend to calm her nerves, Peg hustled around like a marathon runner that morning, making coffee, applying her makeup, yes, even throwing in a load of laundry, preparing for her journey to Pittsburgh with Michele. I had to chuckle, when, some thirty minutes after the initial call, Peg—in black pumps and pearls but still in curlers—raced down 512's cracked sidewalk, got in Michele's gray Grand Prix, and rode away as if she were merely on the way to the grocery store.

Maggie arrived shortly thereafter to manage "communications central" with Mollie, Maura, and me. Alan stayed home with their 2-1/2-year-old son Ben. Our ever-thoughtful Aunt Faye arrived by 9:30 or so, with donuts in hand, to make sure everyone was doing OK.

And we were, for the most part, considering what was happening. Our mood was mellow and introspective, just like the light rain that fell softly that morning—for the first time in weeks, in fact, offering some refreshing relief to the unbearable July humidity. We shared hugs, tears, and some occasional laughter, but mostly we were silent, taking comfort, as usual, in simply being together.

It was definitely going to be a long day. So all we could do was wait, worry, and wonder.

Chapter 42

How was Merrick handling all of this? That's all everyone wondered—both silently and out loud. On July 26, 1986, it was impossible for us to know. But we eventually learned when he shared his deepest thoughts with us and wrote about his amazing heart-to-heart experience:

The days leading up to my transplant were physically uncomfortable, yet emotionally and spiritually exciting. They consisted of little more than reading, praying, watching TV, and trying to rest—due to the intense heat of the summer and the poor condition of my body.

The day I received the call from Dr. Getty, I was relieved, excited, and nervous, yet I sensed a calm that had accompanied me throughout all of my struggle. There were very few times from the initial onset of my disease right through the day of my transplant that I had feelings of anger, despair, and uncertainty. I believe this was because not only did my inner disposition recognize that much of what happened to me was not in my hands, but God's, but also because so many people shared their concern with me throughout my ordeal. Without the tremendous support of my family, friends, and others— many of whom I have never met and can only thank in prayer—I never would have been able to deal with my illness and transplant process with open hands, heart, and mind.

Don't get me wrong. There were moments of fear and frustration. But I realized at the very beginning that no matter what happened, the gift of life was too precious to clutch it in fear of losing it. Only by being willing to accept whatever happened was I able to maintain a sense of wholeness and integrity, despite my physical un-wholeness.

Wow. Is it any wonder why we all marveled at our brother?

I arrived in Pittsburgh by chartered plane that Saturday morning a bit nervous. Having never flown in a four-passenger plane before, I had to remind myself (as I looked out the windows at the thick clouds and fog) that planes really do fly by radar.

When he got off the plane, the poor guy puked.

When I arrived at the hospital via an ambulance that met me at the airport, I insisted on walking into the emergency room—much to the ambulance attendant's dismay. I think the nurse was a bit skeptical as I made my way slowly to the counter and rather emphatically told her, 'Hi. I'm here for my heart transplant.'

Mitch and Fr. Paul, I'm sure, were worried, astonished—and inspired.

After a prayer, a hug from each, and the misty-eyed communication of my love for them and my family, I was whisked off to the operating room.

It was now about 11:15 a.m., and Mitch called us back in Olean with an update. Merrick was being prepped for surgery. The donor heart, he had been told, was coming from McKeesport, Pennsylvania, about thirty miles from Pittsburgh. They would have to do some final compatibility testing on it, and if all checked out, it would be a go.

Sadly, Mom and Michele arrived about ten minutes after Merrick was taken into surgery. "Lord, I'm always a day late and a dollar short," Peg would always comment. This time it was true.

Hours passed, and we were beginning to worry back at 512. Not knowing anything is worse than knowing something is wrong. In the journal, we documented as best we could this medical stuff and any news that would be coming our way. Finally, at 5:20 p.m.—after an entire afternoon of waiting and worrying—we finally found out that Merrick was out of surgery. Mitch told Maggie that the doctors seemed pleased. Merrick's heart had been very enlarged, and they had a tough time removing it. His vitals were good, but he was still heavily sedated. He was being cleaned up, and they should be able to see him in an hour or two.

Mom's reaction at seeing her son late that evening in cardiothoracic ICU—sprawled out, nearly naked, hooked up to a respirator with IVs galore? "Dear Lord in heaven," she wept as she blessed her weary self. "Now I know how the Blessed Mother must have felt after the Lord was taken down from the Cross …"

The news about Merrick's transplant began to spread, both in Olean and throughout western New York.

"The next thing I remember was waking up and looking down at my chest, wondering why it didn't hurt," Merrick eventually wrote about his experience of receiving someone else's heart. *"Then I wondered what those staples were doing there."*

I have many memories of my days in the hospital: The painful muscle cramps caused by the initial massive injections of Cyclosporine. Pounding headaches. Frequent vomiting. The discomfort of dehydration I felt as I lost a total of twenty-nine pounds of fluid.

Merrick was in a daze for just a few days, and we all took shifts visiting him in Pittsburgh for the next twenty days.

Visits from family and friends. Hundreds of cards dangling from my hospital room. The feeling as I walked the hallway for the first time without any support or assistance. The joy after hearing my biopsies were negative. The incredible realization that I was feeling alive *like never before.*

If there's anything that expressed my feelings then—and now—it is gratitude. *I realized as I flew to Pittsburgh that all of what was happening was possible because someone else had to die.*

Somewhere, Merrick and our entire family knew, some family was heartbroken and grief-stricken in McKeesport, Pennsylvania, on July 26, 1986. Yet quietly, courageously, and selflessly, they turned their overwhelming grief into our incredible joy. Thank you, thank you, thank you—whoever you are.

"In his or her death," Merrick wrote, *"I was given the greatest gift of all: the gift of life."*

Chapter 43

Do you believe in miracles? How about the power of prayer? You surely would if you witnessed my brother's amazing gift of life and recovery from near death.

Within just twenty-four hours of his surgery, doctors were calling Merrick's progress remarkable. Although he was still groggy as his anesthesia wore off, doctors were able to remove his respirator and oxygen mask. The swelling in his feet and abdomen was down considerably, indicating that his new heart was pumping much better than the old one had been, and his coloring looked ten times better than the day before. By the evening of the twenty-seventh, all IVs but one were out, and Merrick was sitting up and eating Jello, chicken soup, and apple juice laced with the anti-rejection medication Cyclosporine. Indeed, we believed, a miracle was happening right before our eyes. And all those prayers were being answered.

By Monday, July 28, Merrick was front-page news of the *Olean Times Herald*. The headline summed it up best: "Olean Man Receives a 'Second Chance' with New Heart."

The next couple weeks had numerous ups and downs. But just three weeks after end-stage heart disease nearly claimed his last breath, Merrick Jude Bednar was released from the hospital—armed with a healthy new heart from some unknown but generous soul whom he decided to call "Lucas" (inspired by the name on the travel bag that Merrick always brought to Pittsburgh!), and a multitude of powerful drugs—much to the amazement of his doctors, family, and friends. On that joyous day—Saturday, August 20, 1986—Merrick was reborn physically and spiritually … and so were we, his family.

We planned a relatively simple welcome home party at 512 on that sunny Saturday. And although Mom seriously wanted to find a marching band to mark the occasion, we settled for a little Kenny Loggins ("Heart to Heart" and "Celebrate Me Home," I think) blasting from a boom box, a homemade heart banner hung from the house, and about twenty of us there to greet Merrick as he got out of Mitch and Eileen's car. I assure you that we did celebrate Merrick home. For both him and us, it was a homecoming never to be forgotten.

Yes, indeed. Miracles do come true.

Chapter 44

Unbelievably, within a few weeks Merrick was back at Christ the King beginning his second year of graduate study, literally without missing a beat, despite having a most unusual summer vacation. And life, for the most part, returned to normal by Bednar standards: Mollie and I headed back to college, and Maura was set to begin her senior year of high school. Mom stayed at 512, tending to Grandma Jo, now in her early eighties and beginning to endure some health battles of her own.

A year or so post-transplant, Merrick ultimately had this to write:

…It is sometimes difficult to fully appreciate what my life is now like. I have yet to experience any rejection, although I did suffer with cramps in my back, and fought an expected case of pneumonia. It's difficult to notice the side effects from my medications, mostly because now I look so healthy that people remark about the difference from the frail, sickly-looking young man I was to the healthy, energetic person I've now become. I returned to school immediately, and am now in my next to last year of graduate studies. I am student body president, carry a full course load, work one day at week at a social justice center in Buffalo, and sometimes have trouble keeping up with myself!

I've been able to return to the physical activities that I had told myself I would never again be able to do. I engage in daily calisthenics, jog, lift weights, ride bikes, play golf, floor hockey, and softball, and have yet to find myself unable to do anything I attempt within reason. My days begin at six thirty in the morning and often end after midnight. They are filled with classes, meetings, community prayers, personal prayer, studying, researching, reading, and socializing with friends. But to me, the fact that I am now able to do all of these things is always kept in the perspective of the time when I couldn't be this active. It's important to realize that the quality of one's life is more often determined by a person's inner vision and strength (through their weaknesses) than by the mere physical quality of their life.

I feel extremely blessed and grateful for all that has happened to me in my life. The experience of being ill was a graced time for me—a time of struggle, but a time of opportunity as well. It was an opportunity to reflect on the meaning of life, the importance of love, and the value of each day. Now, restored to health, I sense a kind of resurrection, a transformation in which what I learned while ill colors the enthusiasm and vigor with which I am now able to live my life. As a person studying to become a priest, I see this in terms of God's gracious love for all of us as my life becomes an act of praise. For others who have shared this experience with me, I believe that they, too, have sensed something larger than mere human actions, too. Finally, for anyone who must face a transplant, I would daresay that although there are many obstacles to face, the gift of life received leads you to see everything with a perspective that is imbued with gratitude. I've literally lived from heart to heart and must admit that my 'second chance' is one that I'm glad to have received.

Now, my life will hopefully be a gift for others.

Chapter 45

And what a gift it was.

Merrick's life-threatening illness at such a young age became a life-changing experience for him. I'm convinced it's what inspired his newfound "seize the day" mentality (he took up golfing, traveling, and doing things on the spur of the moment), enhanced his appreciation for *everything* (from food to family to friends to fun), compelled his advocacy for organ donation, and, most of all, cemented his calling to the priesthood. In fact, Merrick's suffering, and his subsequent second chance at life, not only inspired his vocation, it emboldened it. He even wrote about the ministry of suffering and offered some pretty personal and profound thoughts on the topic—especially for a twenty-something:

"Why me?" began my brother's December 1988 graduate school thesis titled, "Suffering as Ministry."

This is a question so often painfully asked again and again by a person undergoing some physical, emotional, or spiritual trial. The human capacity for intelligence and reflection quite naturally seeks to make sense out of our experiences. However, when that experience is the experience of suffering we are many times left feeling helpless and confused. Suffering threatens what we believe about the meaningfulness of life. For persons of faith, suffering questions what is believed about God ... For a person in the throes of some disease, some illness, or ailment that is life threatening, and for all persons who are in contact with such a person, the question of finding some meaning in the midst of their suffering is critical.

The Christian tradition insists on the redemptive nature of suffering ... Yet one perspective that is overlooked is what the suffering person does for others by his or her suffering. The experience of suffering can become ministry to others, not only an occasion of ministry from *others. My own experience of suffering has provided the insights into this dimension.*

Through his suffering, Merrick said,

... the dying and rising of Christ became real for me physically, emotionally, and spiritually. I died to physical activities that had been an important part of my life ... I died to the emotional feelings that accompanied physical wholeness. I also died to the spiritual pride of control, for now my physical condition was for the most part beyond even the control of doctors. Yet, in all this affliction, doubt, and pain, and despite carrying in my body the dying of Jesus, I was not overcome by despair and doubt, nor struck down. In my body, the life of Jesus was somehow mysteriously being revealed. Death was at work, but so too was life. 'Indeed, everything is ordered to your benefit,' says 2 Corinthians, 'so that the grace of God bestowed in abundance may bring greater glory to God because they who give thanks are many.' This verse aptly described much of my journey of suffering. For regardless of how grim things appeared medically at various times, everything always seemed to work out.

By some appearances, it would appear that I lived a charmed life, because I had a habit while ill of coming through situations and circumstances that even amazed the doctors. The result was an astonishing sense of confidence and thankfulness no matter what happened, shared by doctors, family, and friends. It did seem that everything was ordered for my benefit—which led to greater praise to God as I repeatedly insisted that God's hand was directly involved in my illness.

As I journeyed through moments of illness and relative health, I sensed that much more was going on in my life because of my illness.

Talk about turning lemons into lemonade! That's what made Merrick such an amazing person, and such an incredible inspiration. His lessons on suffering taught him much:

There is no question that suffering makes us experience our limitations. It makes us aware of our dependence on others. It makes us appreciate the concern and care of others for us. But it also opens our minds and inclines our hearts to the needs of others. It makes us sensitive to a power beyond our control and to the experience of God's love in a profound way, and to sharing of that love with those who minister to us.

Suffering is unavoidable. It is neither desired nor sought by people. Yet, when one can find the meaning and power of redemption in suffering then it can become an experience of redemption and grace for others ...

My experience of suffering has opened my eyes and heart in a way that whenever something dies a lot, I die a little. It has allowed me to see the connections. It has made me a gentle person with death and with life...

This experience has raised many questions about the meaning of life and the nature of God. It has forced me to grapple with pain and ambiguity, and has been a test of faith. It has taxed my own naïve acceptance of just what the cost of discipleship is and shown me more poignantly than I had ever expected the way of the cross ...

This experience has stretched my faith seeking understanding about the nature of God, the meaning of suffering, the efficacy of prayers, and the power of selfless love ... It has shaped the approach and direction for the rest of my life.

By the way, Merrick aced his thesis and graduated in May 1989 with a master's degree in divinity—with honors, thank you very much—from Christ the King Seminary. He was ordained a deacon (the final step before becoming a priest) in June 1989, and was able to perform the wedding ceremony of his younger brother—me—to my college sweetheart and love of my life, Barb, on November 4, 1989. It was a magical day for me in more ways than one.

Chapter 46

It should come as no surprise that Merrick's suffering had a profound impact on his entire family, as well. None of us realized it at the time, but I now know that if it weren't for all the "bad stuff" he had to endure—and the grace with which he handled it—there's no way our family would be as close as we are today. For at the time when most families, large or small, separate physically and emotionally—in their twenties and thirties— to go their own way, do their own thing, Merrick became our reason for staying in touch and coming together. Ironically, his suffering served to strengthen not only him personally, but us as a family. Indeed, our brother's "brokenness" ultimately created an unbreakable bond that kept our zany family together despite miles, months, marriages, or mayhem. His miraculous recovery, his powerful ministry, and his exuberant zest for life—shown through his twinkling eyes, wide smile, and hearty laugh—made him a beacon to all who knew him. Indeed, through the darkness of all the storms he had endured, Merrick became a transforming light to each and every one of us.

Is it any wonder we all sought opportunities to be with him and celebrate the amazing person he had become?

Chapter 47

With praise and gratitude to Almighty God,
the people of the Church of Buffalo
with Margaret Richardson Bednar and Family
joyfully announce and invite you
to the ordination of their son and brother
Merrick J. Bednar
to the ministerial priesthood of Jesus Christ,
through the invocation of the Holy Spirit
and the laying on of hands by
The Most Reverend Edward D. Head, D.D.
Bishop of Buffalo
on Saturday, the twelfth day of May
Nineteen Hundred and Ninety
at ten o'clock in the morning
St. Joseph Cathedral

May 12, 1990.

What a joyous day for the Bednar family! Of course, we had to tease Merrick about the numerical date of his ordination: *5-12.* How perfect was that?

It was indeed with praise and gratitude to Almighty God that my entire family, along with hundreds of friends, relatives, and supporters, gathered at the magnificent cathedral in Buffalo that glorious May day to witness our brother ultimately prostrate himself at the altar and dedicate his life to God. There had been so many times since 1983, when Merrick's long road to the priesthood was just under way and he drove himself to the Ogdensberg Hospital, that we all seriously wondered if he'd ever live to see this day. So just the majestic sight of our twenty-six-year-old brother processing down the aisle with dozens of other priests and the Bishop of Buffalo brought an instant lump to my throat and tears of joy to my eyes. Merrick's ordination was a grand, music filled, and awe-inspiring experience for everyone present, but a particularly poignant and proud moment in time for my mom and all of us. It was almost impossible to believe that our son and brother—the same kid who swore at the social worker, navigated us across country, stole the toilet paper, and was the man of the house at twelve—was, through the laying on of hands of his fellow priests, now a priest himself. The same guy who, through his life-threatening medical ordeals had taken us as a family to the lowest of lows, was now raising us up to the highest of highs. I remember vividly how Merrick beamed that day, like the Light of Christ that he was, dressed in his stunning new vestments, which were emblazoned with a double-heart logo that he helped design.

Saturday, May 12, 1990: Another "Merrick day" and date that my family would never forget. Followed by still another remarkable day: His first Mass—on Mother's Day, nonetheless—back in our home parish of St. Mary's in Olean. I swear there has never been a mother more proud than mine on that special day and weekend. And she had every right to be.

"This is my beloved son, with whom I am well pleased."

Of course she knew it was a line from the Gospel, but somehow it seemed OK for Peg to be quoting it throughout the weekend. Indeed, with Merrick, she had earned the right.

Chapter 48

Merrick's life as a new priest was a rich and rewarding one. His first assignment was at St. Bernadette's, a wonderful parish in Orchard Park, New York, a suburb of Buffalo just a few miles away from where his lifelong favorite football team, the Buffalo Bills, played. He loved that parish, and the parishioners loved him back. He kept such a crazy pace—with Masses, baptisms, weddings, funerals, counseling, parish meetings, and other aspects of ministry—that often many weeks would go by without us seeing him. For solitude, he'd escape by himself once a week to Burger King for a double cheeseburger and to work on his homilies, which were always topical, timely, and entertaining. He usually wove some craziness from his own upbringing into them.

In his "spare" time, my brother read a lot, hit seemingly every new movie on opening night, golfed as much as possible, and traveled whenever he could—even to Europe one summer as a chaplain. Mom had a fit, given his heart! Merrick also would visit car dealerships on his days off, just for the fun of test-driving the newest models or to wheel and deal for a friend or family member on the hunt for a new lease deal. If you didn't know better, you'd never guess in a million years that this guy full of life and boundless energy had once had a heart transplant! Merrick simply made everything in his own life look so simple—from taking his daily dose of drugs, to traipsing off to Pittsburgh for his periodic check-ups—that it's no wonder that he endeared himself literally to all who came in his path. Given all he had been through in his young life, and the blessings of feeling and looking great once again, Merrick truly was living by his adopted motto of "Carpe Diem!" (Seize the Day!)—the phrase made famous (again) in the early nineties by Robin Williams in *Dead Poets Society*, one of Merrick's favorite flicks.

But no matter how busy Merrick was, we all kept in touch

with him—and he with us—by phone. Whenever we needed a "Merrick fix" we would take a short road trip to Buffalo for a weekend Mass and meal with our amazing brother. And whether it was just a couple of us present, or the whole clan, especially my mom, we were treated like royalty by the parish, simply by being the family of the beloved Fr. Merrick. It was crystal clear to us how much Merrick was loved, and how much of an impact he had on young and old alike.

Indeed, in the first couple years following Merrick's ordination, life once again seemed to settle down at long last for the Bednars. For the first time in about a decade, it seemed, things seemed relatively normal—at least by our standards: I was the happy newlywed, now working in alumni relations at my alma mater. Barb taught in the Catholic schools, so we were really rolling in the dough and living in our first apartment in Rochester! Maura graduated from college in Geneseo, New York, in 1991 and began her business career and adult life at Xerox in Rochester as well. Barb and I were thrilled to have her nearby. Mollie had found her first permanent teaching job, ironically, in Olean—the place where she had vowed years earlier to never live. Michele was in nearby Allegany, where she had been teaching for as long as I can remember. Maggie and Alan were busy building their careers and raising their young family of three in nearby Bradford, much to Maggie's chagrin, while Mitch and Eileen were doing the same in Atlanta. My brother Mike—who had fortunately turned his wild life around in the late eighties by meeting and marrying the Pittsboro, North Carolina, love-of-his-life Vickie—was building a life, a home, and a career in construction in North Carolina, and my brother Mark was busy trying to get his life back in order after a divorce in the eighties, pursuing dreams of his own.

Much to her dismay, my mom remained at 512. "Lord, why does everyone have to move so far away?" she'd ask. She did some occasional substitute teaching, lots of whoopin' it up with her divorced and dumped-on girlfriends (honest to goodness "Golden

Girls") and her "TGIF" club, and began caring more closely for her own mother—my wonderful Gramma Jo, who, now in her mid-eighties was beginning to fail from a series of mini-strokes. Of course, by now Gramma had mellowed from the strict warden she once was into a dear friend and proud grandmother to all of us kids.

But, as has always been the case when things are too normal in my family for too long, something had to give. And so it did, on January 7, 1993.

Chapter 49

I was a few weeks shy of twenty-seven when I first experienced the death of a loved one—someone I really loved, as opposed to someone I just knew and cared about—up close and personal. And considering that it was the death of my eighty-six-year-old grandmother—whom I was blessed to have known very, very well for many years (most of my peers had lost their grandparents when they were kids or teenagers)—I guess I was pretty fortunate. But I sure didn't feel fortunate on that cold January morning (just two days before Maura's twenty-third birthday) when the phone startled me out of a sound sleep at around six o'clock.

From behind the tears, I couldn't tell at first if the voice sharing the bad news on the other end was Mollie or Maura. It was Mollie. I had to call Maura, scare the heck out of her with an early morning call, and share the sad news with her.

Gramma Jo's death was a watershed moment in my family's life—despite the fact that, as she was aged eighty-six, we had ample warning that her death was coming. For eighty-plus years, she had lived a happy, healthy, simple, yet joy-filled life for the most part—despite her fair share of heartache and her nearly life-long habit of puffing on Lark cigarettes. Since 1989, however, Gramma Jo had failed slowly but surely, suffering from a series of debilitating strokes that eventually landed her in and out of the hospital, temporarily in a nursing home (which she hated and managed to get out of), and left her weakened, unable to speak, and in need of daily home health care. But because my mom lived at 512 (more out of necessity than choice) and her sister Pat was a frequent visitor and caretaker during that time, Gramma was able to live most of the final few years of her life in her own home, which she loved. It was the day after Christmas, 1992, that Gramma had to be rushed from 512 by ambulance to the Olean General Hospital one final time, where she would receive the Anointing of the Sick for the umpteenth time in three years and eventually die less than two weeks later.

So Gramma Jo's death didn't exactly come as a shock to us. But what it was—to me, my entire family, and certainly for my mom—was the end of an amazing era, and in a sense, the official end of our childhood. For although we youngest Bednar kids were now in our twenties and doing OK for ourselves, we all had come to realize that Gramma Jo had played a major role in how we turned out as young adults. If it hadn't been for her role that far exceeded most grandparents' influence in their grandkids' lives, we wouldn't have even had a roof over our head or a place to ever call home. And her death hit that point home. As for Peg, now sixty-three, whose heartfelt loss included lots of guilt over the roller-coaster relationship she had through the years with her mother, Gramma's death finally forced her—and all of us—to figure out what she was going to do with the rest of her life, now that her kids and her elderly mother no longer needed a daily caretaker.

Gramma's death also hit home how fortunate we were to have a priest in the family—and not just any ol' priest, but one as remarkable as Merrick. In fact, it was through Gramma's wake and funeral that I first fully witnessed Merrick's ministry in action as teacher, leader, grief counselor, and faith-filled believer. Despite his own personal loss, he comforted his entire family—mother, brothers, sisters, aunts, uncles, and even distant cousins—throughout those sad days and balanced some delicate and a few potentially explosive family relations with great finesse simply by his presence (the collar definitely helped), his peaceful and prayerful demeanor, and his leadership in planning exceptional liturgies. In fact, I'm sure no one was more proud than Gramma Jo herself from her place in heaven on that cold January ninth (yes, Maura's twenty-third birthday) when her own grandson presided over her beautiful and heartfelt funeral Mass at St. Mary's—complete with her own personal choir that traveled from

St. Bernadette's parish as a way to honor Merrick and acknowledge his loss. It wasn't until the end of his moving homily that Merrick's voice finally cracked and gave way to the weight of it all. And yet his momentary tears from the altar revealed nothing but his genuine love and gratitude for his grandmother, the deep sadness that everyone in that church felt—and the profound changes that would be felt well beyond that bitter January day.

Chapter 50

Imagine Buckingham Palace without the Queen Mum, and you have an idea of what 512 without Gramma Jo was like. Her presence was such an integral part of that house for so long—certainly for my entire life—that in many ways, Gramma was 512, and 512 was Gramma. In the minds of the many who loved her, there was no way to separate the two. With the "Queen Mum of 512" gone, the house was hollow. Incomplete. Sad. And surely could never the same.

It was no surprise to anyone, really, that in her will, which this always wise woman had pre-planned many years earlier, Gramma Jo mandated that 512—her only real asset—be put up for sale upon her death and that the proceeds be divided evenly between her six remaining children.

Although it was not Gramma's intention, her will basically served as an eviction notice for my mother, now the only resident of the big, old, and quickly dilapidating house. But somehow, Peg was OK with that.

"Lord, this place spooks me," she had always complained, even years before Gramma passed away. "I always picture Aunt Sade under that window, and now all I picture is Mother in her chair."

Indeed, this house, once full of life and hustle and bustle had become, literally overnight, a depressing and melancholy place. And while only Mom would admit it out loud, it did have an empty, eerie, and downright spooky feeling to it. But spooky or not, it had been the only home Peg had known for more than twenty years. So whether she admitted this or not, moving from there was going to be a dramatic change—for better or for worse—for my mom, and definitely for us. We grew up in that kooky, now spooky, place, and the memories were in every nook and cranny. At least it would take a while to sell the old place—which was a good thing, because it could probably take years to get all the stuff out!

Although she didn't really have anywhere to go, and certainly didn't have lots of money, Peg had one thing that most people in her position didn't have: nine adult kids with the concern, willingness, and now the collective means to find, at long last, a decent place for her to call a home of her own.

I figured it would be somewhere in Olean.

But I was wrong.

"Mom's moving to Bradford?" I questioned with amazement when Maggie called me in late May of '93 to tell me she had found the perfect little ranch house just a few blocks away from hers—and that Mom had agreed to move there. "You're kidding me. This is never going to work … Her life is in Olean."

Never great at making decisions, and unfortunately growing more and more discontented as she grew older, Mom didn't really know where the heck she wanted to be. So her decision literally became a question of, "Where will you be least miserable?" Knowing that she wanted out of 512 and feeling the pressure to make a decision, Mom thought a fresh start in a charming and affordable little house just thirty minutes from Olean and three minutes from Maggie might just be the right place to do it. So she decided, albeit reluctantly, to give it a try.

So in early June of '93—just five emotionally charged, roller-coaster months after Gramma's death—with Gramma's will still in probate and her house still not sold, Mitch and Maggie (with the support of their kind spouses) put up the bulk of the upfront money needed to buy the house at 86 Fiske Avenue in Bradford. The plan was for the rest of us to help Mom foot the monthly bills—supplemented by the Social Security that she finally had started collecting (off her ex-husband) when she turned sixty-two (despite an indignant employee at the Social Security office insulting her by telling her, "Ms. Richardson, you never worked!"). The closing would take place just before the Fourth of July; we'd move Mom in, get her settled in her new digs, and then the second half of 1993 would be far better than the first. And then, maybe, just like a good fairy tale (or at least the ending of a happy story), Mom and the Bednar family could finally live happily ever after.

Maybe.

But then again, maybe not.

Chapter 51

Cancer.

There's probably no other word in the world that is as horrifying.

The insidious disease strikes without warning, like an earthquake, and doesn't give a hoot about what—or who—it tries to destroy in its path.

Even if you're a much loved and much needed priest who's already survived more than your fair share of earthquakes in your twenty-nine years.

Yes, in June 1993, in the midst of mourning Gramma and moving Mom, our thriving heart-transplant-surviving brother Merrick was diagnosed—seemingly out of left field, as is usually the case—with cancer.

They always say bad things come in threes.

But they never say life is fair.

I actually learned about Merrick's cancer inadvertently from Mollie—perhaps the perkiest of all my sisters and, as I jokingly refer to her, my twin. That's because she and I were born just one year and five days apart and shared nearly everything from the time we were kids: toys, friends, fun-loving ways, problems, life stories. In fact, if Mollie were telling this story, it would be nearly identical to what I've written here because our adventures and perspectives were almost always the same. So while my mom never officially had twins, Mollie and I were the closest things to them in the Bednar family. Of course, there was a time—mainly during our high school years—when Mollie (or MiMo as she eventually was nicknamed) had a heck of a chip on her shoulder. Who could blame her, given our upbringing coupled with normal teen angst? But as the sports-loving tomboy eventually blossomed into the effervescent, naturally-pretty girl-next-door she's become, Mollie's happy-go-lucky personality and bubbly demeanor bloomed as well.

Anyway, my sister was unloading golf clubs from the trunk of her car in the driveway of her then-boyfriend's house. It was a warm Friday evening in mid-June, around dusk, and Barb and I had just arrived in Olean an hour or so earlier for the weekend. Mollie, now a gym teacher, fitness guru, and sports enthusiast, had obviously just finished playing a round of her favorite pastime.

"Hi, MiMo!" I blurted as I walked toward my normally cheerful lifelong buddy.

"Hi ..." she replied, her greeting lacking its usual exuberance. "Can you believe the news about Merrick?" she instantly asked, figuring I already knew.

"What news?" I asked.

"Haven't you talked to him?" she queried, soberly.

"Not today ... but what's up?"

She paused momentarily, but then realizing that there's no easy way to say it, just blurted it out. "He's got cancer."

"What?!" I shot back in total disbelief.

It's obviously not something anyone jokes about.

"Cancer? You gotta be shittin' me ..." I think was my automatic, dumbfounded follow-up.

Come to find out, Merrick had discovered a lump under his arm recently, and had mentioned it to his doctors on his regularly scheduled checkup in Pittsburgh a week or so before. While he may have thought it was something serious, he hadn't mentioned anything about a lump to any of us at first—I'm sure because he didn't want to worry anyone. Still, his conscientious doctors, several of whom had now become enamored with the charismatic priest with the inspiring attitude, ordered a full series of tests— CT scans, an MRI, whatever—and had been in touch with him that fateful Friday with some somber news: the transplant survivor had now been diagnosed with non-Hodgkin's lymphoma.

Post-transplant, non-Hodgkin's lymphoma, to be exact.

Cancer of the lymph nodes.

It was a horrible diagnosis, one that even the most hopeful and skilled physicians realized—as did Merrick and all of us, once we learned—may not have a happy ending. Its seriousness was immediately clear when in just days, not weeks, from diagnosis, Merrick was admitted to the University of Pittsburgh Medical Center where he would spend the entire summer of 1993 fighting for his life.

Again.

Chapter 52

For being as sick as he was, Merrick never really looked like a patient, especially a cancer patient. Although confined to a hospital room for the most part, the stylish and handsome priest always showered, shaved (until his platelets got too low), and got dressed (usually in comfy but neat shorts and a fun novelty T-shirt printed with a clever saying or picture). The whole hospital gown thing was a definite fashion faux pas in his eyes. "It's mind over matter," he'd often tell us.

Likewise, Merrick never acted like a patient of any kind, either, at least whenever I saw him. And that was fairly frequently, as my whole family and some of Merrick's dearest friends took turns visiting him throughout the entire summer of '93—often getting lost in downtown Pittsburgh and ending up in the parking lot of the old Three Rivers Stadium. So Merrick rarely was ever truly alone. Despite the poking and prodding, the daily tests he'd endure, and probably feeling lousier than he ever let on, Merrick would never just lay in a hospital bed unless it was absolutely necessary. Instead, he'd sit in a chair, stroll the halls if he could, talk on the phone, and welcome visitors as if they were coming to his house. He always had a smile on his face and a warm embrace for each and every one—and then would proceed to engage in great conversation. The hours would pass, and then he'd ask, "Wanna order a pizza? I'm sick of the food here." Occasional visitors were often taken aback by the doctor's general approval of this, but we frequent visitors got used to pizza delivery guys coming to Merrick's room every now and then.

Quite honestly, when you spent time with Merrick at the hospital that summer, it was often hard to believe that he was as sick as he was, that tumors were growing rapidly inside his body. And what those tumors—or more specifically, the methods used to treat them—would do to his transplanted heart was anyone's guess, and everyone's worry. "What are you gonna do?" Merrick would often ask, nonchalantly. Life continued to give him lemons, but he never stopped making lemonade. Heck, the guy even had to turn the milestone age of thirty confined to the hospital with cancer—and yet somehow he managed to make the most of it. The good people of St. Bernadette's even shipped down "Look who's turning thirty" buttons to help him celebrate.

Believe it or not, there was an ironic upside to Merrick's hospital stays: They gave his family the chance to spend real quality, one-on-one time with our otherwise always-busy, always-in-demand brother. In fact, in a bizarre way, it was kind of fun going to see Merrick. Often times, there'd be rip-roaring laughter coming out of his room, caused by us cracking up about something or other. Other times, you'd engage in some the deepest and most meaningful conversations you could ever have with someone. Or sometimes you'd just be there, together—watching the news, a ball game, or *The Young and the Restless*—drawing silent strength from each other and simply cherishing the moment. If it was a Sunday and he was feeling up to it, Merrick would usually say Mass for us in his hospital room. He always traveled with his "Jesus Kit," as we jokingly referred to it—a small kit with all the essentials for Mass. It never seemed strange to any of us because Merrick would say Mass for us at home on occasion, but looking back, some of the hospital workers probably thought we were a bunch of holy rollers. And when it came time to leave for the night, or to reluctantly return home for the next person's turn to visit, Merrick would always say a short prayer, then we'd give each other a hug and leave with a final, "Love ya."

I think it was on a drive back from Pittsburgh to Rochester that summer when I, deep in thought, began to first realize that some of the most profound, spiritual, and downright wonderful times that I personally—and I'm sure all of my other siblings—ever shared with my brother Merrick had taken place in a hospital with him deathly ill. And yet it was he who remained the beacon of hope to us all.

Go figure.

Chapter 53

As weeks turned into months, Merrick's cancer worsened. Traditional treatments and protocols simply were not working: The initial rounds of chemo didn't do anything except make the poor guy sick. Then, I recall, came talk of radiation. Or more chemo. Or more tests. Who knows? It was all a blur.

"Lord, it's like Merrick's a human guinea pig," Mom would bluntly complain—and then usually get scolded by one of us for being so negative. But, as was usually the case, she was right. Even the doctors couldn't agree on what to do with the ailing priest, since nothing they tried seemed to move the dial at all. And time, it appeared, was not on their side.

As Merrick's cancer worsened and his medical team grew more perplexed, the rest of us grew more weary. We strived to juggle our constant worry with work schedules, visits to Pittsburgh, and, on top of it all, trying to get Mom settled in the new house in Bradford, where she suddenly decided she didn't want to be. Yet through it all, Merrick still somehow remained positive and managed to keep an upbeat attitude, despite his own growing frustration.

How did he do it?

How did that brother of mine manage to remain so mentally strong while physically becoming more weak?

How did the long-suffering patient remain so patient?

In a word: prayer.

And through prayer, Merrick remained spiritually invincible.

For deep down, Merrick believed—he *truly* believed, just like the Gospel that he proudly preached said—that nothing was impossible with God.

Even beating cancer ... when you've already had a heart transplant.

Actually, Merrick's prayerfulness was remarkable—and inspiring—to witness, as Barb and I did on a couple of our visits that summer. One occasion in particular, which I'll never forget, occurred near the end of that long summer. To most, it may not even seem like a big deal.

It was a weekday morning—a Thursday, I think—and we were due to head back to Rochester. We had always made a point to pay Rick a short visit, even on the mornings that we planned to head out. Merrick would usually ask that visitors in general not come to his hospital room much before 10:30 a.m.; that would allow for the doctors' morning rounds, and then give him time to eat breakfast, shower, and get dressed.

I think because of the hassles of parking at the hospital, Barb and I were running a little late that day. So it was closer to eleven as we approached the open doorway of Merrick's room. The patient's bed was freshly made, but he was not in it. As we entered the room, he was seated to our immediate right, wearing his golf T-shirt and khaki shorts, and hooked up as usual to his IV trolley. He sat upright against the wall in a regular chair—not even the oversized hospital recliner that took up much of the space in his tiny room—in silence, eyes closed, his small Bible opened on his lap, saying his rosary. As he noticed us, he simply closed the Bible and placed his simple wooden rosary beads on the portable hospital table.

That was it. But the simplicity of the moment was as powerful as it was profound. Both Barb and I commented to each other on our way out about how that tender sight broke our hearts. And that image has remained with us both for all these years.

It was on a different hospital visit that I learned Merrick also kept a prayer journal, in which he would randomly list his special prayer intentions. He asked me to grab it for him one evening in the middle of watching the national news. There had been a horrible natural disaster—an earthquake, if I recall correctly—in some remote region of the world, and the images on the news of peoples' suffering were horrific. Merrick simply took his pen and added "victims of today's earthquake" to his running list. "Can I take a look?" I asked, curiously. Sure, he offered, and handed me the simple-looking hard covered journal. There was page after dated page in his increasingly illegible handwriting—I would often innocently tease Merrick about how his hands shook as a result of all the meds he was taking—about many of the people and things he'd pray for. I recall some of the listings just prior to his most recent entry: Mom. Mollie and her boyfriend. A patient on his floor who was nearing death. President Clinton. Patience.

"That's really neat ..." I said, again humbled by the quiet quality of my brother's character.

"No big deal," he replied.

Of course, for as much as Merrick prayed, he also knew that he was constantly being uplifted by the prayers of literally thousands of people. As he often stated, heaven was being stormed with prayers on his behalf. As a popular priest, his own parish was praying for him daily, as were the parishes of all of his priestly friends in the Diocese of Buffalo and elsewhere. Even the Bishop would check in on him periodically and offer his prayers and support, and all of us—his family and friends—never stopped praying for him from the days he first took ill all those years ago.

Ironically, we all used to laugh about how, when we were kids and before the family fell completely apart, my mother would make all nine of us get down on our knees around her bed (how weird is that?) to say our nighttime prayers and frequently recite the rosary. Maura would toddle around in her sleeper, the older boys would usually end up giggling while some of us *tried* to pay attention, and Mollie would inevitably zonk out long before we concluded the First Mystery.

But I know none of us, including Mom herself, had any idea

just how important that simple habit of learning to pray would become during our lifetimes.

As a priest, Merrick would often say, "We should pray always, and pray all ways."

And he was definitely a guy who practiced what he preached.

Chapter 54

It had been a hell of a year, but nevertheless, by the time Thanksgiving '93 arrived, we still believed we had much to be thankful for. Specifically, Merrick was still with us, even though his cancer continued to spread and he had spent much of the fall in and out of the hospital. But as the holiday approached, it was looking like he was going to be able to be with us for our first Thanksgiving at 86 Fiske—Mom's new home, and therefore our new home, in Bradford.

When I arrived at Mom's place on the Wednesday evening before Thanksgiving, excited about the thought of all being together again, she was in the front bedroom on the phone, disappointed and in tears, with Merrick. On doctors' orders, she had just learned, he was required to remain in Pittsburgh. His blood counts were dangerously low; it simply was not safe or prudent to discharge him, even temporarily for Thanksgiving as originally planned.

Great. Another Bednar holiday on its way to becoming a Bednar helliday.

"Your brother just walked in," Mom said as I bounced in the room. She was always so happy to see me, especially the older I got. "He's going to be so disappointed."

Mom explained the situation briefly to me, and she was right: I was disappointed. But I was even more disappointed for Merrick.

"Rick," I said as Mom handed me her makeup-stained Trimline phone. "There's no way I'm going to let you be alone on stinking Thanksgiving."

"Don't worry about it," he tried to reassure me. "I'll be fine."

"The hell you will! There is absolutely no way I am going to let you be alone on Thanksgiving," I repeated. "I'm coming down."

"But Barb should be with her family ..." he tried to protest.

"She will be. I'll get Mollie to come down with me. Maura can stay here with Mom and the rest of the clan, and we'll make sure you're not alone. It'll be ... fun."

"Is that what you call it?" he asked, his spirits, I could tell, lifted.

"Yeah, just another Bednar helliday."

And so, I didn't spend the Thanksgiving just weeks after my fourth wedding anniversary with my wife—who absolutely supported my decision—but with my "twin" sister en route (fortunately on a mild Thanksgiving day) to that dreaded Pittsburgh hospital where our cancer-stricken brother remained, fighting for his life. When we arrived, Merrick was dressed but in bed, where he stayed most of the day because he was so weak. Still, we cracked up a lot (whenever Mollie and I get together we burst at the stupidest things), watched football, and helped Merrick—and each other—get through an otherwise depressing Thanksgiving Day.

When it came time for dinner, the cafeteria sent a traditional (but nauseatingly processed) Thanksgiving meal up for Merrick. Mollie and I sat with him while he picked at it, grossed out by the smell. Then the time came that we needed to eat something, too. Since we had grown so tired of the hospital cafeteria food through all our visits this year, we opted for something far more glamorous: the Forbes Avenue McDonald's. It was Thanksgiving, after all.

Mollie and I were just about the only two people on the street—except for a few homeless people—as we walked the three blocks down the hill from the hospital to the normally hectic city street, where the urban and grubby Golden Arches awaited. But, boy, were we disappointed to learn that our Thanksgiving dinner of Chicken McNuggets was not to be: The place was closed. Who knew that McDonalds ever closed?

So it was back to the eleventh floor of the hospital, where we ordered yet another cheeseburger and side of fries.

Still, after eating a cafeteria cheeseburger for Thanksgiving dinner, after leaving Merrick later that night alone in a hospital room, and after checking into a room at the nearby Holiday Inn, I went to sleep that night thankful for this most unusual—and unforgettable—Thanksgiving Day.

And I kept telling myself that by next Thanksgiving, things had to be much better.

Chapter 55

Through the years, my brother Mitch has earned the unfair reputation as the family tough guy: hard nosed, show-no-emotion, tell-it-like-it-is. But deep down, we've all learned, he's as soft as a marshmallow and as caring as they come. That was so evident as Christmas 1993 approached. Mitch summed up what all of us were feeling at that time in a heartfelt letter to Merrick that he wrote, I believe, one sleepless night at the Holiday Inn just a few blocks from the hospital. With just one week to go before Christmas, Mitch had just spent a gut-wrenching day and evening with Merrick and his latest chemo-concoction.

Mitch's uncharacteristic gift was the ultimate Christmas present. In fact, Merrick was so moved by it that he eventually shared it with all of us:

December 18, 1993

As I write this, I am upset that this does not find you in excellent health. Once again you face another life and death challenge, at another inopportune holiday time, in another out of town hospital room.

My holiday thoughts are to make sure that I share with you what you mean to me and your family and friends—and what you have taught me.

Ever since this summer when cancer entered the picture, I have found myself only going through the motions. Constantly distracted during my day to day activities because everyday words, sayings, or songs remind me of you.

Words such as: Inspiration. Miracles. Adversity. Cancer. Courage. Character. Excellence. Risks. Hero.

Over the last fifteen years, most of what I have cherished has involved you. You would encourage and inspire me with keen obser-

vations, gentle humor, and loving advice that rang with truth and insight.

I have not had to look far to see a miracle. One of God's greatest miracles is to enable ordinary people like you to do extraordinary things.

You have put an uncommon touch on even the most common task.

I know things are tough right now. Life seems to give you the test before you have had the chance to study the lesson. I guess the heart sees what is invisible to the eye.

Over the years, as I have visited you in the hospital, I have come across two sayings that have touched me and inspired me and reminded me of your courage and character.

The first is: "I have cancer, but cancer doesn't have me."

The second is: "Never ask a question where God has put a period."

Both of these will help console me for the rest of my life.

You have displayed that courage is the first of human qualities because it is the quality that guarantees all others. Courage is resistance to fear—not absence of it. There can be no courage unless you are scared.

I am so proud of your courage.

You have shown me that good character is not like a talent that is given to us. You have to build character piece by piece. By thought, choice, courage, and determination.

I am so proud of your character.

You have taught me that excellence means doing your very best in everything, in every way. It means going far beyond the call of duty—doing more than others expect. This is what excellence is all about.

I am so proud of how you have lived your life in excellence.

You have pointed out that to try something is to risk failure. And the person that risks nothing, does nothing, has nothing, is nothing.

Only a person who takes life's risks is truly free.

For you to live, you have to risk dying.
I am so proud of the risks you have taken.
I am so proud that you are my hero.
These are my holiday thoughts. You will be in my prayers.
Thank you for sharing your love, laughter, encouragement, and values. They will always guide and inspire me.
Thanks for touching my life, Merrick.

I love you,
Mitch

Chapter 56

Thankfully, we didn't have to wait until next Thanksgiving.

On March 10, 1994, the prayers of thousands were answered.

My phone rang at my weird new job, which I had just started a couple months before and was anything but thrilled about. It was an excited Merrick, and the call was definitely the highlight of an otherwise just-get-through-it day.

"Marsh," he began. "Are you sitting down?"

Oh no, I thought, fearing the worst. What now?

"I'm cancer free," he said, understated.

"What?!" I immediately asked in total disbelief.

I could now all but hear the glorious smile on his face as he repeated what he just said.

"I'm calling to tell you that I am cancer free!"

I get goose bumps even now when I think of the call.

Merrick went on to tell how his most recent CT-scans of his neck, chest, and abdomen—which had taken place just two days before in Pittsburgh—showed absolutely no abnormalities. Not even one. And at first, no one—including his doctors—could believe it. So they double-, triple-, and quadruple-checked the results before sharing them with Rick.

"It's a miracle," he said. "It is truly a miracle."

Then he said the words that were music to my ears: "I am in a complete remission."

"Oh, my God! This is unbelievable …"

And it was—both unbelievable and a miracle. By all normal accounts, and to put it bluntly, my thirty-year-old brother probably should have been dead by now. His lymphoma—which is a difficult cancer to treat under normal circumstances, I understand—had been stubborn from the get-go some nine months before. It never responded to traditional treatments, and rejection of his transplanted heart had always been a serious concern and reality. So if the cancer didn't kill him first, heart problems of some sort very well could have. But at one point, I don't recall exactly when, Merrick had gotten so frustrated and fed up with the attitude of one of his doctors—the lead oncologist, I believe—that he somehow demanded and received a different one that he felt better suited his needs. Call it the power of the collar. Enter Dr. Miller, an incredibly gifted, warm, and empathetic oncologist (make that, female oncologist) who instantly clicked with Merrick (make that Fr. Merrick, as she always respectfully and reverently called him, despite being told by Merrick to just call him Merrick ... and even though she was a good fifteen years older than he). After a thorough and careful review of Merrick's case, Dr. Miller ultimately suggested an experimental treatment plan involving a powerful new chemotherapy approach—personally overseen by her—that could potentially fight back his cancerous cells and return his rapidly diminishing quality of life.

There were no guarantees, but with Dr. Miller came renewed hope.

And that's all Merrick the risk-taker (the one that Mitch praised and admired) needed. So with the help of a certain angel in disguise named Dr. Miller, who surfaced at the time as the answer to countless prayers, Merrick once again took this family from the lowest of lows to the highest of highs—from the horror of a cancer-diagnosis to the thrill of a remission.

Let's just say that the highs with Merrick are a lot more fun.

Chapter 57

It's more than ironic that as a kid, Merrick always loved roller coasters, because as an adult, the dramatic roller coaster that was his life far surpassed the thrills and chills any theme park ride could provide. It was like he was the coaster itself, full of all the ups and downs, and we were the passengers in the cars hopping on for the wild ride.

When Merrick beat cancer, it was definitely a thrilling high for us all—kind of like the exhilarating buzz you get on a coaster after you've ascended slowly and painfully to the top of the tracks and then drop far and fast, screaming in delight as the wind rushes in your face and your stomach remains back at the drop. By the time the ride finally comes to a complete stop, you think, "That wasn't so bad after all."

And so it was with Merrick. In fact, one of his biggest problems or faults (if you call it that) was his knack for making the dreadful things that he endured—like fighting cancer, or having a heart transplant—seem, well, almost easy. Oh, don't get me wrong. It was hell going through them, and no one believed for a minute that those ordeals were easy. But each time Merrick faced a truly life-threatening challenge, he ultimately came out on top and seemingly walked away with barely a scar—or a complaint. So along the way, something ironic—or amazing—had happened: The more Merrick suffered and overcame, the more imbued with gratitude and appreciation he became for everything, as did all around him. In many ways, it was the exact opposite of what you normally expect—after all, most people who suffer just a little complain a whole lot (myself included!)—and this appreciation for all the good that seemed to always come to us out of all the bad was the path that Merrick led us down, just by being who he was.

Call it grace if you will. I do.

So we celebrated Merrick's amazing remission and recovery at, of all things, Barb's and my housewarming party in March of 1994. We had finally saved enough money to buy our first home—a brand new, albeit modest townhouse in a suburb of Rochester. And, sure, we were excited about the house, but welcoming a healthy Merrick filled with energy and vitality (along with the rest of our family) rightly overshadowed that. Our brother looked great with yet another lease on life as he checked out our new pad with enthusiasm. And he was so thrilled about his news—as were we—that he even brought and shared copies of his medical report with us that gave him the all clear. That, along with the Mass he presided over in our new living room surrounded by family and friends, clearly was the best housewarming gift anyone could ever ask for.

Chapter 58

It wasn't long after Fr. Merrick's second miracle that Father Time started to play catch up with my age-defying, party-loving, sixty-something, glamour-gal mom. Oh, Peg had always fought growing old every step of the way—from her unique beauty routines to her lifelong obsession with wearing high heels—but as we'd seen with Merrick, the spirit may be willing, but the body can be weak. And I'm certain that those crazy high heels that Peg wore, I swear daily for some forty-five years, were part of her downfall.

The first time I really even paid much attention to the fact that my mom was aging was at a small party we had in mid-June '94 at her house to celebrate both Mollie and Maura finishing their master's degrees in the same year, Mollie's in education, Maura's an MBA—somehow achieving them despite all the Merrick turmoil. True to form, Peg and her sister, my dear Aunt Pat—who both, literally, have always marched to the beat of their own drum—tried to lead in good fun a playful march around the house to "Strike Up the Band" in honor of the girls and their accomplishments. (Only in this family.) By the time the music stopped, Mom was noticeably limping and complaining about how incredibly painful her right leg felt. None of us really paid too much attention to it, but we did tell Mom that she should have that leg checked.

And then in an instant—the following Thursday evening around eight o'clock, as Peg was getting out of a cab (naturally) in her own driveway—my mom took one step that catapulted her unwillingly down the path of old age.

She fell.

Actually, Peg didn't even trip on anything, despite the couple of drinks she had downed at dinner, primarily to help relieve the pain she had been enduring for weeks. No, she fell because her femur, the largest bone in her body that had been killing her for months while she wished away the pain, finally gave way. It shattered, due to advanced osteoporosis and years of arthritis in her legs. And down Peg went, screaming in excruciating pain.

Hard to believe, but the idiot cab driver didn't even do much to help. But fortunately Mom's nice neighbors across the street were puttering in their yard, saw the whole thing, rushed over to help, and called 911 and Maggie.

The next thing I know, Maggie was on the other end of my phone, calling from the Bradford Hospital, telling us that Mom was in the emergency room, and it was looking like she'd need surgery.

After surviving Merrick's ordeal that began the June before, we had all been dreaming of a much calmer summer of '94. But it was clear that those dreams came to a crashing halt with Mom crashing on the concrete.

I think it was finally at this point when Barb—now married to me for almost five years—realized that what I had told her before we got married was true: There is never a dull moment in this family.

And that there is no family quite like the one she married into.

Chapter 59

By the time we made it to the Bradford Hospital the next day, my sixty-four-year-old mom was in traction—and unbearable pain—and the doctors were planning surgery to help rebuild her femur with rods and pins. There was talk of a wheelchair, and of the aggressive therapy that would be needed to get her back on her feet again—both literally and figuratively—given her advanced age and her years of not taking good care of herself.

Unfortunately, all those years of hard living—whether by choice or circumstance—had finally caught up to our dear mother. No matter how hard you try to dodge it, they always do.

And although she hadn't always taken great care of herself, you couldn't help but feel terrible for Peg. For one thing, she was rarely, if ever, sick. Just like that "Dr. Mom" TV commercial that says moms hardly ever are! She had long hated doctors and hospitals in general, so it was quite startling to see her as a patient, flat on her back, heavily medicated and in a hospital gown.

Ironically, if her son the priest was among the best patients ever, the priest's mother was among the worst. She never liked to follow orders, she didn't think doctors knew what they were doing in the first place, and long before this unfortunate incident occurred, Peg had constantly griped, "Lord, if they don't cut it out of you, they'll burn it out of you."

Still, after surgery to rebuild her leg and a week or so in the hospital, the doctors decided to send Peg to a rehab facility in, of all places, Erie, Pennsylvania—you recall, one of the places we lived in residence at the Parade Street Ramada Inn some twenty years earlier during the longest summer of our lives. Wow, had life come full circle!

It took a lot of convincing and a fair amount of arguing, but Peg reluctantly—and I mean reluctantly—agreed to go to the Erie rehab facility, which she hated even before she got there and complained about nonstop. Then we spent most of the summer of '94 juggling schedules and traipsing back and forth to Erie to see and support her.

"She's going to do all she can to get better," we finally all convinced ourselves, "because she's too damn stubborn and proud to use a wheelchair permanently."

We couldn't have been more wrong.

The good news was that by the time the summer ended, and after several weeks of physical, occupational, and recreational therapy, Peg had recovered enough to return home to Bradford. But that wheelchair had become her crutch ... and a very visible sign that she needed help (or attention). So rather than doing all she could to get rid of that sucker, like we first thought she would, she came to rely on it more and more. I'd often tease her, in fact, about the way she'd whip around the kitchen in one fell swoop from fridge to counter to sink, that she had gotten so good maneuvering the thing that she should enter the wheelchair Olympics.

As the weeks and months went by, whether intentionally or not, the wheelchair-dependent Peg demanded a lot of collective attention: from Michele doing her grocery shopping and running her errands; to Maggie hauling her to church; to Alan doing anything and everything around her house and pushing her up the long and windy ramp at her favorite watering hole, which she still liked to frequent. To help out as much as we could, Maura, Mollie, Merrick, and I would visit as frequently as possible and would always try to stay for Sunday dinner, which Mom still loved to prepare (from the wheelchair, of course).

And when did I finally realize that Mom wasn't terribly concerned about drawing too much attention to herself in a wheelchair? I recall the moment exactly: When my brother Mark got remarried (in a civil ceremony, which upset Peg to no end) to his delightful girlfriend Debbie in October '94 and my mother danced all night long at their reception in her wheelchair—with balloons attached to it and a light-up glow stick around her neck.

Wheelchair or not, Peg was still the ultimate party girl.

Nevertheless, between Peg's redefined life and Merrick's ongoing health issues, it was like my entire family was on some out of control, emotionally exhausting seesaw during the mid-1990s. If Merrick was up, Mom seemingly bottomed out. Whenever our high maintenance mother was on the upside, our awe-inspiring brother was low, low, low.

How were we to know that this was just "Act I" of the topsy-turvy mother-son adventure on which my family was now embarking?

Chapter 60

I dare say that most thirty year olds don't give a hoot about their bone marrow, much less think about it daily. Most are too busy contemplating their budding careers, their student loan payments, and their sex lives.

But within days of my thirtieth birthday, I was obsessing about my bone marrow—and a whole lot more.

As I approached the big three-oh that year, things were looking calmer and brighter than they had been in a while, as thankfully both Merrick and Mom had held their own throughout most of 1995. Upon serious advice from his doctors to lighten his load for his health and well-being, Merrick made the difficult decision that fall to leave his beloved St. Bernadette's and take on a less stressful position as chaplain at a Catholic high school, still in the Buffalo area. It was a bittersweet farewell for him, but he was genuinely excited about his new ministry. And Mom, while still relying on that wheelchair for mobility, had made strides with her therapy and was seriously making a go of her new life in Bradford. Moreover, at Christmas that year, Barb and I had surprised our families with the exciting news that after six great (but Bednar intense!) years of marriage, we were expecting our first baby (something I had always promised Barb from the time we got married: "By the time you're thirty, we'll have a baby!"). We were thrilled and delighted about our news, as was Merrick, who was the only person we told in advance of the Christmas Day announcement. Actually, even Peg took it pretty well, all things considered. She always did have a soft spot for little babies—and the role of mothers.

So the new year—and January, the month I hate the most—was off to a great start. But as Bednar luck would have it, by the time my thirtieth birthday approached on the twenty-ninth, Merrick ended up back in Pittsburgh, feeling weak and fatigued yet again. His team of doctors was running all sorts of tests to determine what was ailing him this time. Consequently, he spent most of January and early February in and out of the hospital—and ended up missing the small surprise birthday party that Barb and my family threw for me. Could I really be thirty?

Ironically, it was on another holiday —make that "helliday," (Valentine's Day 1996)—when Merrick called each of us on the phone from Pittsburgh (as he always did, since only a few of us had e-mail at that time) to personally share his latest news: The test results were in.

He had been diagnosed with myelodysplasia.

Myelo-what?

Myelodysplasia. A pre-leukemic condition.

Leukemia? Merrick's now got a form of leukemia?

 How could this happen? Why did this happen? Those were two questions that seemingly everyone—except Merrick—asked as we received this horrible news. Yet in a way that only Merrick—who had already knocked on death's door twice before in his thirty-two short years—could, he calmly and faithfully explained as much as he had learned earlier that day about how, simply put, his blood cells and platelets weren't doing their job anymore, nor were they being produced in a normal fashion. And, he realistically went on to say, it looked like there might be a way out, but that it wasn't going to be easy: He'd need a successful bone marrow transplant to live.

A bone marrow transplant? You've got to be kidding. How much more over the top could poor Merrick's life get?

But sadly, it was no joke. And yet, amazingly, through his spirit-filled words and compassionate tone, Merrick shared this most devastating news about his own life and made it seem, once again, like it was just a minor problem. That's because he genuinely was more concerned about how tragic news like this would affect those he loved than how it affected him.

Always the guy who could find the silver lining in every black cloud, Merrick pointed out the good news in all of this: The odds were on his side that with eight siblings, there probably would be a perfect match.

"It's going to be me," I told him emphatically. "I know it is." Not only did I feel it immediately, but, as Bednar luck would have it, Barb and I were about to have a baby. What's a little more stress? I also knew that it made the most sense, medically speaking. I had done research on heart transplants years before for a college writing project, so I knew that age, sex, and blood type were important factors in successful organ transplant matches. I just assumed it worked that way with bone marrow transplants, too—although I had no clue how one really happened.

My siblings and I would find out soon enough. Within a week or so each of us received a letter from Doctor Miller confirming the horrific news about Merrick and informing us that a bone marrow transplant coordinator would be working with us to coordinate the necessary blood tests, to find out which of his eight siblings might be a suitable match for Merrick.

Chapter 61

As I had suspected (and wished for) from the beginning, it turned out to be me.

But since Merrick had always been in a class all by himself, he truly had no *perfect* match. I was off by one antigen, I learned—whatever the heck that meant—so I was Merrick's *closest* sibling match. Our brother Mike was next closest (he and I were perfect matches, we then learned through this process), but since I was younger and closer in age to Merrick, I emerged as the best candidate.

And what an awesome privilege it was going to be—although I readily admit that as the family wimp who had never even spent a day in the hospital, I was a bit freaked by the thoughts of huge needles invading my body. In fact, as friends and co-workers learned that I was going to be a bone marrow donor, they treated me as if I were some type of selfless hero. But that certainly wasn't the way I viewed it. Merrick was the hero here; I was just the lucky one—out of my entire family and all the other people who would have jumped at the chance to help this much-loved and admired guy—who actually got to do it. Leave it to Merrick, though, despite the life or death fight that lay ahead of him, to somehow shine the spotlight on me through all of this.

Deep down, I have to admit, I was extremely proud of the fact that I had could help Merrick in this way. We had been through so much together from the time we were kids—heck, he was Batman and I was Robin—so to me it was only right that I would now turn into "Donorman," as he and my family started to affectionately refer to me. Plus, he had given so much to so many—including me—through the years, that I was thrilled to be able to do something this important for him.

Of course, from the time I learned that I was his best match, I prayed and prayed that all would go well—for Merrick, and, selfishly, for me—because, despite being proud, I was scared. Scared mostly that my bone marrow could end up killing him … but I'd be lying if I said that I wasn't scared that something bad could happen to me as well. As a soon-to-be new dad, I guess I was a bit overwhelmed by everything that was happening in my life all of the sudden. Hello, thirty!

Anyway, our pre-transplant journey began, ironically enough, on April Fool's Day, 1996. I hopped a three o'clock flight (courtesy of Maggie's frequent flyer miles) that early spring day from overcast Rochester to rainy Pittsburgh, cabbed it to our "regular" Holiday Inn in Oakland, and met Merrick, who had arrived earlier that day, in the hotel lobby. You'd never know by looking at his handsome face, warm smile, and Buffalo Sabres hat that cancer was consuming him—although he had definitely lost some weight since I had seen him last.

After our standard greeting—the Bednar hug—we sat in the hotel lobby, waiting for Mike and Vickie to arrive. They were resolute about driving up from North Carolina to provide support for tomorrow's pre-transplant evaluation. The wait provided Merrick and me with that rare luxury of talking face to face, alone, for seemingly the first time about what we were getting ourselves into. I didn't realize it at the time, but it was another one of those vivid moments that stay with you for a lifetime.

I don't recall every word we said, but after some light-hearted conversation and some serious cracking up, there were three things that Merrick said that evening that really sank in:

"What you're doing for me is incredible," he said in all seriousness, "and I'll never forget it." He looked me in the eye. "But if it doesn't work, it's not your fault."

There he was again, thinking of others—me—before himself.

"It's gonna work," I defiantly assured him.

He then told me, "Also, if anything does happen, I want you to write a letter to the president of the hospital, thanking him on my behalf for all that the people here have done for us through the years."

Merrick knew I liked to write, and he liked my way with words.

"Of course I will," I assured him. "I'm your vice president, remember? But nothing's going to happen."

But in that moment, I was heartsick about this thought—and reminded yet again how filled with gratitude that brother of mine was, even as he faced the reality of his own demise.

"And one last thing," he told me, shaking his head.

"You've really gotta write that book ..." referring to the book about our family that I had begun on a lark the year before.

I looked him straight in the eye. "I'm gonna. I promise."

"Then let's do it!" he exclaimed, playing off the new "Just do it!" Nike ad campaign of the time. As we arose from our lobby chairs, we double-handed high-fived each other, which we did a lot, then intertwined each other's hands. We held our grip on each other for a few seconds, squeezed, and looked right into each other's eyes, as if we were telling each other, "We're gonna get through this."

Just then, some Carolina sunshine walked into the lobby from the pouring rain.

It was always great to see Mike and Vickie, and today was no exception. Ever since marrying Vickie in 1987—and Merrick blessed their marriage as a newly ordained deacon in 1989—our eldest brother had turned his life around: saying goodbye to booze and drugs, working steadily, reconnecting with his family, and revealing his true and wonderful inner core—all thanks to his "Miss Vickie." Like her, Mike was simply the kindest, most caring, most giving person you could ever meet. And despite our assurance that they did not have to travel from their tiny town of Pittsboro, North Carolina, to the "concrete jungle" (as Peg always called it) of Pittsburgh, Mike and his wife insisted on driving ten hours that day and would have it no other way.

As we ate dinner in the hotel restaurant and our conversation grew more serious, Mike made it perfectly clear why.

"I wasn't there for your first transplant, bro, and I kick myself for that," he said in his longtime Southern drawl. "But I'm going to be with you every step of the way for this one. Vickie and I both are."

Both Merrick and I told Mike not to worry about the past. Things were very different then, and he was in a very different place. No one ever held anything against him. But Vickie told us how guilty Mike has always felt about that.

After dinner, we took Merrick back to the nearby cathedral, where he always stayed whenever he had to come to Pittsburgh. (I was crashing with Mike and Vickie at the Holiday Inn.) As the rain continued to fall, we chatted a bit longer in his guest suite about what lay ahead tomorrow with the pre-transplant appointment. Since we were all exhausted and had a big day ahead of us, we called it a night fairly early. Before heading back to the hotel, though, we held hands and bowed our heads as Merrick led us in an impromptu but moving prayer. Then he gave us each a yellow laminated prayer card—"I've got one for everyone," he told us—which he said was the prayer that he was relying on these days, and believed we all should. It was the beautiful prayer of St. Francis deSales, which read appropriately enough:

Do not fear what may happen tomorrow.
The same loving Father who cares for you today
will care for you tomorrow and every day.
Either He will shield you from suffering,
or he will give you unfailing strength to bear it.
Be at peace, then, and put aside all anxious
thoughts and imaginings.

Funny, I slept better that night than I ever thought I would.

Chapter 62

In typical Bednar fashion, we were almost late for our 9:00 a.m. pre-transplant appointment because Mike's car wouldn't turn over. He had flipped the inside light on in the parking garage the night before, and inadvertently had forgotten to turn it off. Oh, great.

We were sweating bullets thinking we'd be late, but fortunately the garage attendant broke protocol and actually jumped Mike's new Pontiac Bonneville for us. Thankfully Merrick had had the good sense to call a cab from the cathedral and had planned to meet us at the hospital from the get-go.

As we parked in the garage and hustled through the drizzle to the hospital lobby, the pit in my stomach grew bigger and bigger. Here we go again, back at this damn hospital where I vowed I would never return.

If I felt this way, how must have Merrick felt? Where did he get the strength to do this?

I asked myself that over and over.

We spotted Merrick, shared a brief and light-hearted laugh about our car woes, and then followed him to the suite of offices where our appointments that day were. We arrived with literally not a moment to spare, and the words on the wall in big lettering all but kicked me in the gut: Pittsburgh Cancer Institute.

Is this for real?

Do we really have to go in?

I think I'm the one who's going to be sick.

Chapter 63

Yes, we had to go in.

The heavy woman behind the sliding glass check-in window wasn't even that friendly. But I can hardly blame her for hating her job.

The waiting room was larger than a regular doctor's office, and as I looked around I was sickened and saddened. Dear God in heaven. Do all these people have cancer? Of the dozen or so seated there early that morning, I wondered who was silently suffering with this awful disease, and who there was silently suffering alongside them. I'm sure all the other people in the room were wondering the same thing. It was a very sobering place, and none of us said much.

I was actually relieved when we were called in to a small meeting room, where we would spend the next four to five hours meeting a few nurses, the doctor who would do the transplant, our transplant coordinator, a social worker, and even a hospital finance person. Dear God. As if it weren't bad enough, someone actually has to pay for this misery.

And then they draw your blood. "We need several vials from the donor and the recipient," we were told.

I wasn't expecting this. I thought all my blood had already been tested two months before.

Did I tell you I hate needles?

But I was doing this for Merrick, and I'm not as wimpy as everyone thinks I am.

I just bruise easily.

From there, everything became surreal—like something out of a movie. I brought a pen and pad, because all I really knew is that I knew nothing at all, would be asked a million questions afterwards by family and friends, and would probably not remember much, except how depressed I was that all this was real. Yes, despite feeling surreal, this was very, very real.

By the time I hugged Mike, Vickie, and Merrick tightly later that evening at the Pittsburgh airport for my flight back to Rochester, I was whipped, worried, sad, frightened—but also excited and energized—about what I had learned that day, and what now awaited us in just a few short weeks.

Chapter 64

Thank God I was a good student who was used to taking good notes. The information we received that day was dizzying, alarming, and amazing:

"Patient and donor are HLA identical except for a mismatch as HLA-A due to AXB crossover."

Translation? Merrick didn't have a perfect match. We're nearly identical except for one antigen. I was the best chance he had for a successful bone marrow transplant.

The reasons for a transplant?

Merrick's marrow was failing, it wouldn't get better by itself, and the good priest was now transfusion dependent.

I'm no doctor—but I realized that was clearly not a good thing.

Has anyone with a heart transplant ever received a bone marrow transplant?

To the best of their knowledge and research, no. Merrick would be a first, making this an experimental process—and of benefit to others.

Kinda cool, I had to admit. I never thought I would be part of medical history—although I wished none of this were happening.

What are the risks?

Graph-versus-host disease (kind of like rejection, except it's not an organ), other toxicities, unpredictable infections, organ failure. There's a 20 percent mortality rate associated with graph-versus-host disease, meaning one-fifth have a chance of dying within the first hundred days.

My heart sank at this news.

Bottom line?

This was not elective surgery. Without this transplant, Merrick would die.

My heart sank even farther.

But if all went well, Merrick's cancer could be cured—and he could have a quality life with virtually no limitations.

'Nuf said.

After listening intently and asking numerous questions, Merrick unbelievably and enthusiastically proclaimed "Let's do it!" as he once again gave me the high five.

I could tell he had confidence in the mild-mannered, reassuring, and brilliant young doctor, Dr. Baker—a colleague of Dr. Miller's—who was telling us all these things, and who, in no small coincidence, had an aunt, we learned, who was a member of St. Bernadette's parish back in Buffalo!

Then we talked through the entire process and timeline with the transplant coordinator, Mary, whom we'd been dealing with by phone and liked right away. She was businesslike but friendly, and extremely empathetic. She had a dry sense of humor, too, which goes a long way with us Bednars. It was Mary who briefed us on all the details: the timing, the need for "reverse isolation" for the patient, the massive pre-transplant chemo, the donor collection process, "Day Zero" (the day of transplant), the first hundred days post-transplant. Mary even gave us a tour of the special bone marrow transplant wing of the hospital. I understood the need to see it, but this was one tour that did little to excite any of us.

In fact, the place still haunts me.

Somehow, I think it always will.

Chapter 65

All healthy people who have ever felt sorry for themselves should be forced to spend a day in UPMC's bone marrow transplant unit (or if they'd rather, the hospital's cardiothoracic intensive care unit). After spending an intense ten hours there watching someone they love fight desperately yet valiantly for his or her life, they should be forced to catch the nine o'clock hospital shuttle down the steep and bumpy hills of Pittsburgh to the Family House—a group home of sorts for those in need of a comfortable yet inexpensive place to stay—where they try to momentarily escape their sick brother's, or son's, or husband's, or mother's brave battle with some awful illness.

It's enough to break a heart of stone, and make your insignificant troubles seem like a day at the beach.

I think of it as an exercise in perspective shifting.

But it's something more as well. It's a deep, powerful, introspective experience—one that, by no choice of our own, my brothers and sisters and mother and I had seemingly done so many times in ten years that we'd lost count. But that moving experience, as painful as it is, hits home what's really important, and brings you closer than you ever thought possible to yourself, your loved ones, and your God.

I guess that's one of life's—or at least my life's—most profound ironies.

And so, like it or not, my family spent a lot of time in that bone marrow transplant unit in May 1996.

It's a month—and an experience—none of us will ever forget, most especially Merrick and me.

Chapter 66

I'm not sure if it was Merrick or Maura who had the great idea to resurrect the journal—the old red hardcover bookkeeper's log that we bought at CVS in the Olean Center Mall ten years earlier to track Merrick's heart transplant. Heck, if we had known from the get-go how valuable that journal would become, we would have bought a fancier one! Merrick had held onto it all these years, and it was actually fun to re-read the entries from a decade before.

It many ways, it seemed like a lifetime ago. In other ways, it felt like yesterday.

Clearly, so much had changed in the past ten years. But I think even Merrick would agree that no one person had changed as noticeably during that time than our baby sister Maura—now an extremely talented, fast-rising, over-achieving twenty-something in the mid-nineties corporate world of Xerox.

As the saying goes, "You've come a long way, baby." That was certainly true with Bednar Baby Number Nine.

Being the baby of any family always has its advantages—and disadvantages. With Maura and her birth order in this clan, I can honestly say there were far more disadvantages than advantages to being the youngest. Since she was only four when it all hit the fan, so to speak, Maura remembers absolutely no normalcy in her childhood—precisely because there was none. From getting run over by a car at age four, to being "kidnapped" or frequenting occasional bars at age five with Mom as she plotted to get us out of foster care, to traipsing around the country at age six, seven, and eight (usually while fighting one of her older siblings for the front seat), Maura's childhood was anything but a little girl's fantasy. Is it any wonder then, as a youngster, she was precocious, self-centered, and stubborn? Of course, she also could be as sweet and loveable as a puppy, and was as cute as a button with dark hair, dark eyes, and a big heart—characteristics that endeared her to young and old, especially Mom, her older brothers (except me at the time!), and her Uncle Kenny.

By eight, nine, and ten, Maura was like every little sister on the planet: totally annoying to her young teen siblings (read: Mollie and me). In fact, she fought with the two of us all the time (I even have a few scars to prove it!), all but lived on penny candy and junk food, and was a total grub who hated taking showers. Quite a switch from the glamour gal she is today, I assure you. As a young teen, she was much more into her girlfriends than her family, and suddenly discovered clothes, makeup, boys—and mischief. It was enough to get her in trouble from time to time with both Mom and Gramma Jo.

Amazingly, even as a young girl, Maura was both book smart (probably because on our cross-country trips we'd drill her on the state capitals and other senseless trivia) and street smart—simply because she learned to be to survive. Since she was so bright, Mom had her skip kindergarten when we lived in Eldred and enrolled her in first grade, despite never having spent a day in preschool. Academically Maura thrived, despite always being the youngest person in her class, and continued to do so at every grade level despite all the turmoil in our lives—finishing both eighth grade and ultimately high school as the class valedictorian.

By then, Maura had begun to use her brains wisely for the most part—and also had learned a lot about life's do's and don'ts by watching and learning from her older siblings' successes and mistakes. So while it usually was a pain in the butt having eight siblings watching over you like a hawk most of your life, in the end it worked to our little sister's advantage.

In addition to her brains, Maura had something else working in her favor: her looks. As she matured, a natural beauty emerged, and she quickly learned how to accentuate it. Of course, those good looks attracted lots of guys—but, unfortunately, the pretty young thing didn't always use her God-given brains to separate the good from the not so good. Most, at least the ones I know about, fell into the latter category.

But give or take a bad choice (or twenty!) in guys through the years, by the time Maura headed off to college in the fall of '87—a year after Merrick's heart transplant had changed us all—she had a good head on her shoulders and had outgrown much of her teen angst, replacing it with a warm and friendly personality. Armed as she was with a trifecta of brains, looks, and personality, it was clear to all that she was bound to go far—which she has, both personally and professionally.

So by the time of Merrick's bone marrow transplant, our baby sister was indeed all grown up. She was now a wonderful young woman whom we all adored and admired. Literally, in the past ten years, she had evolved from the supporting kid sister role she played during Merrick's first transplant to a leading role as his competent, efficient, and indispensable executive assistant this time around—using her "get it done" ways to take care of things big and small for her sick brother.

In that E.A. role, which Merrick valued and she cherished, Maura made the first entry of Merrick's second transplant in the infamous journal, simply titling it "ten years later ..."

Sunday, May 12, 1996
5:00 p.m.
Room 829

- *Mother's Day!*

- *Merrick's sixth anniversary of being ordained.*

- *Back in Pittsburgh, this time in Montefiore Hospital ....*

- *Merrick has been here since last Monday (5/6).*

- *Received his last dose of chemo today and started FK506 (Tacrolimus, to replace Cyclosporine). Feels as good as can be expected, a little nauseous and some leg cramps. Still has his wonderful attitude and sense of humor. The nursing staff loves him (as usual).*

- *Martial is being a great trooper! As donor, he receives two shots of a drug called Neupogen every morning for four days to increase his white blood count—causing general achiness, fatigue, and headache… Barb was "pitsy" when she left yesterday (her sister Cathy picked her up to head back to Rochester). Baby Bednar's on the way in three months!*

- *Martial and Maura are with Merrick; Mitch is due in town this evening, and the rest of the troops come down tomorrow and Tuesday. If all goes as scheduled, on Tuesday Martial checks in at 8:15 a.m. for the "harvest" of peripheral stems cells—a procedure that will take approximately four hours—and then Merrick will be infused shortly thereafter. The side effects of chemo will be at their worst then.*

- *Lots of well-wishers and prayers from back home. Cardinal O'Hara sent four hundred-plus cards (which Merrick was so touched by), St. Bernadette's took up a special collection for him, and the new Bishop of Buffalo called to offer his prayers and support.*

What the journal didn't say is that, no matter how you slice it, there are far better ways to spend a special anniversary or, if you're a mother, Mother's Day. We all just clung to the hope that next year at this time, everything would be OK.

Chapter 67

Tuesday, May 14, 1996
Day Zero

I was sooo ready for Day Zero, the day of transplant, to arrive—obviously for Merrick's sake, but also for mine. After the initial blood draws upon my arrival in Pittsburgh, several days of Neupogen shots (a drug that would increase my white blood cell count) from a visiting nurse, and daily needle sticks to check my blood counts, I definitely wanted the needles to stop.

Actually, the more shots I got, the better I became at getting them. Sure, I winced at each and every one of them, and it kind of burned as the drug was injected into my arm. But I purposely never complained, because in light of all that Merrick had already gone through—and what he had ahead of him—I knew that twenty needles or so in my arms in five days was a very small price to pay compared to all that Merrick had to endure.

While it may not have been the most fun I've ever had, physically speaking, donating my bone marrow was a huge high on other levels. I awoke early that morning more excited than nervous, although I couldn't eat a bite. I showered and donned the navy blue "Just Donate It!" T-shirt that my longtime pal MaryAnne McCormick had embroidered for me. She sent Merrick a matching "Just Do It!" one, which he wore that day as well. Before going to the hospital's outpatient check-in, Maura and I paid a short visit to Merrick's room, where we held hands and he led us in one of his beautiful impromptu prayers. I was so in control, I didn't even cry when I hugged him! We just high fived each other, and off I went—excited about this amazing life (and life-giving) experience that had finally arrived.

Either at check-in—or maybe it was days earlier when I had to sign my donor consent form for this medical research study and review all the risks—I was asked a bunch of questions that made me glad I led a pretty wholesome life, relatively speaking. Things like "In the past ten years, have you injected any drugs with a hypodermic needle?" "Have you had multiple sex partners?" and the like. After answering all the questions "correctly," I was taken to what looked like a regular hospital room—just around the corner from where Merrick was—where a pheresis nurse, who reminded me pleasantly of my delightful sister-in-law Debbie (Mark's new wife of two years at that point), awaited. I lay down on the bed, and before long had two big needles in my now black-and-blue-and-bruised arms—where they would stay for about six hours. As I had been told, my harvest was a new, more sophisticated, less invasive one than a traditional bone marrow harvest, where you're knocked out cold in an operating room. Officially, I was undergoing a "peripheral stem cell harvest." With the nurse by me at all times, one needle basically drew all my blood out into a tube, which traveled to a centrifuge. The centrifuge somehow (don't ask me how!) spun my blood and separated my stem cells from my white cells, red cells, and platelets. The stem cells—which basically looked like thick blood— were bagged, and everything else amazingly was returned to my body through the other line that went into my other arm. The whole thing blew me away.

Of course, we turned this whole procedure into an event, as the Bednars always seem to do. As the process started, Mom, Maura, and the rest of the family rotated between sitting with me and with Merrick, who was being pre-medicated for his transplant, which would take place later that day. I think everyone was more concerned about how I'd do through all of this than Merrick! I had Maura call Barb, who I had purposely sent home to Rochester a few days earlier to keep her stress level down— considering she was carrying my child! She was so relieved to hear my voice, and couldn't believe how well I was doing. "It's not that bad," I assured her. I even told her I was watching an old episode of *Charlie's Angels* on TNT or some other channel. She couldn't believe it.

Neither could I.

The nurse continued to check my levels and did her job to ensure that all was fine. I even had Mollie call Merrick, hold the phone up to my ear (since I had to lay flat and could not use my arms), and I assured him I was fine. (He was worried about me too!) I surprised everyone—including myself. I knew this was a significant medical procedure, but I was confident that everything would be fine.

The minutes, and then the hours, ticked by slowly. I eventually grew more uncomfortable—primarily from just having to be in one position for hours—but I eventually managed to doze a bit. Every so often, someone would bring me a milkshake to sip on because I had to keep my calcium levels up. (Gotta love those milkshakes!) The next thing I knew, several hours had passed, and I was done.

They took my cells to the lab for one final check and to count how many they collected. Now there's a fun job! One thousand one, one thousand two, one thousand three ...

I felt weak and woozy, and was very light-headed, so I had to wait a while before getting up and going to Merrick's room for the transplant. When I walked in the unit, and then into a darkened Room 829 some thirty minutes later, my whole mood changed, as had everyone's. It was not long after I arrived that Maura picked up the journal and began writing:

2:40 p.m.

- *The infusion has begun! The pheresis from Martial went extremely well—lots of stem cells, 13 percent of his blood. He's tired and drained, but overall doing fine.*

- *Merrick is doing well, a little tired from his pre-meds for the platelets. The infusion should last about forty-five minutes … Heather (his nurse) and all the others are taking great care of him. Dr. Miller and Mary have stopped up a few times to inquire on both … Almost all of the family is here. Martial and Merrick have their "Just Do It" and "Just Donate It" T-shirts on, as well as the girls ("Test Your Faith … Daily"). Even throughout all this, we are having our usual "photo shoots." We have to catch this medical first on film! … So far, so good!*

3:30 p.m.

- *The infusion is complete—the engrafting has begun, and will take place over the next seven to ten days.*

By now, I was physically whipped and suddenly emotionally drained, having sat by Merrick's bedside holding his hand throughout the entire transplant (which in many ways looked like a blood transfusion), not really saying much at all. Neither of us did. After the awesome—in the truest sense of the word—but somewhat anticlimactic forty-five minutes, Maura offered to take me back to the Family House to rest. I kissed a sedated Merrick gently on his forehead, and walked out the door.

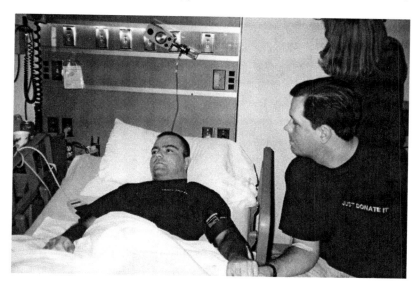

I don't think I even made it around the corner to the elevator when the weight of it all finally hit me like the proverbial ton of bricks. With one simple and sincere, "How you doin'?" from Maura, the lump in my throat and quiver of my chin gave way to huge tears that I tried hard to fight back, simply because of the busy elevator and congested lobby I had to walk through. But by the time we got outside and got in Maura's car in the parking ramp, I was crying like a little kid on the playground who had just been beaten up. Like a parent would care for that whupped child, Maura did everything in her power to try to make me feel better. She eventually got me back to the miniscule room at the Family House we had been sharing that week, helped me calm down and get control of myself, and even snuck a Diet Pepsi and a Little Debbie Swiss cake roll up to me from the kitchen.

"Mitzi's gonna have my head!" I blurted, half delirious, referring (inaccurately) to the person in charge of the Family House who forbade food and drinks in the rooms.

Once I finally lay down, and seemingly seconds after my

head hit the pillow, I fell into a deep, deep sleep and Maura gave Barb a call to tell her I was OK, as I had instructed.

But before long, my much-needed power nap was rudely interrupted by the obnoxious ringing of the phone on the night-stand right next to my twin bed.

I answered it, not even pretending to be awake. It was Mary, the transplant coordinator.

* * *

5:15 p.m.

- *Word from the nurse that Martial will need to undergo pheresis again tomorrow—they only got 5.75 million today. (They were shooting for ten.) Round Two tomorrow ...*

Chapter 68

To put it bluntly, Round Two sucked.

I must have cried out all the courage, strength, and bravado that I had displayed the day before, because it was nowhere to be found for Round Two. In fact, I hadn't even returned to the hospital that evening before because I was such a mess and didn't want Merrick to know that I had, in an instant, come completely unglued. I was so mad at myself! I had to get my act together! How could Merrick be so strong when he's got the hard part—and I'm so weak despite having the easy part?

It's not that I didn't want to do it for Merrick, or that I wouldn't. I think it was just the fact that I had convinced myself that it would only be once (despite being told in advance it could take two or even more collections), that all would go well (which it did), and Merrick would get better, just like that. What I hadn't counted on was the intensity of the whole emotional aspect of the transplant process. I had been so focused on getting through the physical—the needles, the drugs, the procedures, for both for Merrick and me—that it wasn't until that part was over and done with (or so I thought) that I realized that was the easy part. The hard part is looking your dying brother in the eyes, holding his hand while you hope and pray that your marrow dripping through that bag will not only make him better but won't kill him. Until you go through it, there's no way to prepare yourself for the emotions stirred within. At least that's how it was for me.

So, shortly after receiving word from Mary that I was definitely going to need to donate again in the morning—and get two more extra painful shots of Neupogen that evening—there was a knock on my door. I figured it was Maura, who already knew I had fallen apart once, checking back in on me. But it wasn't. It was Mitch, who had just learned I had to do this again in the morning, and knew damn well that his thirty-year-old little brother needed a shot in the arm of a different kind.

Like the good coach who knows how to rally one of his players who's really down on his luck, Mitch touched my heart that evening with his sincere praise for what I had done, his empathy for what I was feeling, and his absolute confidence in me—when I had more doubts than anyone.

The next morning, I showed up at the pheresis room again— but this time nervous, uptight, and emotionally drained. And wouldn't you know that instead of the nice nurse who reminded me of Debbie, there was some mean one who had trouble getting the huge needles into my veins? She poked and poked my now seriously bruised up arms and still couldn't get one in my right arm. So she took my right hand, squeezed it, and stuck the five-inch steel needle right into the only bulging vein I apparently had left. I winced painfully as tears dripped down the sides of my face onto the pillow, and let out a yelping, drawn out *"Ouuu-ch!"* as Maura watched—desperate but unable to help.

Shortly after that, Dr. Miller came in to check on me. With one look and a quick chat with Maura or Mollie, who had also come in to check on me, she could tell I was a different person from the day before. She told me she would give me something called Ativan to relax me.

Thank God for Ativan.

The next thing I remember was waking up six hours later and learning that they had collected all they needed.

Thank God!

My job as donor was now complete—and the old Martial was back in no time at all.

Chapter 69

- *The transplant is officially complete. Martial underwent pheresis again yesterday (with the help of a drug called Ativan!) and got enough to reach the ten million stem cells target ...*

- *So far Merrick is doing as well as can be expected. Lots of well-wishers and greetings from back home sure help!*

- *Now that Martial has recuperated from being Donorman, he's become Media Man.* The Times Herald, Buffalo News, *and Buffalo TV and radio stations have done some nice stories on Merrick. Martial spoke with the hospital PR guy today who informed him that his phone has been ringing off the hook with inquiries of Merrick's condition.*

Chapter 70

Sunday, May 26, 1996
Pentecost Sunday
Day Twelve

- *What a week!!!! Starting with the good news: Merrick's counts are up today—he has a count of one hundred four neutrophils, forty-one thousand platelets, and eight hundred white blood cells. The neutrophils are the disease-fighting parts of the white blood cells. He has to reach five hundred before he can be discharged. But today is the first day he's had any, so that's encouraging!*

- *Merrick is doing pretty well today, but he had a hell of a week. Hopefully, the worst is over! His fever shot up last Monday and Tuesday to one hundred five degrees. The doctors weren't sure if his heart was rejecting (thank God his heart is fine) or what the source of the fever was. They were treating him with antifungals and antibiotics, which, unfortunately, caused major body shakes, convulsions, and tremors. He had Mitch, Mom, and Maggie very scared, but they were troupers and stayed with him throughout, taking turns crashing on the couch (and Mitch munching on Junior Mints!) The fever broke on Thursday and has been normal since. Merrick's throat is still sore, his eyes are bloodshot, and he's still retaining fluid, but slowly and surely he's back on the upswing.*

- *Other than that, Mrs. Lincoln, how was the play?*

Chapter 71

Friday, May 31, 1996
Day Seventeen
6:55 p.m.

- *What a glorious day! Merrick, Martial, and Maura are sitting in the rectory of the cathedral, unpacking Merrick in his "home away from home." He has been discharged on Day Seventeen! It's truly a miracle! The nurses and doctors gave Rick a going-away cake and sang, "For He's a Jolly Good Fellow." Dr. Baker and Dr. Miller were beaming!*

- *We took a cruise in the White Ghost (a/k/a Maura's new Acura Vigor) to Squirrel Hill on a beautifully warm and sunny day. First stop: Revco (so Rick can get some "beauty supplies"!)*

- *Merrick feels good and is hungry for pizza, of all things!*

- *His neutrophils are over eighteen thousand and his myelodysplasia is completely cured!*

- *Unbelievable!*

- *Martial and Maura packed up Room 829— that floor will never be the same! I'm sure the nurses will feel rather bored without all of the Bednars running around!*

- *We're making the round of calls right now— Maggie and Mitch still can't believe this!*

- *"Is this a managed care decision?!" Maggie the health-care expert demanded to know.*

- *Plans are for Rick to go to the clinic twice a week on Mondays and Thursdays ... I'm sure he will continue to improve with each passing day.*

- *For any non-believers, they need to look no further to see the power of prayer at work!*

Halleluiah!

Chapter 72

Saturday, June 1, 1996
Day Eighteen
1:20 p.m.

- *June has started off much better than May ... Merrick is getting stronger each day. We just went down and met the Bishop of Pittsburgh, who was here at the cathedral for an ordination. Merrick is full of energy and life today (isn't he always?) and now making plans for Lucas' tenth anniversary ... Then he, Martial, and Maura are off to see the matinee of "Mission: Impossible." (How appropriate!) What a beautiful day!*

9:00 p.m.

- *Merrick is certainly feeling better! We went bombing around to a bunch of car dealerships, to the movies, to 6:00 p.m. Mass, and to Union Grill for dinner. Merrick has more energy than Maura and Martial combined!*

"Turn that up," the car-loving priest instructed me as our kid sister chauffeured us around that sunny Saturday from one Pittsburgh car dealership to the next in her gorgeous new white Acura—just to check out the latest models for fun. "I love that song!"

And with the sunroof open and the windows down, we blasted Jon Secada's latest—"I'm Free"—from Maura's excellent sound system.

Indeed, we wanted the whole world to know that Fr. Merrick Bednar was once again free.

Chapter 73

All of the sudden, the summer of 1996 was looking sunny again for Merrick and for this family—which was quite amazing, considering what its outlook had been just a few short weeks before. Not to sound selfish, but this was really great for Barb and me, considering we were now just two months away from becoming parents for the first time. Thankfully, Barb had had an excellent pregnancy thus far, despite all the stress in our lives since we had shared our happy news at Christmas.

So instead of illness and possible death, our thoughts turned happily to new life that summer, for good reason. In addition to the upcoming birth of our new baby, we now had the rebirth of our brother.

Even though Merrick had to spend his first hundred days post-transplant—roughly the whole summer—living at the cathedral in Pittsburgh so he could be seen and monitored in the bone marrow clinic two or three times a week, and even though we all knew that things could change on a dime's notice, Merrick's spirit and optimism was contagious. "Carpe Diem" became the guy's spoken motto now, and he had every intention to live by those words. As he quickly started feeling better and gained more energy, he'd keep himself busy each and every day by walking, golfing, writing, or, heck, even shopping. In fact, one day when Mollie was there for a visit, he wanted her to go to the mall with him before they went golfing. He was on a mission that day: to buy all of us—his immediate family members—a copy of Celine Dion's "Because You Loved Me." It was his thank you gift, he later told us as he made a point to give it to each of us personally, for getting him through his transplant. I daresay most people would only think of this song as a love song to a significant other. Not the ever-grateful Merrick. He said the lyrics spoke straight from his heart.

People who knew Merrick well—like all of us and his close friends—along with all those who he had only known for only a short while—like his medical team, the teens he counseled back at the high school in Buffalo, and people at his former parish—truly marveled at the thirty-two-year-old wonder priest. Not just because of the suffering he had endured and overcome, but once again *how* he had done it. Merrick energized, amazed, and inspired—in many more ways that I'm sure I'll ever know.

But we did learn of one way that summer, as Merrick improved enough and was given the OK to come home to Mom's place in Bradford for a weekend visit. He was so touched by a letter and special gift from two former parishioners that he had received just days before that he couldn't wait to share it with us:

July 19, 1996

Dear Father Merrick,

We hope that this letter and the accompanying gift find you in improving health and good spirits.

A few months ago, we began writing songs together as a natural extension of our musical friendship. Recently, we decided to write a song for you that captured, on behalf of our parish, the influence you have had on all of us. That influence, among other things, embodies an incredible sense of faith and eternal optimism. In searching for a proper metaphor to convey those characteristics, we decided upon a flame—or more specifically in this case, "The Torch." Your example to this parish is the torch that our song refers to and urges us all to takes its light and pass it on. We believe that is exactly what is happening. Most of us would consider ourselves very fortunate to have such an influence on those around us. We wrote it in hopes that it may contribute, in a very small way, to your recovery, which we understand is progressing nicely …

We hope your recovery brings you back to visit St. Bernadette's real soon.

With our warmest regards and get well wishes,
Jay and Ralph

And then my brother popped a cassette into Mom's boom box, which played a stirring song titled, "The Torch" that basically set his life and ministry to music. The lyrics were simple … powerful … stirring. Merrick's tears showed us how touched beyond belief he was by this remarkable act of kindness—we all were. And yet, despite the outpouring of affection and support he received from those two gifted and giving musicians—and so many others—Merrick remained humble and filled with gratitude.

The guy was unbelievable. I stood in awe of him. And because of my bone marrow that now flowed through his body, we had a bond that, quite honestly, is impossible to put into words.

Two things became clear to my family as Merrick's check-ups were getting better and better: That I had damn good bone marrow (thank you very much!)—and that a celebration was definitely in order, Merrick-style. And we wasted no time planning one. Ironically, way back at the start of this most unusual year—before Merrick had been diagnosed with his latest cancer—we had talked about a big celebration in 1996 to mark the tenth anniversary of Rick's heart transplant. Merrick instantly had suggested a Mass of Thanksgiving in memory of Lucas and his family. We all loved the idea and started brainstorming ideas, but no one ever said another word about it after Merrick's diagnosis in February—for obvious reasons.

That all changed the day Merrick got out of the hospital. The eventual invitation, which Merrick wrote, said it all:

With praise and gratitude to Almighty God
And in celebration of the power of prayer,
enduring faith, and your companionship
Please join Fr. Merrick Bednar and the Bednar Family

at a Mass of Thanksgiving
to commemorate the tenth anniversary of his heart transplant
and the success of his recent bone marrow transplant
Sunday, July 28, 1996
2:00 p.m.
St. Francis of Assisi Parish
Tonawanda, New York

Reception to follow

And on a gorgeous summer Sunday—exactly ten years and two days after receiving a heart transplant, and just two months after receiving a bone marrow transplant—Merrick once again brought his entire family together, along with three hundred fifty other people, including several priests and the Bishop of Buffalo. This time, we packed a hot church for an unforgettable and uplifting Mass celebrating one extraordinary life. Of course, Merrick being Merrick—and always putting others first—made sure the whole congregation sang "Happy Birthday" to my mom, whose August first birthday was just days away. Of course Peg loved that!

Merrick's own words, printed in the program he titled "A Celebration of Life and Love," summed it up best, I think:

During the last ten years, I have received the blessing and grace of your prayers and love in countless ways. I am profoundly humbled by the presence of each of you in my life. With many others, each and every one of you here has in some unique way been an instrument of God's healing power in my life. To each of you, I offer my deepest gratitude through prayers of praise to our incredible God.

Again and again, I have asked myself how—or better, "why?"—I should be so abundantly blessed by God to experience such an out-pouring of kindness and concern. I know that who I am as a person and priest is largely a tribute to the power and strength of the loving people who have formed, shaped, influenced, and nourished my life. I simply try to give others the love and respect that I have received. You have made a remarkable and lasting difference in my life. Your presence in my life is the face of God's love. It also is the source of my faith in God, and the wellspring of my hope. It is the energy and grace God blesses me with to be his priest and your companion on the journey of faith. It is indeed the power of the Cross.

As each of us struggle daily to lift high the Cross of our lives, God's grace lifts and transforms the burden of the cross by seeing to it that we are never left to carry our cross alone. You have been my Simon, sharing the way of the cross with me through degenerative heart disease and cancer. In doing so, you have led me toward salvation—to a healing that has been more miraculous than the mere physical; indeed, one that is emotional and spiritual as well.

This Eucharist is being celebrated in loving memory of "Lucas" Bednar. It also is being celebrated for you—my family, friends, members of my parish and high school communities, priests, sisters, doctors, nurses, and supporters. All who have offered healing, encouragement, and strength. To each of you I say thank you. And to each of you I promise my prayers that God may bless you as abundantly as He has blessed me.

Chapter 74

Blessed.

Indeed, that's what Merrick and all of us felt that joyous summer day—and what Barb and I felt again just fifteen days later—on Monday, August 12, 1996—when we held our beautiful new baby in our hands for the first time.

Actually, we felt blessed *and* relieved—considering Barb had endured nearly twenty-four hours of increasingly hard labor pains, one false alarm visit to the hospital, an intense all-nighter that showed us both firsthand that they don't call it labor for nothing, and the maximum two hours of pushing, all before her doctor decided they'd have to take our stubborn little baby, who didn't want to arrive naturally, by C-section.

"Are you OK with that?" I asked my wife, worried, as it had been one of her biggest fears during pregnancy.

By that point, a grateful Barb couldn't thank the doctor or the anesthesiologist enough.

And so, after they prepped her for surgery and had me don a hospital mask and surgical attire, I entered a cold, sterile operating room for the first time in my life to witness the most amazing miracle of life: the birth of a child.

"Are you OK, hon?" I immediately asked my doped-up wife who was lying on an operating table with surgical draping around her stomach.

"I'm fine," she instantly responded, as if having surgery were an everyday occurrence. Obviously, the anesthesia was doing its job.

It seemed like it was only minutes later when the lead surgeon started saying, "We're almost there, we're almost there ..."

"What is it? What is it?" I asked excitedly, barely able to contain my enthusiasm.

Nearly everyone—except Merrick—thought we were going to have a girl.

"It's a boy!" she finally proclaimed, as she raised the most incredible human life from Barb's abdominal area.

"A boy!" I beamed. "It's a boy, Barb!"—who by this time had been through the wringer and back.

One of the nurses took the boy—our baby—over to a different area of the O.R. to run some quick tests, clean him up, and swaddle him in a striped hospital blanket. I followed her, looking on in awe.

"Is everything OK?" Barb and I both needed reassurance.

"Everything's fine," the nurse replied. "Here, you can hold him," she told me, as she placed the tiny little thing in my arms. And as I held him awkwardly for the first time and looked at this delicate creature's beautiful face, I beamed. "He's beautiful ..."

As I stared at him, I then added with pride, "He's got my nose, Barb!"

We brought the beautiful and now whimpering baby over to his mother, who was now being sutured on the operating table, to hold. "He's so beautiful ..." she exclaimed, overcome by tears of joy.

It's a moment like nothing we've ever experienced before. Time seemingly stood still while we just stared at the miracle in front of us.

"What are you going to name him?" someone on the surgical team finally asked.

Barb and I had selected both a girl's name and a boy's name in advance so that we'd be prepared when the big moment arrived. We hadn't shared the names with anyone, either. We both really loved the first name, but it was Barb who had ultimately suggested the middle name—in light of everything we had been through, and because of the amazing role model this person would be to our son.

"Alex Merrick," I proudly announced.

Chapter 75

"How on earth did you do this nine times?!"

I'd always ask my mother that question any time I spoke with her during those initial sleep-deprived days and weeks after Alex's birth. It's not that I didn't love my son, but I quickly realized that nothing fully prepares you for the dramatic changes a little baby brings a new parent's life—or the sheer amount of work it is to care for a child.

"I don't know …" Peg would quip. "Lord, it's no wonder I'm half nuts."

And for the first time, I began to think she was right. I mean, becoming a parent—and I was "just" the dad, after all—is overwhelming, even in the best of circumstances. From the moment you hold that child, and from the moment he wraps those beautiful little fingers around yours, you're hooked. You feel love like you've never felt it before. You literally hold innocence and goodness and potential and dreams right in the palm of your hands. Along with all that, though, you worry more than you ever thought possible—*Will he be cute? Will he be smart? Will he be liked? Will he be a good person? Will he stay healthy?*—and inherit a whole new world of pain, both real and perceived. It wasn't until I became a parent myself that I began to see my mom's life in a whole new light—to appreciate that when Peg would say (as she often did), "You don't know what it's like to be a mother," I really didn't. Her pain—and joy—were magnified with each child she brought into this world. It literally was life times nine.

Becoming a dad—of only one child—also cast new light for me on my father, who by now hadn't been a part of my life for some twenty-plus years: A small part of me could *almost* understand how all those kids could put anyone over the edge. But the bigger person in me wondered how any father—no matter how sour the relationship with his spouse—could ever all but abandon his own flesh and blood. It's something I'll never understand, no matter how hard I try. Yet one of my life's most profound ironies is that the absence of a father in my life somehow has worked to make me a better dad to Alex. And the person I have to thank most for making me a loving, caring—albeit imperfect—dad?

My loving, caring, imperfect mom.

Go figure.

If I've gained any parental wisdom through all of this, it's that life rarely makes any sense. And that being a parent is definitely the most difficult—and important—job on the planet.

Anyway, our life clearly had been blessed by the birth of Alex, and his life was literally blessed on September 22, 1996—his mom's thirtieth birthday. Alex was baptized by our own family priest who, of course, was our child's namesake and the natural choice as godfather as well: the incomparable Uncle Merrick.

Given all we had been through that year alone, having my reborn brother baptize my newborn son—in the chapel of my alma mater, nonetheless—exceeded the mere magnificent. It was another one of those miraculous moments that seemed to punctuate the story of our lives.

Once again, life was good.

How long could it last?

Chapter 76

Unfortunately, not long enough.

By the time Thanksgiving rolled around that year, the bottom started falling out.

Again.

What gives with Thanksgiving and this family? It's amazing that any of us can even tolerate that holiday—let alone like it. And yet we do!

This time, it was double trouble. Thank God it had nothing to do with my newborn son—Alex continued to be Barb's and my primary source of joy and happiness. But sadly, it was both Mom and Merrick. And it was serious.

To be totally honest, Mom's woes actually began a bit before Alex was born. Having never fully recovered from her shattered leg two years before and still relying on that wheelchair for mobility, and having those issues magnified by a history of poor circulation and varicose veins in her legs, she started developing some painful open sores in the lower part of her legs. At first, she just doctored them herself (big surprise there). But throughout the fall they started growing more and more painful and began to burn and ooze. Peg was not only grossed out by them, especially as they soaked through her heavy bandages, but she'd literally be in tears from the excruciating pain whenever you'd call on the phone. And you could tell that it was no act.

After not being able to wish them away, and since they were definitely cramping her get-up-and-go style, Peg agreed to see the doctor—a dermatologist she liked in Olean. Although he wanted to do all he could to help, it was obvious to him that Peg had developed several venous ulcers, which, we all learned quickly enough, are extremely difficult to treat.

In the two weeks between Veteran's Day when she rode with Michele to Rochester for a weekend visit at my house, until the time we came to Bradford the evening before the Thanksgiving holiday, Mom had become a very sick woman. She was in non-stop pain, had completely lost her appetite and at least fifteen pounds, and had developed a very serious infection in her body. We convinced her that she had to call the doctor again the day after Thanksgiving, and she agreed.

Meanwhile, just a day or so before Thanksgiving, Merrick—who returned to the Buffalo area in the fall and was doing his campus ministry work at Cardinal O'Hara High School on a limited basis—started feeling lousy: vomiting, fever, general fatigue. Taking no chances, his doctors in Pittsburgh ordered him to come to the hospital immediately. I think he drove himself there, and was promptly admitted.

Of course, we instantly started talking about who would go to Pittsburgh once again for the holiday. But Merrick (being Merrick) was more concerned about Mom—and about me being a new dad—so he insisted that all of us spend the day as originally planned, with Mom in Bradford, and that I, in particular, spend my baby's first Thanksgiving with my three-month-old child, my wife, and our families. We all reluctantly agreed, but Maura and I had decided that we would drive down to Pittsburgh first thing on Friday morning while our other sisters tended to Mom.

Needless to say, it was another weird Thanksgiving day.

We arrived at the hospital on Friday by 11:00 a.m. or so, and spent the entire day just keeping Merrick company. Rick looked OK—by now his hair, which he had lost months before, had started to grow back—but he was chronically fatigued, and was hooked up to a heart monitor. The doctors decided that they would run all sorts of tests on him—of course, not until Monday, after the long holiday weekend—to determine what might be wrong. But they weren't going to let him leave, given his unique medical history.

As usual, we shared some laughs with Merrick, but spent most of the day talking with him about Mom. He was as worried about her as we were, and he hadn't even seen her in several weeks. He had no idea how bad she really looked. We had learned by phone, though, that she had checked in with her doctor that day and had scheduled an appointment to see him on Monday. That was a relief.

By the time Maura and I reluctantly left Merrick late Saturday morning for our dreary late November trek back to Bradford (and then ultimately on to Rochester), it was hard not to be bummed out by the precarious situation that both our brother and our mother found themselves in. The season to be jolly was now upon us in full force, but we were anything but. Merrick always said it's harder to be the one *watching* the suffering than *enduring* the suffering. I wouldn't go that far, but I've got to admit that neither is much fun.

It was around two o'clock when we pulled Maura's Acura into Mom's snow-dusted driveway. When we entered the house, we found it eerily silent. That's because our sick mother was just lying on her bed, so weak and out of it that she simply didn't have the strength to get up. It was then that Maura and I decided, whether she liked it or not, that we were taking her to the emergency room.

After alerting the troops, somehow maneuvering our weak mom into the car, and then spending seemingly forever in the Olean General Emergency Room, I think it's safe to say that our Thanksgiving holiday that year had indeed become an official Bednar helliday. With first our brother and now our mother in the hospital at the same time—a couple hundred miles apart, nonetheless—our worst fears were seemingly coming true. And to top it off, winter was on the horizon, with a forecast of some harsh, cold storms like we've never seen before.

Chapter 77

Even though it kicks off my least favorite month of the year, I've always loved the new year—the fresh start it brings, the hope for good things to come. And considering that 1996 had been a year full of enough Bednar melodrama to last a lifetime, I think my entire family was more than happy to ring in 1997. I know I was.

And it did start off with a bit of hope. After spending nearly three weeks post-Thanksgiving in the hospital, Mom certainly was not well, but she was stable enough to be discharged a bit before Christmas—provided she accepted some short-term assistance for her infected leg from some visiting nurses and agreed to meet with a highly regarded vascular surgeon that her caring dermatologist tracked down in Buffalo. She couldn't bear the thought of surgery, but with prodding from all of us—and the right nudging from Merrick—she agreed to go for a consultation. When she heard the cold hard truth from the stereotypically abrupt surgeon that she was seriously at risk of losing the lower part of her right leg if that horrific infection and now open wounds were not operated on, she realized there was no other option.

Her surgery was scheduled for January 8.

Merrick, too, had been released in December—despite no clear diagnosis about what had caused him to feel so lousy. On the surface, it seemed the doctors basically just treated his symptoms, monitored his weekly blood work, and ordered him to take it easy, which he tried to do for the most part.

Unlike Thanksgiving, we were at least all able to be together for Christmas—making Alex's first a special one particularly for Barb and me. And the Sunday after, on the feast of the Holy Family, Merrick said Mass in Mom's living room for four generations—including our now ninety-something Aunt Faye and

Uncle Kenny, who still lived in Eldred, and whom we all still adored all the more after all these years. For as many times as we had a private Mass led by Merrick through the years, none of us ever tired of them. He blessed us all, gave a weak Mom the anointing of the sick in advance of her upcoming surgery, and prayed for health and wellness for all of us in the year to come.

Unfortunately, it took less than two weeks for the new year of hope to turn into the new year from hell. And as Bednar timing and Bednar luck would have it, everything started falling apart on Maura's twenty-seventh birthday.

Chapter 78

At first, it seemed like Mom had weathered her surgery quite well, all things considered. Michele had driven her to the hospital in Buffalo, where she was admitted the day before surgery as planned. Merrick, of course in his collar, met them for all consults with the doctors and pretended to feel better than he really was feeling. His presence was reassuring—and quite honestly secured some extra attention and VIP treatment for Mom. The power of the collar at work.

On the eighth, Mom went in and came out of surgery seemingly OK, and by that evening, Merrick and Michele had made the round of calls to all of us scattered around New York State and the country that Mom was out of recovery and back in her own room where she would remain for several days. She sounded doped up as we said hello to her on the phone, but that was to be expected.

By the morning of the ninth, however, Mom had shown no sign of post-surgery improvement. And throughout the day, not unlike the January weather, she began taking a turn for the worse. Her breathing had become very labored, and by early evening—just as Maura finished a casual birthday dinner out with me and cake back at our house—we got a call from Merrick that Mom was being moved to ICU for observation. It was troubling news to be sure, but we all remained calm. "Just say some prayers," Merrick told us.

Twenty-four hours later, as Mother Nature unleashed her fury with an infamous lake-effect Buffalo blizzard, the effects of the physical storm my mother had been enduring for months finally gave way like an enormous avalanche.

Peg crashed, big-time—and the crash cart in the ICU was her only hope.

Chapter 79

In the middle of the night, Peg's monitors started going ballistic, and it didn't take long for the ICU nurses to realize that the new patient in the unit was having a heart attack. Within moments, the staff jumped to action—and literally jumped my battle-worn Mom with the paddles, God knows how many times. The poor, frail thing was barely breathing. She was not getting enough oxygen. "Get her surgeon here, stat!"

By the time the phone rang at my house and startled me out of my deep sleep, it was early Saturday morning—about six-thirty—and still dark. The hospital had contacted Merrick, who had raced over in the ensuing blizzard, hours earlier. He was now calling to tell us the horrible news that Mom had worsened since entering ICU, had been intubated in crisis mode, was now breathing with the help of a respirator, and was being sustained by a feeding tube through her nose. Officially, she was listed in critical condition.

Oh, my God. How can this be? Not our Peg. She's always been invincible.

If she hadn't been moved to ICU on Friday, Mom surely would have died that night. Her normally unhealthy—but now seriously weakened and undernourished—body simply could no longer withstand the trauma it had endured from a significant surgery forty-eight hours before.

And to add insult to injury, the blizzard that had roared in off Lake Erie in the past twenty-four hours had now, like some awful omen, put the entire Buffalo area in a state of emergency. Nearly two feet of snow had fallen in the past twenty-four hours. There were sub-zero wind chills, blowing and drifting snow, and complete whiteout conditions.

But no blizzard was going to keep us from getting to our mother.

Chapter 80

By late morning, Maura and I had decided that we were going to brave the treacherous New York State Thruway from Rochester to Buffalo. Barb would stay home with Alex, we decided, and Michele was already en route from Olean, riding with Maggie and Alan in their Ford Explorer, which was locked into four-wheel drive the entire way.

After far too many whiteouts to count, the two of us made it in Maura's white Acura to the virtually shut-down city of Buffalo in about three hours—which was more than double the time it normally takes—but in one piece. Not bad, considering the lovely January weather.

We had decided to all meet at the home of our friends Teri (Tilly) and Mark Chapman, who lived just a few miles from the hospital. Mollie had arrived the night before. Teri—our childhood neighbor and dear friend since seventh grade, along with her husband of several years, Mark—knew our family well. Upon hearing the news about Mom, they had automatically invited us to gather at their home and stay the night there, rather than in a hotel. Their little Cape Cod surely would burst at the seams with six extra adults there, but we took them up on their kind offer—never thinking their home would become a virtual Bednar bed and breakfast for as long as it did.

From Teri's, we fought the twenty-plus inches of snow and bitter wind chills once again and trekked to the hospital for the first time. After making our way from the freezing parking garage to the dreary but warm main lobby, we took the elevator to the fourth floor, where we met up with Merrick in the ICU waiting room, where he had spent nearly the entire day.

It was always good to see Merrick, no matter what the circumstance, and this time was no different. He was always such a calming and reassuring presence, especially in times of crisis. And of course, he definitely knew a thing or two about hospitals. After the day he had, he seemed whipped and worried, but perked up a bit as we all arrived.

After filling us in again on the happenings of the past twelve hours or so, Merrick did his best to brace us for what to expect when we eventually would make our way in twos into the intensive care unit to see our seriously ill mother. But, I soon learned, nothing he—or her doctor who also briefed us in advance—said could have done that.

Chapter 81

It was a heartbreaking sight. One I'll never forget for as long as I live.

There she was: My one-time invincible mother, lying in a dark and busy intensive care unit. Battered, bruised, and still partially covered in dried blood from the emergency surgery that was done on demand earlier that day to save her life. Now breathing with the help of a machine. Being nourished through a feeding tube. Monitors and IVs all over the place. Her eyes were glassy, but open. If I didn't know better, I would swear she'd been beaten to a pulp by a vicious gang.

"Oh, Mom ..." I sobbed instantly as I turned the corner into her tiny area and my eyes connected with hers. Could she see me? Could she hear me? Could she understand?

Obviously, she could say nothing. But her eyes told me was still fighting.

And yet, for all the sixty-seven-year-old had already been through in the past several days alone, she wasn't even close to being out of the woods. The doctors were very concerned about the amount of blood Peg had lost, her dramatically weakened heart, and the lack of circulation to her lower leg. The surgeon even brought up the eventual possibility of amputating part of it if things didn't improve.

That, we all knew, would kill her.

From that point on, the month of January became a blur—one bitterly cold, snow-blinding, mind-numbing blur. Peg remained in ICU for days, then weeks, and all of her kids—including Mike from North Carolina and Mitch from Baltimore, along with our dear Aunt Pat and good pal Teri—juggled demanding jobs, relentless winter weather, and our hectic real lives to keep vigil with Mom to see how or where this would all end. It was nearly impossible to explain the whole thing to colleagues or acquaintances who couldn't possibly appreciate the situation—or our commitment to each other, cemented through trials such as these. But despite the tragic circumstances, we once again took comfort in our time together, whether sitting alone at Mom's bedside in her tiny unit, grabbing a burger together at the nearby Perkins, or simply crashing for the night at Teri's.

The uncertainty and limbo we found Peg and ourselves in made for a sad, sad time. It was a cruel but fitting coincidence that Toni Braxton's "Unbreak My Heart" was the number one song in America at that time, playing incessantly on every radio within earshot. In fact, by the night of Mollie's bittersweet thirty-second birthday on January 24, after a day when they had planned more surgery on Mom's leg but opted against it at the last minute because of her still weakened state, I distinctly remember Mollie, then Maura, breaking down in the car as the mean-spirited snow flew at our windshield and then that sad song came on the radio yet again. "Turn it off," Maura wept, as we crept our way through the blinding snowstorm to Merrick's rectory for pizza and Mollie's birthday "celebration." Heck, Merrick didn't even get to the hospital that day because of the lousy weather—and the progressively lousy way he had been feeling.

Unbreak my heart.

We all wanted that to happen quite desperately. But Merrick needed that to happen quite literally.

Chapter 82

Valentine's Day 1997.

Another heartfelt and memorable one—but for all the wrong reasons.

The year before, of course, Merrick had called us on Valentine's Day to tell us the alarming news that he needed a bone marrow transplant. This year, Mollie called to tell us the alarming news that she and Teri had just barely gotten a very sick Merrick on a plane that blustery Friday morning from Buffalo to Pittsburgh.

What a day to learn—as we did several hours later—that your brother is in heart failure.

There's no doubt in my mind that Merrick knew how sick he was before boarding that plane. But that's exactly why he was so determined to get to Pittsburgh, where he had complete faith in his medical team: He knew how serious his situation was.

The only good news—if you call it that—was that just days before Valentine's Day, Mom had been moved from ICU to a regular hospital room. She was by no means well, but the feeding tube they had inserted some five weeks before and remained in her side had provided enough nourishment first to get her off the ventilator she was on and then help her regain enough strength to continue fighting for her life. While we juggled weekend visits, Merrick had visited Mom almost daily until the day before Valentine's Day, when he called her and said he wasn't feeling too great himself and that, after checking with his doctors, he was going back for a quick trip to Pittsburgh for another check-up. "Don't worry about me," he told her. "You just keep on getting better."

So once again, Mom was in one hospital, and Merrick was in another—a couple hundred miles apart. The rest of us literally started a scheduling calendar to see who could be with whom when, as we spread ourselves as thin as humanly possible with the support and understanding of our incredible spouses and own families. It was quite a feat, I assure you. Thank God there were a lot of us, or we could have never done it.

Two days after Merrick was admitted to the cardiac floor of Presby—a floor that flooded us with memories from 1986, despite having been renovated since then—Mitch and Eileen drove from Baltimore, where they were now living, to Pittsburgh to check in on Merrick, as the rest of us tended to Mom in Buffalo. Not long into their visit, with virtually no warning, Merrick suddenly coded. His monitors set off a panicking alarm and a flurry of instant activity. Within seconds a team of doctors and nurses rushed to Merrick's bedside and booted Mitch and Eileen out of the room.

The two of them stood outside his hospital door, stunned— in shock, worry, and disbelief—as the team on the other side of the door did all they could to save our brother's life.

Chapter 83

First Mom. Then Merrick.

Yes, unbelievably, it was the second time in two months that a crash cart was used on someone in my immediate family.

It's hard to believe that we didn't lose Merrick right then and there. Not only was his heart barely functioning, but because of that, he had gone into kidney failure as well. But through the grace of God and the expertise of the medical team working that day, our thirty-three-year-old brother was jump-started at his bedside.

While he was still out of it, Merrick was moved almost immediately to the cardiothoracic intensive care unit, where he would now need to be "scuffed" (I think that was the term) regularly: that is, undergo a form of dialysis since his kidneys weren't working—all because his heart was barely pumping. It had all happened so quickly, or so it seemed. By the time Mitch could even call to let us know all that was going on, our normally cool, calm, and collected brother was anything but—for good reason.

Of course, the absolute gravity of Merrick's situation didn't fully sink in for real to me, at least, not until Maura and I made our first weekend trip from Rochester to Pittsburgh the following Friday—with, of course, a stop in Buffalo first to check in on Mom, who had been making some progress but who was now sick with worry over Merrick.

We eventually made our way to the CT-ICU, took a deep breath, and entered the unit where visitor access is strictly limited.

"We're here to see Father Merrick Bednar ..." we told the nurse, a friendly, slightly heavy woman with red hair.

"Oh, we love him here ..." she began, and then told us in her Pittsburgh accent a bit about how Merrick was doing since being rushed to the unit five days before, and how the staff all thought the world of him. After chatting for a few minutes, telling us how excited Merrick was to see us, and then leading us to his private area in the horrifying, suffering-filled unit, she told us, "I'm so glad you're here. Your brother is *very* sick."

Chapter 84

This was all just too far-fetched to believe. Like some ridiculous, unbelievable, over-the-top storyline from *The Young and the Restless*.

Merrick in heart failure—again. Mom living off a feeding tube—and still in need of more surgery on her leg. The two of them communicating by phone, hospital room to hospital room. The rest of us shuffling off to Buffalo, to Pittsburgh, to home, to wherever the need was the greatest, the most urgent, the most life-threatening.

This went on, and on, and on. Not just for days, or even weeks: January. February. March. April.

Seasons changed. The nasty snow finally gave way to icy rains, then eventually to subtle signs of spring.

Valentine's Day gave way to St. Patrick's Day and then to an early Easter. Of all the strange holidays we had experienced as a family, that one had to take the cake for being the most unusual. Maura and Michele ate Easter dinner at a Buffalo Applebee's after spending the day sitting with Mom. Mollie spent another holiday eating in the Presby Cafeteria alone. At least I spent Alex's first Easter with my son and wife at her family's house, but feeling like no matter where I was, I was in the wrong place at the wrong time. I don't even know where the rest of my family was that holiday.

Despite the seriousness of it all and being stressed out of our minds with worry for months about both Mom and Merrick, I know I personally got to the point where I would barely share details about any of this outside of my immediate "need to know" circle. As for work, I don't know how any of us kept from being fired during that time—not because we missed that much work, but because of the mental distractions we were all dealing with. And as far as our home lives—especially for those of us who were parents—all I can say is thank God for our spouses. For months, Barb had become a virtual single parent on weekends—not because I didn't care about Alex, but because all I did was travel to one hospital or another seemingly every five to seven days.

By mid-April, we got a bit of encouraging news. After more than three full months in an acute hospital setting, Mom and her leg had finally improved enough to be moved to a skilled nursing facility—still in Buffalo—where she would receive daily physical, occupational, and recreational therapy. Although nowhere near being fully recovered, this was the first bit of positive news we had seemingly had since this whole tragedy began at the start of the year.

Merrick's news, on the other hand, just seemed to get worse and worse. During the past couple of months, he had been moved in and out of CT-ICU several times and, unbelievably, had learned that he was in need of—yes—another heart transplant. It had finally been determined that Lucas, his now nearly eleven-year-old heart, had deteriorated to a point where it simply wasn't doing its job anymore. Of course, considering all it had endured—years of anti-rejection drugs, two battles with cancer, several rounds of chemotherapy, and the fight of its life during a bone marrow transplant—no truer words had ever been spoken when Merrick, at his tenth anniversary Mass, proclaimed that it, like a Timex watch, had "taken a lickin', but keeps on tickin'."

But that still didn't make it easy news to take. In fact, so much had changed since 1986 when Merrick had his first heart transplant. Not just the technology and success rates—but, most importantly, the large number of people who needed new hearts and other vital organs and the far fewer number of available donors. The statistics were frightening. And when Merrick told us that he was on the B List—meaning that all those on the A List came before him—it was even more frightening. So everyone just prayed all the harder for Merrick. He had been through so much, he'd come out of this one, too. He had to.

"I'm not afraid to die," he told me candidly during a late April visit. "I just want to live."

Amazingly, as Merrick continued to fail physically, he continued to minister as long as he could to all those around him, regardless of their faith, or lack thereof. Whenever he heard that a donor heart had become available for another on the cardiac floor, he'd go and bless that person and pray with him or her while they awaited surgery. And when those patients' family members were struggling with worry or fear, he'd talk to, counsel, and pray with them as well. It was an amazing—and uplifting—site to behold. In many ways, Merrick had become the wounded healer.

By the time Ascension Thursday—forty days after Easter—arrived in early May that year, Maggie had been in touch with Merrick's dear nurse friend Ann (who had been on his cardiac team since 1986) by e-mail. Maggie, who by now had built an incredibly successful career in the health care information field, knew hospitals, health care, and how the system worked. She alerted us all that Ann was extremely concerned about Merrick's health, clinically speaking: his blood pressure, his swelling, his kidney failure. They all told signs of impending doom.

I was doing marketing communications at a hectic HMO at the time, and had asked a dear and trusted colleague, who also happened to be a nurse, to interpret some of the clinical information in the forwarded e-mail. I could barely make sense of it.

"Martial," she told me after reading the email. "You need to go see your brother this weekend."

Even though it was going to be Mother's Day Weekend—Barb's first as a mom—Barb absolutely agreed that Pittsburgh was where I needed to be. In fact, she was on the phone with Merrick when I walked in the door that Ascension Thursday evening from Mass, telling him that I'd be heading down in the morning. He seemed pleased, even though he told me I didn't really need to come.

I drove the five hours to Pittsburgh that Friday, and this time met up with Mollie there. By now, a very weak Merrick was back in CT-ICU. (For a short time, they had moved him to the cardiac floor.) He didn't look good, nor did he talk much. Selfishly, my sister and I were horribly disappointed on Saturday morning when we learned that someone else had just received a new heart the night before. We were in the waiting room and observed with jealousy one family's miracle in the making.

Damn. Why couldn't that heart have been Merrick's?

We sat by our brother's bedside for two long days, hoping and praying for another miracle. Although he spent most of the time sleeping, Merrick did share with us that his doctors were now talking to him about the last resort: the possibility of placing him on an artificial heart until a donor heart came along.

Some poor people in the unit were on them, and it was a pitiful sight to behold.

"What are you gonna do if they really want to do it, Rick?" I asked, worried and heartbroken by the thought of this desperate measure.

"Let's just pray I don't have to make that decision," he replied as he looked me straight in the eyes. I knew what his answer was.

Mollie and I went to Saturday evening Mass, where I urgently pleaded with God to help both Merrick and Mom. We then returned to sit with Merrick for as long as the ICU nurses would allow us—until 9:00 p.m. or so. He was half asleep as I reminded him that I'd be leaving first thing in the morning because it was Mother's Day. "Tell Barb 'Happy Mother's Day,'" he mumbled almost inaudibly.

"I will," I said, as I kissed him good-bye on the forehead. "I love you, Rick."

I cried myself to sleep that night in the silence of the tiny room I had at the Family House. Then I cried on my long ride back to Rochester that sunny May morning, making a pit stop in Buffalo to wish Mom a happy Mother's Day. By the time I arrived home, with flowers and gifts in hand for Barb, my wife's first Mother's Day was more than half over. Thanks, Barb, for your understanding on that one.

PART III

May 12 • Might • Magnificence

Chapter 85

May 12, 1997.

A sunny, warm, glorious spring Monday.

A good sign for a great day; after all, it was the seventh anniversary of Merrick's ordination.

I had a feeling that this was the day our prayers finally would be answered.

Perhaps everything *was* going to be OK.

But then, May 12, 1997, turned into the worst day of my thirty-one years of life.

I was exhausted, worried, and stressed out of my mind. Work was terrible. The phone had been ringing all day. "I need this." "Can you get me that?" "I hate to bother you, Martial, but can you make tomorrow's meeting?"

Eleven a.m.

Maura called to tell me that she just talked to Maggie in Pittsburgh. Merrick had a good night. She stayed late with him. He was talkative and laughing quite a bit. Quite a switch from the Merrick I left Saturday night. I was pleasantly surprised and encouraged.

Four twenty-five p.m.

I'm on one line, but getting paged throughout the building by the receptionist. Over and over.

"Martial Bednar, dial the operator, please. Martial Bednar, dial the operator."

Thirty seconds later. "Martial Bednar, dial the operator. Martial Bednar, dial the operator."

Obviously, someone needed to reach me. I ended one call and dialed the receptionist.

"Hi, Darlene. It's Martial."

"I think your wife's on the phone ....."

"My wife?" I asked, confused. "I just hung up with her."

Nine Ms and a Mother Like No Other

"I think it's her ... Isn't your wife's name 'Maura'?"

Maura never pages me. My heart sunk into the huge pit already in my stomach.

"No ... that's my sister. I'll take the call."

And then the God-awful nightmare began.

In tears, Maura told me that Maggie had just called her again. "Merrick's in cardiac arrest," she said. What the hell does that mean?! Maura wasn't sure; she was as confused as I was. The room started to spin. I had to get out of there. Panicked and terrified, I told my colleague that I needed to leave for the day, rushed out of the office and jumped in my car, heading for home.

"Hail Mary, full of grace, the Lord is with thee ..." I repeated over and over during my frantic journey home on that picture perfect spring day. "Please God," I pleaded out loud, "let everything be OK."

This couldn't be real. It was all a bad dream.

"Hail Mary, full of grace ..."

I pulled in my driveway at 603 Strand Pond Circle, to be greeted by my wife in the doorway, holding my beautiful nine-month-old son, Alex Merrick, in her arms. It's a moment frozen in time—a dreadful, hideous, vivid moment that I'll never forget as long as I live.

One look in her eyes, and I knew it was over.

"I'm so sorry ..." she said, holding back her own tears and sadness, trying to be strong for me and our son.

"Is he dead?" I questioned, at first in complete denial. Then I demanded: *"Is he dead?"*

Her silence and tears spoke volumes.

"Noooooooo!" I wailed as I collapsed to my knees in the doorway, tears pouring from my eyes like they never had before. I was numb and shaking as if overcome by pneumonia, and Barb pleaded with me to get up. "You're scaring Alex ..."

Oh, my God: My beautiful son. Alex Merrick. Born nine

months earlier, to the day. Merrick's godson. Baptized by Merrick. Alex will never know his wonderful Uncle Merrick.

In an instant, our whole world changed.

Life became a blur, suspended in time.

Chapter 86

Breaking the devastating news to my sick mother that her cherished son had died was indeed the most heart wrenching and difficult moment of my life. To this day, it chills me just thinking about it, yet I recall the gut wrenching episode as vividly as yesterday. Here was a woman who had spent four months in the hospital fighting for her own life. She was now in that rehab center in Buffalo fighting with all her might to get better. She had not seen Merrick since the day before Valentine's Day, when he had to rush to Pittsburgh yet again in heart failure. She had spoken to him—hospital room to hospital room—just the day before, when her deathly sick son called to wish her a happy Mother's Day and tell her he loved her. She told him she'd call him back because she had to vomit. She longed to see his face and hold his hand, and prayed with all her might for his recovery as well as hers.

Together, Maura and I somehow managed to drive to Buffalo, grief-stricken and in disbelief—trying to connect with the rest of our siblings by mobile phone and, despite our despair, figure out how we were ever going to break this news to Mom. Yet we knew we had to get to her before she saw the eleven o'clock news, since Merrick—as a young, dynamic priest with a medical history that had been chronicled in the press during the past decade—had become, for better or for worse, a bit of a regional celebrity. Surely, we knew, his death would be a newsmaker. So Mom needed to know before all of Western New York did.

We met up with a devastated Michele and Mollie (with her boyfriend, John) in the nursing home lobby, along with a couple of Merrick's dear priest friends from St. Bernadette's who had already heard the news and had come to lend their support to us—and to Mom. For a good thirty minutes or so, we gathered in a downstairs conference room to cry, hug, talk, grieve—and plan. We were all truly frightened about what this news would do to Mom in her fragile state—not only emotionally, but physically. We contacted the head nurse, shared the awful news with her, and asked to have a nurse present with us in case the horrible news literally caused Mom to go into shock or have another heart attack. The nurse agreed that these were legitimate concerns; Mom had made some progress, but was still incredibly frail. Before we headed upstairs, Fr. Nugent, the pastor at Merrick's first parish, led us in prayer for the repose of Merrick's soul and for strength and courage in the hours and days ahead.

The moment we all walked into her room—by now it was 8:15 or so—Mom sensed quickly that something was wrong. Her initial surprise and delight turned quickly to despair as she saw four of her kids and two priests file unexpectedly into her room, especially on a Monday evening when most of us had just visited the day before. There was already another priest—another friend of Merrick's who had heard the news—in the room, visiting with Mom. He, of course, did not say a word about the news.

"Dear God, what's wrong?" she asked. But then—as we made a beeline directly toward her to embrace her—Peg's powerful maternal instincts provided the awful answer to her own question. *"Oh no. No! Not Merrick! What's wrong with Merrick?!"* she demanded in a panic.

"Mom …"

We huddled on the edge of her bed in the dingy and dimly lit room and hugged her and each other as tightly as we possibly could, sobbing. All these years later, it still tears my heart out just thinking about how devastated we all were.

At first, the words wouldn't come. They simply wouldn't come.

The three priests simply stayed back and looked on in silence, most likely praying.

Finally, never letting go, one of us—either Maura or Mollie or Michele or I—finally got the words out: "Mom, Merrick died this afternoon." Upon hearing the dreadful words, our poor mother wailed and started violently thrashing her head back and forth in complete denial, not unlike what we all did when we first heard the devastating news. "No, no! I just spoke to him yesterday." Then, seeing the priests, she begged, "Father—please, please—this is my son ..."

The priests—especially Fr. Nugent, whom my mother adored and he, too, through the years, had grown to adore her back—were an unbelievable source of strength for Peg and all of us. Despite his own grief, the good priest embraced Peg and assured her that her son had been freed from suffering and had now gone to his Heavenly Father. He led us all in more prayer, and comforted us as best he could with his wisdom and caring, grandfatherly way.

We spent the rest of the evening consoling Mom and each other in that nursing home room—talking by phone to the rest of the family and a few close friends—and ended up leaving a bit before midnight, after Mom had been given a sedative and had finally fallen asleep.

Drained emotionally and physically, we invited ourselves to Teri and Mark's to crash overnight yet again.

Thank God for good friends like them, especially at times like this.

Chapter 87

After lying awake for hours in the spare bed in Teri's basement, I finally dozed off—only to awake early the next morning feeling like I had been through war.

Please tell me this was all just a terrible nightmare.

I replayed the past fifteen hours or so in mind.

I realized, dreadfully, that it wasn't.

Merrick—my brother, my friend, my buddy, my mentor, my hero—was dead. Dead. Dead, damn it! And it felt like part of me, quite literally, had died with him. Initially, I felt like I had somehow let him down. If only I had been a perfect match …

Would that have changed anything?

I had never felt so sad. So empty. So angry. It was a horrible pain I had never felt before. My thoughts turned naturally to my final visit with Merrick just days before. As I thought hard about how deathly sick and weak he was, and then about the possible artificial heart and more surgery and no quality of life, his words kept coming back to me:

"Let's just pray I don't have to make that decision."

Over and over, those words kept running through my mind.

"Let's just pray I don't have to make that decision."

It was slowly becoming clearer to me. My prayers hadn't been answered, but Merrick's prayers had been. And not coincidentally, on May 12—the seventh anniversary of the day he devoted his life to God. This remarkable fact could not be overlooked … or be more overwhelming. There it was again: five-twelve. That simple number with lifelong meaning to this family. This all brought such meaning to Merrick's death—and his life—for us all, one that's impossible to fully explain. It was as if Merrick was finally set free—free from all the physical suffering he had endured so willingly for nearly half his life—and, through his death, he was somehow telling us that everything really was OK.

My spirit wanted to believe it, but at that moment, my heart wouldn't let me. The hurt, loss, and pain were too real. But, ironically, that was about all that felt real. In all honesty, everything else seemed quite surreal. I think it started when I went upstairs. The morning news was on the TV, and sure enough, short clips about Merrick's death—complete with file footage from previous stories that had been done on him through the years—were all over it. Channel Two. Channel Four. Channel Seven. But we were drawn to the TV like a bad accident: You really don't want to look because it's so awful, but you feel compelled to do so anyway.

This can't be. It just can't be.

Our sadness was palpable, but there were many plans and decisions to be made. Where will the funeral be? When will it be? What about a wake? Who will handle the arrangements? How do we make sure Mom is taken care of? How do we get Merrick's body from Pittsburgh to Buffalo?

Our heads were now spinning as much as our hearts were aching.

It looked like Michele, Mollie, Maura, and I would need to make most of those decisions that day. Mom was simply not able to do anything. Mike, Mark, and Mitch were desperate to get to Buffalo as soon as possible from their homes in North Carolina, South Carolina, and Maryland. And we had only spoken briefly by phone with Maggie since Merrick died (although we had spoken to Alan, who had spoken at length with her)—and we all were very worried. Maggie—our self-assured spitfire dynamo of a sister—had flown into Pittsburgh from some business trip or another, and spent most of the day of May 12 with our brother. She was in CT-ICU, by Merrick's bedside, the moment he started to crash—that's how Maura got that initial confusing call, literally as it was happening. Knowing Maggie, I'm quite certain she stayed in the unit as the medical team did what little it could to help Merrick, but to this day, I have never asked my sister any more details about his death. It would be too painful for her—and, quite honestly, for me. Yet, in a way, I'm sure Maggie feels privileged to have been the one person there. I don't think I could have handled it.

Some things are just better left unspoken.

The surreal day continued as we made our way back to the nursing home—as if we weren't depressed enough—to check on Mom, who had been placed on some sedatives for her nerves. We were still worried about how, in her weakened state, she'd be able to get through this. But there was no way she would not be present for everything, she told us.

Then the normally beautiful woman added brokenheartedly, "And I look like an old hag …"

That's when Maura and Mollie assured her that they'd do all they could to doll her up.

By early afternoon, Merrick's dear friend Father Jim O'Connor joined us at the nursing home. Fr. Jim was a wonderful priest with a hearty laugh and infectious spirit whom Merrick had hand-picked to preach at his funeral Mass and be the executor of his will. Clearly he was an important person in Merrick's life, and the good priest became my family's rock, grief counselor, funeral planning guide, and dear friend, through the difficult days ahead.

After comforting Peg and all of us, it was Fr. Jim who drove us to the funeral home that had been recommended to us by another priest. The experience there was not only surreal, but painful and horrific. It's not so much that anyone did anything too wrong, but I've always thought you had to be a different breed to be an undertaker—and my first real experience on the receiving end with one proved me right. Somehow, anyone who gets enthused about showing off different models of coffins freaks me out a bit and always will. Plus, I discovered that it's at that moment—when you're in that awful room looking at those coffins—that you finally are forced to accept the fact that your loved one isn't coming back. That's certainly when it hit me.

Thankfully, Merrick made much of this easy for us. The ultimate planner—who had knocked on death's door more times than any thirty-three-year-old person should ever have to—Merrick had a small planning book, we learned, that he had given to Fr. Jim for "when he needed it." That's how we learned Merrick's wishes for a simple casket, a simple headstone, and a burial spot at the St. Bonaventure Cemetery in Allegany, near Gramma Jo's grave and as close as possible to the ninth tee on the nearby golf course.

It was no coincidence that, after checking, the undertaker learned that there was *only* one grave left in that entire area of the cemetery—and it was on the end, the closest one to the tee.

Even in death, the golf-loving priest's influence was something at which to marvel.

We also discussed with Fr. Jim some of the details of the funeral Mass—the scripture readings and music, most of which Merrick had pre-planned. Indeed, Merrick had prepared as much as possible for his death—thereby ensuring, just as he had done with all liturgies throughout his ministry, that he put his own unique stamp on the final liturgy of his life.

The next forty-eight hours literally became a blur. That's because there were two wakes to honor Merrick. And honored he was: We soon learned that it was tradition for a priest to lie in state in his church so that mourners could come to pay their final respects. At first it seemed strange; I had never been to a wake in a church. But then, after a five hour wake at St. Francis Church, where Merrick had officially been in residence for the past eighteen months, on that already bittersweet Wednesday, May 14—one year to the day that I had given Merrick my bone marrow—we realized that it was also necessary because there were so many people coming to pay their respects. It was completely overwhelming. People of all ages arrived even before all of us siblings got to see each other or Merrick in his coffin for the first time. We got Mom there with the help of a personal aide (and, only in this family, with a hospital bed—yes a hospital bed—in the church, just in case Mom needed to lie down). Hundreds of people came, and then stayed for a special memorial Mass that evening that was being said in Merrick's honor.

I had always hated wakes—who doesn't, right?—but by being on the receiving end for the first time I finally understood why they are so very important: They transform and uplift.

The power of it all moved my whole family: the kindness of people in general, many of whom we never met; the amazing stories about how Merrick had touched lives in ways we never knew; the beautiful Mass and music; the wonderful homily delivered by another one of Merrick's dear friends, Fr. Bob. It gave my entire family the strength to continue on despite our grief in the hours and days ahead.

Indeed, it was the spirit at work.

If we thought that first wake was overwhelming, nothing could have prepared us for the wake the next day at Merrick's priestly home, his beloved St. Bernadette's, now adorned with flowers galore—the place where he indicated he wanted his funeral Mass held. We had learned the day before that we needed an hour or so together as a family in advance of the wake to grieve and pray together. But it was maybe fifteen or twenty minutes before we simply gave in and had the church doors unlocked to let the crowds of people who had already gathered outside enter. For hours and hours and hours—eight or more—my entire family, including my mom and all our in-laws, personally greeted and/or talked to literally every person who came to grieve alongside us. They just came and came and came, some waiting in a line for hours to pay their final respects. Young school kids. Old parishioners. Friends from far and wide. High schoolers from Cardinal O'Hara who took turns as honor guards at Merrick's coffin throughout the entire day. Priests and nuns galore. Former classmates. Our co-workers. The news media. The wealthy and powerful. The poor and the needy. People we had known for a lifetime. People we didn't know at all. All joined together in sorrow over the death of our amazing brother—their priest—whose life ended far too soon, but who touched us all personally and uniquely.

To say we were profoundly uplifted, moved, and humbled simply does not do it justice.

During those two days and of those hundreds—if not thousands—of mourners with whom I spoke, the words of my dear and wise Uncle Kenny are the words that, looking back, still resonate the most. My ninety-one-year-old great uncle, who in many ways had been the closest thing Merrick and I ever had to a father, walked up to me—the young nephew whom he had helped nurture from a carefree and irresponsible little boy into a caring and responsible thirty-one-year-old man. As I stood near the coffin of my beloved brother, whom he had also help nurture into the incredible person he had become, Uncle Kenny placed his wrinkled but firm left hand on my right shoulder and tenderly shook his arthritis-filled finger at my lowered head, which was drowning in tears that were rolling down my face.

"I told your mother," he began in his stern but compassionate voice, "and I'm gonna tell you the same thing." He paused, and pointed to Merrick's casket.

"He worked his entire life for this moment."

I lifted my head slowly, painfully, until my watering eyes met his. It was the first time in my life I had ever seen my Uncle Kenny cry.

"He worked his entire life for this moment," he repeated.

Then he gave me a big hug.

Chapter 88

Merrick's actual funeral was unlike anything I have ever experienced, or likely ever will again.

Our hearts were heavy on that cold, rainy May morning. Yet they were about to be moved during an unforgettable funeral Mass that was not about death. It truly was about celebrating life.

One magnificent life.

Again, my family and I were overwhelmed but deeply moved by the crowd of a thousand or more who packed the church—especially in light of the thousands of people who had already come to the two wakes. There also were a hundred or more clergy who came to honor their brother priest, along with an additional nine on the altar, including the former Bishop of Buffalo who had ordained Merrick and the current Bishop at the time, who presided over the Mass. It was an incredible honor, and to this day, we remain deeply touched and grateful. As my siblings and I processed in, with Mike wheeling my mother who had almost miraculously risen to the occasion throughout the tragic week, our burden was lifted by the collective love that filled St. Bernadette's Church.

Merrick would have been embarrassed by all the attention, but thrilled beyond belief with the beauty of the liturgy and the music provided by a full choir. It was a stunning, mighty, and humbling sight as the priests and two Bishops processed in the church, vestments flowing, while Merrick's anthem—"Lift High the Cross"—was sung in all its majesty. The Bishop personally and graciously welcomed each of us in the family and recognized the large show of support and love from all over the region. And the scripture readings that Merrick had selected were made all the more meaningful by the wonderful readers, both dear friends of my brother.

Despite the thousand mourners, there was utter silence throughout the church when it came time after the Gospel of St. Mark for Fr. Jim to preach the homily. Fortunately for us, the good people at St. Bernadette's were recording the entire Mass, so we now have an accurate record of it.

"Where does one begin?" Fr. Jim began. "What words can express the love that we have in our hearts for Fr. Merrick Bednar? Someone who we love very much, and someone who we know continues to love and pray for us even now. I'm sure now that Merrick in his place from heaven is praying that we'll all have the strength that we'll need ..."

"I think the best words are 'thank you.' Thank you, God, for the life and the gift of Fr. Merrick Bednar. Thank you, Lord, for the privilege of having Merrick as a son, a brother, an uncle, a nephew, a priest, and a friend. Thank you, Lord, for the time that he lived among us, and for the ways he inspired us to live our lives to the fullest."

Fr. Jim's incredible twenty-minute homily felt like it lasted all of two minutes. He spoke from the heart—personally, spiritually, eloquently—about Merrick, and yet his voice never cracked even once, despite dealing with his own grief over losing a dear friend.

"... Merrick did not give up. It was not in his nature to do so. He did not lose the battle for his life on May 12. He won all that was most precious to him ... We can only begin to imagine the joy and the peace that he now has."

As the priest spoke of the Gospel Merrick had selected, he restated its main message, and applied it to Merrick. "For those who love, all things work together for the good."

In light of the date of Merrick's death on such a meaningful day, he asked, "Could we have a clearer sign from God of his love for his priest and servant? Seven, in Biblical terms, is the number for completion. For perfection. For wholeness. And this is no

coincidence. For there are no coincidences for people of faith
..."

Fr. Jim continued. "We can never again doubt the influence
and the impact one human being can have in other people's lives
when that human being authentically lives and loves other people. We all witnessed how one person—one priest—could touch
the lives of so many through all the people who came through the
lines these last two days."

Then Father suggested two ways that everyone present could
honor Merrick: "The first thing we can do is consider organ
and tissue donation. If it wasn't for the heart of that person that
Merrick called Lucas, we would have never known Merrick and
his ministry among us as a priest these last seven years."

An amazing fact. Thank you again, Lucas, and your family.

"The second thing we can do is live each day of our life to
the fullest."

"Well, Merrick," his friend concluded, "Thank you for all
that you have taught us about what is most important in life:
family, friends, faith, love, courage, strength, miracles, character,
excellence, and risk-taking. We have all been blessed with your
presence in our lives."

"Well done, good and faithful servant," Fr. Jim concluded.

"The applause says it all," the Bishop said after Fr. Jim's moving homily. "We thank Fr. James O'Connor for evoking the
memory, the wonder, of the life and priesthood of Fr. Merrick
Bednar. And we thank Fr. Bednar for making such a magnificent
tribute possible."

Wow. It felt as if the whole church had been uplifted, and
Merrick was right there among us. And after Communion, the
musicians who wrote "The Torch" for Merrick a year ago performed it for him one final, powerful time. We—along with the
whole church—were in tears.

My only regret about the incredible Mass was that I did not
have the courage to stand before everyone after "The Torch"

ended and deliver the eulogy I had written during an all-nighter two nights before. I knew as I wrote it that I did not have the strength to do it, and I didn't want to be a maudlin mess. So my remarks were printed in the program that the parish staff produced. But at the last minute, Mitch asked Fr. Bob—who had delivered the beautiful homily at the memorial Mass following the first wake—to read it from the altar, which he did spontaneously yet eloquently.

They were my words, from my heart, but not from my mouth:

One year ago today, I had the awesome privilege of doing something for our beloved Merrick that connected me with him in a way like no other: Give him my bone marrow. Now, on behalf of my entire family, I feel compelled to put in writing the words I only wish I were strong enough to proclaim in front of all present today.

Actually, words cannot begin to express what's in my heart—and I'm sure, what's in the hearts of everyone who loved him. Merrick's presence in our lives was such an amazing gift. And how lucky, proud, and blessed Michele, Mike, Mark, Mitch, Maggie, Mollie, Maura, and I are to call him 'brother,' Peg to call him 'son,' and all of us to call him 'friend.' He touched each and every person he knew in his own special and unique way—whether it was through his heartfelt words, warm smile, endearing laugh, gentle touch, incredible strength, or unshakable faith.

It has been said, and Merrick believed, that there is a reason for everything. God's calling him home on such a beautiful day ... gives even more meaning to the shining example of Christ's presence that he was in each of our lives. Despite the excruciating pain and loss that will forever be in my heart, I take comfort in knowing that he's enjoying the everlasting life he so richly deserves, with no more pain and suffering. I ask that you do the same ...

Fr. Bob concluded my remarks with my words of thanks and

gratitude on Merrick's behalf for the love, support, and prayers that so many had given my brother and my family for so long. When he spoke the final words, "We love you forever," followed by "Martial," the only thing you could hear in the standing-room-only church was the sniffles of seemingly the entire congregation.

Seated in the front row with my mother and siblings, I kept my head down throughout the entire reading, never lifting it until I could regain some composure.

After a prayerful pause, the Bishop stood, looked my way, and said, "Martial, we thank you for that magnificent message, and we thank Fr. Bob for reading it so meaningfully."

One final tribute followed—remarkably, by the Bishop himself, who clearly also had been moved like so many others by Merrick and the remarkable celebration of his life that we were all experiencing. He told a captive congregation a personal story that obviously had affected him:

"Last year, when I was here for confirmation at St. Bernadette's Church," the Bishop began in his dry and serious tone, "Fr. Bednar was here and after Communion, all of those who had been confirmed stood up on top of the pews. I was quite confused … Things for the most part around St. Bernadette's are done in a very orderly fashion, and I thought 'What is going on?'"

The congregation chuckled at the normally serious Bishop's amusing storytelling.

"Then they reached out their hands—Fr. Merrick was sitting right there where Msgr. Nugent is sitting now—and they all recited this poem that they had composed in his honor. Then he stood up, was going along, and extended his hand to all of them. You may know that's reminiscent of the film *Dead Poets Society*."

"Well, there wasn't a dry eye in the place, because I think everybody here knew there was nothing of the dead poet about Merrick. And there's no dead poetry about him, either. His life sang—and sings—more beautifully than any lyric. His life more beautiful than any song."

By the time the Mass concluded, nearly two hours after it began, it had indeed felt like Merrick's life had been celebrated, not mourned—which is exactly what he wanted. Even the sad burial and the additional tears that followed later that day couldn't change the fact that, even in death, our brother could continue to amaze and inspire.

By the way, the poem to which the Bishop was referring, we later learned, was actually the song "The Torch." As I understand it, when the song was sung during the Confirmation, the teens in the church stood on the pews, extended their arms, and saluted Merrick—just like the awesome scene in *Dead Poets Society* when the students salute their beloved teacher, played by Robin Williams. Amazing stuff—of which Merrick, I assume out of humility, had never told any of us.

Chapter 89

For the first several days and weeks after Merrick's death, I thought I'd never be able to laugh again. Consumed by grief, the beautiful late spring and early summer days of 1997 bore down on me like a dead weight, the nights an endless nightmare. The pain and loss cut deeply at my spirit, and nothing—absolutely nothing—felt like it would ever be right again.

With the help of Barb and my nine-month-old son, I somehow managed to go through the motions of work and daily life, but I didn't want to talk to a soul—unless they were grieving along with me—let alone see anyone in person. The tears wouldn't stop flowing, and were triggered easily and without warning by anything even remotely related to Merrick: a song on the radio, a lunch at Burger King, a trip through the Delta Sonic carwash, and—of course—anything having to do with Mass, particularly if presided over by a dynamic and vibrant priest. I felt like such a hypocrite. How could it be that despite what I *proclaimed* to believe—that Merrick was in a much better place—I still felt cheated, robbed? My entire family had been, my son had been, all who knew Merrick had been. In fact, the whole world had been. It all hurt more than I could ever imagine.

As the weeks turned into months, spring into summer, that sharp and cutting loss slowly began to give way to a few laughs here, a few smiles there—and ultimately a dull ache that is always there and still surfaces from time to time without warning. There were days—and I know there always will be—when that terrible void of Merrick's physical absence—his smile, his laugh—overwhelms me: his birthday; the anniversary of his ordination, his death, his transplants; holidays, and sporadic, out-of-left-field days will forever serve as bittersweet reminders of my amazing brother's powerful role in my life. But through the grace of God, I somehow started to cope with it a bit better as time went by.

Time, as they say, really is a friend. For it takes lots of time, along with cherished memories and a whole lot of faith to ease that indescribable sense of loss, that hole in your heart that scabs over but never fully heals. In the end, I think I've figured out that that's about the only recipe for overcoming grief. Sadly, it took me the entire experience of Merrick's death to learn this firsthand, and to realize that it's impossible to fully "get over" the death of someone you love. You never do. And once you've experienced the whole awful thing up close and personal, you feel the pain of other people's losses a whole lot more. At least I do.

Leave it to my brother to teach me so much, even in his death.

Of course, Merrick touched so many lives in such a short amount of time and at such a young age that his death brought about numerous heartfelt consolations for my entire family, both tangible and intangible, months and even years after his death. All are cherished deeply and serve as a constant reminder of just how blessed my family and I have been, even in Merrick's death. Yet I remain keenly aware that most people who lose a loved one, and who hurt just as badly as we do, never receive anything even close to this.

Ironically, the many tributes that have honored Merrick since he's been gone—things often reserved for an influential bishop, mayor, or celebrity of some type—would definitely have embarrassed the humble priest, who in his life on earth tried hard to model Christ (as a plaque dedicated to his memory states) by "lifting high his Cross and showing us how to carry ours." Indeed, in ways both simple and profound, my brother Merrick was a vivid example to us all about how to live life with integrity and intensity, and how to die with dignity and grace.

That's quite a gift.

That's quite a legacy.

Chapter 90

As painful as it is to lose a beloved brother, they say that losing a child, no matter what the age, is the most horrific loss of all. It's simply not the natural sequence of life. It's so not right—and the pain is so deep—that there's not even a word to describe what you are, let alone how you feel. You're not a widow. Or a widower. Or an orphan. I imagine it's like you're all of them, all at once, rolled into one. That's why I never really thought my mom—in the horrible physical condition she was in—could ever survive the devastating death of Merrick.

Yet once again, my mother like no other proved us wrong.

To tell you the truth, I don't even know how my mom made it through the two long, nonstop days of wakes followed by the emotionally exhausting funeral—"on loan" from the nursing home, in a wheelchair nonetheless, weak, undernourished, and sickly looking. Yet she did. And whenever I did glance over to see her, surrounded by a personal health care aide in bright red pants and throngs of mourners extending their sympathy, she was more composed than I. It was another one of those times—much like when Merrick had his heart transplant, or when she hauled us around the country with no money in her pocket—that her unspoken mantra of motherhood—to be her strongest when her family was at its absolute weakest—transcended any human boundaries.

Taking Mom back to that depressing rehab facility in Buffalo the day after we buried Merrick and then saying good-bye to her again was nearly as heartbreaking as five days earlier when we had to walk into that room and tell her that her beloved son had died. After getting her settled for bed that first evening back, all we could do was tell her that we loved her, that we'd call and visit as much as we possibly could, and that she needed to work hard with the therapists to get the hell out of there.

Looking back, I really think Merrick began pulling some strings in heaven, because, much to our surprise, my mom's physical condition suddenly began to improve—quite dramatically, in fact, given the near-death condition she has been in just months before. She underwent physical therapy (which she preferred to call "physical torture"—a sure sign that she was beginning to feel better), occupational therapy (her favorite of all therapies, since she liked the male therapist and got to do the laundry!), but usually passed on recreational therapy. ("Lord, why do I want to sit around and play bingo all day?") And with the help of some potent anti-depressants, her spirits seemed better than any of ours, given the horrible loss we had just endured. Almost miraculously, she began looking healthier, less gaunt, and even was interested in wearing makeup again. We were all thrilled, and by mid-July—just two months after Merrick's death—we heard words from Mom's doctors that we never thought we'd hear:

"We're going to discharge your mother."

Chapter 91

"What are we going to do with Mom?"

In her healthier, spunkier days, Peg would frequently yet sarcastically pose this rhetorical question out loud to anyone within ear shot—"taunting" us kids about their self-perceived, pain-in-the-you-know-what mother.

But now, the question was no joke. We seriously didn't know what we were going to do with her. When Mom had been so sick, she insisted that we sell her home in Bradford since it was a significant financial drain, and it was clear then that there was no way she could be alone—*if* she ever got out of the hospital and nursing home. Plus, ever since moving to Bradford, she had always griped about how much she hated it there—despite truly loving the charming ranch-style house.

"Lord, I'm homeless," she would only half-joke. But it wasn't far from the truth. She had no home. She had no car. She had no husband. She had no money in the bank. She seriously would have been in dire straits at age sixty-seven—as many elderly people with health scares living only on Social Security find themselves—if it weren't for the fact that she now was the mother of eight adult kids, all earning a decent living, who collectively would never let her down.

Deep down, she knew darn well that few parents are that fortunate.

Of course, it was Michele who sheepishly stepped up to the plate first and offered to take Mom into her Olean home. Logically speaking, this made sense for a lot of reasons—Michele was single, lived in Olean, and had a one-story home—but there's simply no such thing as logic when dealing with my mother. So we all knew this had to be a short-term arrangement. That's because in many ways, despite their complete love for each other, Mom and Michele were polar opposites. "Lord, it's like you're the

275

parent and I'm the kid," Mom used to flippantly say to her first-born daughter, who tended to her every need. But as was usually the case with her flippant remarks, they were 100 percent true. Peg had always been the laid back, undisciplined party girl, while Michele was the orderly, ultra-disciplined, rule-following good girl. The two of them together in the same small house would not be healthy for either of them. It would do them both in.

Don't get me wrong: We were all overjoyed that Mom had managed to pull herself up the mountain and regain part of her life. It truly was the first good thing that happened to our family in 1997. And at first it seemed like Mom was overjoyed about it as well. But despite improving physically, it became clear quite quickly that the past six months had indeed taken its toll on her in other ways. Apparently, getting better physically—while about as challenging as climbing Mt. Everest—was the easy part.

Getting better every other way was a whole different story.

Chapter 92

Gratitude.

It's a funny thing, and fleeting, too. It's easy to feel grateful when you're feeling down and out and then, all of the sudden, life treats you better than expected. It's not so easy to feel grateful when you're just OK—not great—and life throws a few zingers your way.

It's also perspective: Is the proverbial glass half full or half empty? With Merrick, the glass was always half full. With my mom—especially after losing Merrick—the glass was definitely half empty.

Of course, there's a part of me that can understand why. Peg had been through so much suffering and heartache that it was only natural for her to be hardened and become bitter by it all. And yet, because she did survive such profound struggles, it seems that she would be incredibly grateful just to see the sun rise on a daily basis. And at times she truly was.

For instance, Mom was deeply touched and grateful beyond words for the outpouring of love and support that came her way from near and far over the death of Merrick. The letters and cards she (and we) received, I know full well, helped sustain her—and us—in the darkest days and months following Merrick's death. And then came numerous tributes and consolations that honored us all and touched our hearts deeply.

There was a moving editorial about Merrick in the *Olean Times Herald* just days after his death that proclaimed "… the thousands of people who attended his Mass … and the countless thousands of others whose lives he touched, would say their lives are richer for having known him in his thirty-three years. Most people who live twice as long don't have half the impact he did."

Wow.

Then there were special memorial Masses in Pittsburgh,

Olean, and Buffalo shortly after his death. There were "Fr. Merrick Bednar" scholarships created to honor him at three different schools. The students and staff at Cardinal O'Hara High School—where he spent only a short amount of time in late 1995 and early 1996 before his bone marrow transplant—honored him with a beautiful memorial Mass and by re-dedicating and renaming the school chapel after him. St. Bernadette's—his priestly home—honored him by dedicating, with the Bishop present, a whole new wing of its elementary school in his name and commissioning an oil painting of him to grace its entranceway. A street was even temporarily named after him, several years after his death, as was a golf tournament (which probably delights him to no end!). Not to mention several heartfelt memorial services, dozens of Masses, and literally the prayers of thousands that have raised Merrick and my entire family up over and over again. All of these are beautiful and touching tributes. All of them serve as a powerful reminder of the incredible impact our brother had in his mere thirty-three years on this earth.

Simply put, it's impossible to put into words the profound gratitude Mom and my entire family felt about these unbelievably kind and generous expressions of sympathy.

Our family, too—under Maura's and my coordination—decided that we ourselves had to devise a way to permanently honor Merrick, since for so long he was the reason we came together and stayed together. "We're not going to be a family that just sees each other at funerals," we agreed.

And so, the first Merrickfest was born: an annual family gathering held in Merrick's memory each summer right around his birthday and the anniversary of his heart transplant, designed to both remember and celebrate our beloved brother and all that he'll forever mean to us. The first Merrickfest, hosted by Mitch and Eileen in Baltimore in the summer of '98, was a wonderful, spiritual, and uplifting experience for us all—and something we've continued every year since in one way or another. The highlight of the weekend—full of family, food, and fun—is the Mass said in Merrick's memory by our dear friend, Fr. Jim O'Connor, the keeper of Merrick's ordination vestments.

Oh, how my Mom loved those weekends and would always give thanks for the love of her family.

But sadly, those weekends were only once a year. And even though she had so much to be thankful for, as she got better physically, she allowed the negatives of her life to outweigh the many positives.

For one thing, Mom hated her newest living situation. After spending a couple of months or so with Michele, she reluctantly agreed to move into an income-based, independent-living senior apartment building in Olean—ironically just two blocks up from 512. "Lord, after all these years I'm still living on Henley Street," she'd moan. Her actual second-floor apartment was small, but clean and new—and we made sure that it was nice, cozy, and inviting. Michele, Mollie, and Maggie all lived in the area, and made sure that Mom had groceries, got to Mass and her many appointments, and got out as much as possible. And Maura and I visited frequently from Rochester. But despite all this, being among others her own age on a daily basis, and making friends easily, Peg complained endlessly about living there. "Lord, I live at the old folks home," she'd remind us whenever we'd visit. Or she'd answer the phone with two simple words: "Mental Institute." Sure, we'd share a laugh at her sardonic sense of humor, but it was clear that Peg was overcome by negativity and despised living alone—which she could never fully distinguish from true loneliness—and could not get out from underneath it.

Instead of doing things to exercise her sharp mind and recovering body, Peg would pass her days eating more than a woman in her late sixties should have (donuts and ice cream bars were staples in her kitchen), drinking more than a woman in her sixties should have (at home each evening it was a cold beer or a glass of sherry), and watching more TV than anyone in their right mind should have (too much news and talk show garbage, along with an overdose of *Murder, She Wrote* and *Law and Order* reruns). She also complained more than she should have, pontificating to anyone within earshot on everything from the news of the day to the lack of washers in her apartment building. She barely slept, and continued to rely on her wheelchair to get around—which meant the blood flow to her legs would continue to worsen instead of getting better. And although she never stopped praying and never missed Mass, she could even find something to complain about there: "Lord, it's freezing in this church," she'd say about St. Mary's.

Throughout the late '90s, we all tried—seemingly in vain—to help, entertain, and make Mom as happy as we could. But if I've learned anything in life it's that no one can *make* anyone else happy. For sure, happiness comes to those who not only seek it, but embrace it—despite what life throws your way. Surely that's how Merrick lived. In fact, that's what our mom had taught us—whether knowingly or not. So it was sad, very sad—and frustrating as all hell—to see this wonderful woman who had survived so much and somehow molded nine kids into happy adults, becoming an unhappy and opinionated woman consumed by negativity and bitterness in her golden years.

Of course, you don't have to be a rocket scientist—or an MD, either—to realize that Mom's unhealthy attitude surely didn't help her physical condition. In fact, coupled with her unhealthy diet and lack of exercise (thank God she had finally given up smoking after surviving 1997), it's amazing that she progressed as well as she did. But with a health history as complicated as hers—high blood pressure and cholesterol, poor circulation, years of smoking, and giving birth to nine kids, just for beginners—it came as no surprise that her doctor ultimately decided in 1999 that she needed her gall bladder removed to help alleviate some new digestive problems. It was at that time when we were reminded that Mom's digestive problems were likely not just caused by greasy food agitating her bum gall bladder. No, an MRI revealed that an abdominal aortic aneurysm inside her (first discovered in Buffalo during her 1997 health crisis) had grown considerably in the past two years. This "thing," we were told, was like a bubble on a tire that could burst without warning.

And kill her.

"There's no way I'm going under the knife again!" Peg proclaimed to her doctor, and all of us. Of course, she—and we—knew all too well what happened the last time she underwent major surgery. "I'll just throw some holy water on myself and ask God to take care of me." Of course, Mom was serious. So was I as I prayed to God that he would somehow heal her—body, mind, and spirit.

In all honesty, Peg really was caught between a rock and a hard place—and ultimately, her doctor agreed, the decision was hers to make (or not to make, as was the case), plain and simple. So no surgery it was, and he'd just continue monitoring the growth of the aneurysm and treat his patient's symptoms.

Gratitude.

I guess Mom still was grateful to be alive, even though she had a funny way of showing it.

Chapter 93

We were overdue for some drama, and in typical Bednar fashion, it arrived on the day that we were planning a party for about a hundred and twenty-five people.

It was August 3, 2001—the weekend of our fourth annual Merrickfest. Maggie was hosting this year, and in typical Maggie fashion, she took our initial plans for a simple Friday night get-together with family and friends to the max and invited more than a hundred friends and supporters of Merrick to her beautifully restored home in Bradford for an outdoor extravaganza complete with a five-piece band, a hired bartender, valet parking, and pony rides for the kids. We don't call her place the Copeland Cabana for nothing.

Definitely over the top by Merrick's standards, but normal by Maggie's.

Because of our three previous wonderful Merrickfests, my whole family had come to look very forward to these annual gatherings that brought us all together to remember and celebrate Merrick's amazing life and ministry. This year was no different. Maura, who had been living in Arlington, Virginia, for a few years by this time, was particularly excited, as she had begun seriously dating a guy earlier in the year and was using this special weekend as the perfect opportunity to introduce him to her one-of-a-kind family. Early Friday morning, Mollie, Michele, and I headed to Maggie's to help with the set up for the outdoor bash. Maura, who had arrived the night before, had spent the night with Mom in her tiny apartment in Olean and planned to take her to an appointment with her doctor in Bradford, and then join us to get things squared away. Mom had seen her doctor the day before, but he wanted to do an ultrasound of her digestive tract because of the persistent bout of trouble she'd been having with vomiting, literally whenever she ate. The ultrasound was to take place at 8:00 a.m. at the Bradford Hospital.

I was inside displaying some special Merrick mementos when Maggie's home phone rang. Since the music was blaring (it always is at Maggie's house), I could barely hear at first. It was a distraught Maura.

"Marsh, I need some help up here," she said, sounding very worried. "They want to admit Mom."

"What?!" I asked, confused.

"They want to admit Mom. She's been throwing up all morning, and she looks like hell. I almost had to call an ambulance to get her here this morning … I could barely get her in my car. And I'm supposed to pick up Greg at the Buffalo airport this afternoon. Can someone get up here and help me out?"

"Where are you?" I asked.

"In outpatient admissions," she told me.

By this time, my other sisters had gathered in Maggie's family room and realized something was up. "I'll be right up," I said.

I told the others what Maura had just told me, and Michele and I decided that we'd go down to help Maura, find out what was going on with Mom, and report back to them. The hostess and Mollie would stay and continue the party prep.

Fortunately, the Bradford Hospital is only about a half mile from Maggie's house. Michele had taken Mom there for her doctors' appointments many times, so she knew exactly where we had to go to meet up with Maura. When we got to outpatient admissions less than ten minutes from getting off the phone with Maura, we were perplexed because our sister and mother were now nowhere to be found.

"Maybe she's on the second floor," said Michele, who knew her way around the Bradford Hospital. Down the nearest elevator we went.

When there was still no sight of Maura or Mom, we asked the woman seated at the reception desk, "We're looking for Peg

Richardson, a woman in a wheelchair. She's supposed to be here …"

"Oh, I think they just took her to emergency," she said nonchalantly.

Emergency?!

Michele and I shared the same "You've got to be kidding me" look. Our nerves and anxiety level shot up instantly, and we bolted back down the elevator toward the ER, which we had walked right by on our way in.

After exiting the elevator and nearly running through the long, sterile looking and smelling hospital corridor, Michele pushed the button on the wall to her left to open the automatic doors to the emergency room.

And from the moment those doors opened, it was as if we had entered our personal non-stop *ER* episode. For just like the television show, it overflowed with all the elements of "must-see TV": the fast pace, the heightened drama, the moral dilemmas, the dramatic cliffhangers. But the Bednar version of *ER* didn't resolve itself in a mere sixty minutes. Instead, ours was more like *ER: The Mini-Series*.

Or perhaps the worst reality show imaginable.

Chapter 94

The double doors burst open to reveal Maura standing at the ER desk. Our normally put-together sister looked whipped and worried, her runny mascara a telltale sign of the rough morning she had endured.

"Maura, what is going on?" I asked, almost afraid to hear the answer.

"Dr. Martinez is on the phone to Pittsburgh," she summarized as she dabbed her eyes with a tissue. "Mom's in one of the units. He thinks her aneurysm is leaking, and could burst. He's trying to arrange a mercy flight to Pittsburgh. There's no way they can operate on her here …"

The room started spinning at a dizzying speed.

Dr. Martinez was a surgeon—not a primary care physician—who, for some reason, had taken a keen interest in and liking to my tell-it-like-it-is mother. He was the same surgeon who had removed her gall bladder a few years before, and he truly got a big kick out of her at that time—especially when she told him how cute she thought he was, and that she wanted to get back on her feet so that she could "do the rumba" with him. The fact that Mom liked him was quite amazing, considering that she couldn't stand most doctors, and usually let them and everyone else know it. Of course, the fact that Dr. Martinez (who reminded me a bit of Ricky Ricardo) had a wonderful bedside manner and was Catholic went a long way with Peg. So she continued to "doctor" with him, as he had also been monitoring her aneurysm for the past couple years.

"Can we see her?" we asked the nurse at the desk, as Dr. Martinez remained on the phone at the end of the desk trying to make the impossible happen for a seventy-two-year-old high-risk patient on Medicare.

Maura led us to the small, cluttered space around the corner where Mom lay on a gurney with a nurse at her side, a blood pressure cuff strapped to her arm, and an oxygen tube up her nose. Her coloring was terrible, and her wrist area was still bloody from where they had inserted the IVs for fluids and other medications.

It's always sobering to see anyone in that condition, let alone your own mother. It was weird just to see her—a woman who for years barely lain down fully to sleep most nights—lying down at all. I instantly got a lump in my throat … and instantly was reminded of that horrible moment when I first saw her in the ICU in Buffalo more than four years before.

"Hi Mom," I said softly, stepping up to her and gently caressing her face and hair.

"Martial," she replied, softly, sweetly. She was alert, but her eyes were glassy and the drugs they had given her had made her remarkably calm. "I don't want to die … I think I'm dying …"

I instantly teared up. "You're not going to die," I instantly assured her, though not totally convinced myself. Then she saw Michele, and said the same thing.

"I don't want to leave my kids …" she mumbled softly, almost as if she were drunk.

By then, Dr. Martinez stepped back into the unit where Mom was, and said a few kind words to Peg. We then went out to talk to him, while the nurse stayed with Mom. The doctor told us the seriousness of the situation: that the CT-scan showed that Peg's aneurysm had grown to six, seven, possibly eight centimeters—anything beyond five is usually catastrophic; that her symptoms and the distress she felt led him to believe that she was in immediate risk of the thing bursting; and that she was simply too high-risk of a patient for him to attempt to remove the aneurysm in his small, rural hospital. That's why he had, indeed, somehow managed to get a medical transport via jet—yes, jet—to Pittsburgh; ironically, to the very hospital where Merrick had experienced so many health care miracles, yet ultimately breathed his last breath.

A paramedic team was being dispatched to transport Peg from the hospital to the Bradford airport.

Good Lord! We had started the day festively preparing for a party. By early afternoon, we were calling the rest of the family—who, amazingly, were nearly all on their way to Bradford for the Merrickfest—telling them to race to the hospital if they want to see Mom alive.

Definitely not the day that we had planned. You'd think we'd know by now that life is funny that way.

Chapter 95

What are the chances that Mom would get to see nearly all of her family—her kids, their spouses, and her grandkids from all around the country—on what was looking increasingly like the last day of her life?

The rest of the gang (except Mark and Debbie, who were now living in Myrtle Beach), arrived at the hospital in just the nick of time—Mike and Vickie, Mitch and his family, Maggie and her family, Mollie and John, and even Barb—just before the ambulance had gotten there to shuttle Peg to the piddly little Bradford airport. We each got to see her briefly, kiss her, tell her we loved her, and then watch as they loaded her, strapped in some sort of straightjacket contraption to hopefully keep that aneurysm from bursting mid-air, into the ambulance on that hot August day. It made me want to bawl my eyes out when she weakly asked, "What about the party?" as they loaded her in the back of the vehicle.

Then we all hopped into our cars and followed the ambulance the ten or twelve miles to the remote and kind of spooky Bradford Airport. It felt like some sort of funeral procession.

And then there we all were, my family, standing at a wire fence that separated the tiny Bradford airport terminal from its one runway. We waited, watched, worried—and prayed—as a small medical jet, which had been sent from Pittsburgh, made its way down the runway with my mother in it, along with two paramedics and her "baby girl" traveling companion, Maura, by her side. I couldn't help but think of their mother-daughter journeys some twenty-five years earlier. It really was "You and Me Against the World" all over again—and one of those bizarre, surreal, and profound experiences that seem all too common in my family.

And in some strange twist of fate, I caught the whole scene

on video, as I happened to have thrown my camcorder in the backseat of my Honda CRV to use that night at the party.

The party. We were now maybe two hours away from a hundred people or so showing up at Maggie and Alan's house to celebrate. In the confusion and emotion of the day, there was no thought or no way to get in touch with everyone who was planning to attend. So, in honor of Peg the party girl, we decided at the airport that the gathering would go on. Some of us—Mike, Vickie, and I—would drive immediately to Pittsburgh to meet up with Maura and keep vigil with Mom, in light of what could potentially happen. The rest would stay—awaiting word from Pittsburgh, spreading the word about Peg—to ultimately be uplifted by the friendship, support, and prayers of so many who loved Merrick, Mom, and all of us.

Oh, there was one call that was made that afternoon from the hospital: Maura, in tears, had reached Greg, that new boyfriend of hers whom she was so anxious to have meet the family, before he boarded a plane from Boston to Buffalo. She gave him the whole rundown on the day's unbelievable events, and told him not to come because the plans, obviously, had changed a bit. I'm sure he must have thought either she's trying to dump me, or this girl and her freakin' family are completely nuts.

Now how's that for trying to impress the new man in your life?

Chapter 96

It was an extreme case of déjà vu.

I vowed I'd never step foot in that Pittsburgh hospital again after Merrick's memorial service there in 1997, and yet there I was, four years after his death, on the very weekend we were supposed to be celebrating his life, visiting my suddenly seriously ill mother.

Everything had changed since I had last been there, and nothing had changed. It was another muggy summer night, just like my first trip there fifteen years earlier. And Merrick's presence was everywhere: in the busy parking garage, in the hectic emergency room entranceway, up the escalator to the main level. Despite the years and the remodeling that had taken place, I still knew my way around that hospital as if I were visiting 512.

By now, Mom had been admitted to the hospital through the emergency room some four hours earlier. The doctors ran numerous tests and did their own CT-scan of the aneurysm. There was some good news, if you call it that: the state-of-the-art medical equipment at Pittsburgh indicated that the huge "bubble" on Mom's primary artery leading from her heart to the rest of her body was not quite as large as Dr. Martinez had feared. And her vitals had stabilized a bit. So rather than rush her into emergency surgery to remove it—with the very high risk of losing her on the table—the doctors decided to admit her and do their own complete work-up on her. But since it was Friday night, that would have to wait until Monday. So from emergency, they found a room for her on the seventh floor—the cardiac wing.

The *exact same* floor where Merrick spent the final months of his life.

Indeed, Merrick was with us.

Maura, Mike, Vickie, and I tended to Mom throughout the

evening and into the next day. She was weak and vomited quite a bit, but reclaimed her feistiness in between her bouts of puking:

"Lord, I can't hack this place. It's where I lost my son …" she moaned. "This place is too big … I hate Pittsburgh …"

After talking with the doctors, we realized that they felt that Peg was in no condition to withstand a major surgery right away, given her age, her weakened health, her history of poor circulation, and her poor nutrition from months of being sick. If they could strengthen her, they reasoned, they would be willing to attempt to remove the aneurysm, which had become the root cause of her immediate physical problems.

The four of us tried to make Mom understand that it was a miracle that she was even alive, and that this is definitely the best place to try to get better. But she would hear nothing of it.

"I want out of here," she kept demanding to all with whom she came into contact. "I'll just keep taking the medicine that they've given me …"

So despite the high drama that brought Peg to Pittsburgh, basically coding two days after she arrived, and numerous conversations with doctors, nurses, social workers—and even members of Merrick's old medical team—who tried to convince her to stay, my stubborn mom ended up discharging herself less than a week after arriving by jet on the verge of death.

Have I mentioned that my mother was like no other?

Chapter 97

It was mind over matter, or so it seemed. For the first couple weeks after returning to her tiny apartment in Olean, Peg—a woman never afraid of a good battle—had it in her mind that she'd simply fight her physical demons and resume her normal life. She set out to convince everyone—most of all herself—that the huge bubble inside her was not going to get the best of her, and that making the decision to not have surgery in Pittsburgh was the right one.

The spirit was willing, but unfortunately, Mom's body was weak. In fact, in about fifteen days, my suddenly underweight mother had lost about fifteen more pounds—and aged about fifteen more years right before our very eyes.

Now knowing that Peg was truly a human time bomb who could basically explode at any minute, we were all gravely concerned about her and did all we could to be with her. Michele, who lived just a couple miles from her, would call Mom's apartment several times a day to check in. When Peg didn't pick up the phone the morning of August 30, my sister sensed instantly that something was wrong. So she raced from her classroom that she was busy preparing for a new school year to Mom's place.

Michele's instincts were right: she found Peg completely zoned out in her wheelchair, in some sort of spooky, almost comatose state.

Panicked, Michele didn't know what to do. So she called Maggie—the most "medical" of all of us—who advised her to get help to get Mom in the car, and then get her as fast as she could to Dr. Kellogg, Mom's primary care physician, in Bradford. Maggie would call his office to inform him that they were on their way. When they finally did arrive there after what seemed like a very long ride, Dr. Kellogg took one look at Mom and admitted her immediately to the Bradford Hospital in serious condition.

It was right before Labor Day Weekend, and Barb and I were looking forward to attending a friend's beautiful wedding and elegant reception at Oak Hill Country Club in Rochester. Needless to say, we didn't make it. Instead of partying at Oak Hill, we spent the weekend in the Bradford Hospital, believing once again that this was the end for Mom.

Chapter 98

"Lord...If it weren't for bad luck, I'd have no luck at all."

That was another one of Peg's infamous sayings, and it sure seemed to be the case in early September 2001. In addition to all of her recently diagnosed problems related to her aneurysm and poor circulation, Peg's situation had begun to snowball: She was now dehydrated, malnourished, running a high fever, and had developed a bowel obstruction—which, given her weakened state, was quite honestly life threatening. Everything somehow was interconnected, and nothing seemed to be working correctly. It was as if she was simply falling apart, slowly and painfully.

Michele, Maggie, Mollie, and I—along with Peg's dear sister Pat and brother Jeep and all of our respective significant others—kept vigil at the hospital with Mom, and spent a lot of time just waiting in her cramped room or in the hospital lounge for news of any kind. Amazingly, after being admitted in serious condition—and all of us dropping everything after receiving calls that this could very well be it—Peg somehow stabilized just enough for the doctors to get her symptoms under control. And while she'd never really improve, she'd get to a point where she did not require acute care—meaning no keeping her in the hospital. So it'd be time to discharge her. At that time, no one had any idea that this unbelievable cycle could—or would—continue for very long.

After this most recent episode, Peg's doctors had to recommend a rehab facility—just temporarily—for Mom to get her stronger. Otherwise, there was simply no way her body could sustain much more. But although she was physically weak, Peg remained sharp as a tack—and as feisty as ever. "I don't want to go," she argued. But with some tough love from all of us to help her understand that there was simply no way to get better without some rehabilitation, she reluctantly agreed to go to a nearby facility in Cuba to try to get stronger. She was admitted there on September 10, 2001.

Needless to say, watching this tragedy in my Mom's life unfold was beyond horrible. A slow and painful demise—and being stuck in some god-awful nursing home, even temporarily—had always been Mom's worst nightmare, and the worry and stress of her situation in the past month alone weighed heavily on each of us kids. And while, as we always did even with Merrick, we tried to maintain our normal lives of work and other less important commitments, it was overwhelming to say the least.

And then September 11 arrived.

I was at work that sunny Tuesday morning, and, like all of America, I watched in disbelief at what ultimately unfolded live on the office television screen. Like nearly everyone in the world, I was aghast. The sights and sounds hit me hard and I was frightened, sickened, and in complete shock over the unimaginable tragedy that I was witnessing as if it were a movie. My thoughts instantly turned to my own family—Barb and Alex, as well as my mom and brothers and sisters, who, thankfully, all were safe—along with the victims of the worst act of terror in American history.

Ultimately, the weight of all the tragic events that were happening in my own little world at that time—coupled with the tragic events of that horrible day in America—caught up with me, and I think I came as close as I ever have to completely losing it. It happened without warning, and in the strangest of places: I was in my car, driving home from work on the Friday after 9/11. I was in moderate traffic, with horns blowing, nerves frayed, and NPR on the radio detailing more of the horrors of 9/11. Then, for no reason at all, I started trembling—no, make that shaking—and felt freezing cold. My head started to spin, and I became lightheaded—like I was going to pass out. Then I started sweating and panting for air. Fortunately, I somehow managed to pull into the parking lot of a car repair shop. I frantically whipped my car into park, rolled down the window to get some fresh air, loosened my tie, turned off the news—and started sobbing uncontrollably for a good ten minutes. I finally managed to stop hyperventilating and calmed down enough to drive myself home, but the whole episode completely freaked me out. I had originally planned to drive back down to the Olean area to see my mom—for the fourth or fifth weekend in a row—but after I told both Barb and Michele about my panic attack, they both insisted that I stay home and try to relax.

Clearly, the stress that knocked on my door that day was typical of the anxiety and stress my whole family was feeling at that time. The worry over Mom, the effects of 9/11, the craziness of work and everyday demands. It was simply too much. Surely, it couldn't go on much longer.

But it did.

In fact, it went on and on. By early October, Mom had crashed a couple more times—thus, going in and out of the hospital, usually through the emergency room and always in crisis mode, which meant we'd all fly out of wherever we were and rush to the hospital with the fear that this was the end.

Of course, it had now been two months since Mom's initial crisis; she had barely eaten a thing in all that time, as her body simply would not keep anything down. And with no nourishment, she had no strength, which compromised virtually every system in her body, which meant she could not fight infection, which meant she kept getting sicker and sicker. It was an awful, vicious circle. So now, in addition to worrying about that huge aneurysm that could burst at any moment, we had to worry about Peg literally starving to death. But that simply was not an option, so her doctor at first inserted a temporary feeding tube up her nose. But when she wasn't getting any stronger, he told her that she had to have a tube inserted surgically so that she had a fighting chance. With her options pretty bleak at this point, Peg reluctantly agreed.

The surgery was to take place on Columbus Day 2001, and once again many of us—Michele, Mike, Vickie, Maggie, Mollie, Maura, Greg (whom we finally all met!), Barb, and I—traipsed into the Bradford Hospital on that cool and sunny fall day to be with Mom before her scheduled surgery. But it was clear as we entered her tiny hospital room that morning that she was doing even worse than usual. She had been vomiting, which we had become used to, but today she was literally panting for air. "It's probably just nerves," the clueless nurse said. But we knew Mom well enough to know that this was more than just a routine case of the jitters; it didn't take a genius to see that the poor woman could barely breathe. As we collectively tried to calm her, Mom's breathing became even more labored. We insisted that the nurse take her pulse-ox (which, given all our experience in hospitals, we knew was her blood oxygen level). The number, as we suspected, was alarmingly low. Mom's nurse instantly got the charge nurse, who tried to draw blood for a more accurate reading. "I'm afraid I'm going to have to ask you all to leave the room," she told us. And from the hallway where we stood, we could hear Mom screaming in agony as the nurse poked and poked and poked at her—trying desperately to draw blood from her very superficial veins. When she couldn't do it, she called the hospital's top phlebotomist, who had a heck of time as well, but finally got some blood from a weary and worn-out Peg.

From there, things started spinning out of control yet again. Peg's blood work showed that, among other things, she definitely had not been getting enough oxygen and that her potassium level was dangerously low.

Obviously, they weren't going to be able to do the surgery for the feeding tube. Instead, Peg was hooked up immediately to an oxygen unit, and then was rushed to intensive care. Clearly, the poor thing was sicker than sick—and had it not been for us, her small army of advocates, she might have had a stroke or a heart attack in bed while awaiting surgery that day. By the time they got her in the ICU and her regular doctor got there, she had crashed yet again. This time, though, our deteriorating mother needed an emergency tracheotomy to help her breathe, or, we were told once again, she would probably not make it much longer.

The automatic doors of the intensive care unit shut, forbidding anyone to enter. So with heavy hearts we all shifted to the ICU waiting room to worry and wait.

It certainly made for an unforgettable Columbus Day. Is it any wonder why I dreaded when people at work would ask, very innocently, "How was your weekend?"

"Good, " I'd lie to most.

Chapter 99

One heartbreaking look into Mom's bloodshot and teary eyes— lying there helplessly in another ICU with a tube in her throat, IVs in her arms, and a machine helping her breathe—and it was clear that her worst nightmare was indeed coming true. She was living her purgatory, ironically, as she always had joked that she would, too afraid to die. "I don't want to leave my kids," she'd often say. And her kids, I know firsthand, simply were not ready to let go.

With each passing day, things got bleaker and bleaker, Peg would come closer and closer to dying, and we tried bracing ourselves as best we could for the inevitable. And then, somehow—to everyone's amazement: her doctors, her kids, herself—Peg would manage to recover ever so slightly, just enough to breathe on her own, for instance, or ultimately get the feeding tube that would sustain her, and raise the bar one tiny notch, where it would plateau for a while, yet never trend upward. It's as if she was being forced to play some sadistic form of the limbo—testing how low her life could possibly go without hitting rock bottom, and challenging her to hold it there as long as she could.

It's almost impossible for anyone who didn't witness it to believe that this over-the-top game went on and on and on. Not for several weeks, or even a few months. No, this heartbreaking cycle of decline—watching my once beautiful and vivacious mom vomit daily, burn with fever, lose bowel control, gasp for air, develop urinary tract infection after urinary tract infection, fight pneumonia repeatedly, suffer endlessly, and ultimately wither away to nothing—lingered on from the fall of 2001 into the bittersweet holidays of that year, then into winter, then spring, then summer, then, yes, fall of 2002. All the while, she'd go back and forth like a ping-pong ball between the godforsaken nursing home—a place where no one ever wants to be, a place where everything stinks, literally, from the hallways to the food to the view to your options—to the in-a-crisis emergency room, and, if she were lucky, to the third or fourth floor of the Bradford Hospital to recover from the latest infection or ailment. Even her favorite doctor, Dr. Martinez, began referring to his long-and-hard-suffering patient as the Energizer Bunny.

Sadly, throughout all this, life went on for everyone else but Mom. While we were absorbed and overwhelmed by the enormous stress of caring about and tending to her, the world didn't seem to give a hoot that our dear mother was dying. There were bills to pay, work to contend with, kids to raise, and even a few special events that popped up—such as Maura's engagement, which happened shortly after Mom's initial scare at the Merrickfest and, ultimately, her wedding a year later in the fall of 2002. How's that for "Bednar timing"? There was absolutely no way to prepare Greg for the situation he was about to enter. Although Mom rallied slightly in the spring of 2002 and committed to being better for her baby's wedding, it never happened. Maura and Greg were married near Boston on September 27, 2002—as Mom listened in from her hospital room on speakerphone, while Alan held a cell phone to the speaker in the church. It definitely ranks as one of the most beautiful but bittersweet days a family could ever endure. Yet it was a celebration we all desperately needed.

For me personally, I spent nearly that entire year driving back and forth from Rochester to Bradford to visit Mom—trying to do my part to help out Michele, Maggie, and Mollie, who were by her side nearly day in and day out. I'd drive three hundred miles a weekend, usually in silence, thinking and praying hard about Mom and life in general. I'd arrive and simply sit by Peg's side while she mostly slept, or hold her hand, give her a kiss, and tell her I love her—each time convinced when I'd reluctantly pull out on Sunday, sadder than the time before, that this would be the last time I'd see her. Quite honestly, it was horrible and exhausting for us all—and there were times when I thought I would simply drop and couldn't take it anymore. But whenever I'd complain that this couldn't go on much longer—for Mom's sake and ours—Barb would always remind me that there would come a time that I would be grateful that I did exactly what I did. In fact, the longer this ordeal went on, the more I came to realize how fortunate we were to have this time. For as awful as things were for Mom, the time she lingered in limbo was a gift to all of us who knew and loved her. For it gave each of us the precious gift of time to set aside the stupid stuff, mend any fences, and make sure she knew just how much we loved and cherished her.

And we did. In fact, for Christmas 2001, all of her kids and grandkids gave her a "Journal of Love" containing nothing but personal and heartfelt messages proclaiming our love for her. It touched her heart deeply—even though she joked (as best she could) that she felt like we were giving her eulogy! One thing Peg never lost through her horrible ordeal was her sense of humor. And on my thirty-sixth birthday in January 2002, I sent Mom a balloon bouquet—she always loved balloons—simply to brighten her day, and thank her for bringing me into the world.

I'm not exactly sure when it happened, but at some point throughout her relentless suffering, Mom changed—or, to put it more accurately, was transformed. Gone was the bitter woman who complained incessantly and fought everything tooth and nail. In her place was the same loving, caring, and gentle mother I always knew—but mellowed, forgiving in all things (including her ex-husband!), accepting of whatever came her way, and, yes, dare I say, content. At peace.

I didn't realize it then, but it clearly was the grace of God at work.

Mom's newfound qualities were tested in a big way in May 2002 when she received a call from my brother Mike. Still living in North Carolina, he had been making monthly trips up since the fall with his wife Vickie to support Mom and us. Mike, a master carpenter by trade, had been suffering from a bad back for a couple of years. He had been seen by several doctors, all of whom chalked up his back problems to years of hard manual labor. One afternoon, while installing the trim in a new home, he sneezed hard and instantly doubled over in excruciating pain. From his cell phone he called Vickie, who ultimately took him to the emergency room. Later that day, after a series of tests and x-rays confirming that he had broken several vertebrae with a single sneeze, Mike's life changed forever.

In the midst of all this going on with my mother, my eldest brother was diagnosed with multiple myeloma: bone cancer. And Mom was the first person Mike called. No matter what your age, isn't Mom always the one you call when you're in need?

Of course, Mom's whole ordeal—coupled with the onslaught of Mike's bad news—transformed all of us, too, and I distinctly remember one epiphany that I experienced. After sitting all Saturday morning and afternoon with Mom, we'd usually go to Mass at four o'clock for a break. There was one Mass in particular, ironically at Michele's parish—Little Bona's, my parish as a kid—where the priest gave a powerful homily that seemed like he intended it just for me. The priest had just experienced the death of a very dear friend who had been suffering from cancer, and talked about how profoundly life changed for his friend and all who knew him after his sudden and serious diagnosis. He talked about how the paradigm of life changes dramatically when we know someone is dying. We do away with all "the stuff" that bogs us down in our relationships, he said, and replace it with only the things that matter. Because when it's all said and done, it's the love that we'll remember. Nothing else.

"Think about how different life would be if we treated everyone as if we knew they were dying," he challenged. "What a gift that would be."

It was then, throughout all the tragedy and dark clouds that surrounded my family and me, that I knew I was one of the lucky few who had been given the gift.

Indeed, the paradigm had changed.

Chapter 100

Peg was always a larger-than-life character who never played by the rules that everyone else did. A lifelong Frank Sinatra fan, she'd always tell us growing up that "My Way" should have been our father's theme song. Ironically, I always thought, it could be hers—especially now. The woman never stopped doing things on her terms.

Seriously, Peg had by now cheated death so many times that I began wondering if her long-running half-joke about death—an emphatic "I'm not going!"—was no joke at all. Maybe that's why, deep down, I never let myself fully believe that it would actually happen. But when Mom had become so weak that she couldn't even mumble my name on the phone as Michele or Mollie held it to her ear, despair finally overpowered any remaining hope that I could muster. We all sensed the end was approaching, but when the calendar hit December 1, 2002, I told Barb that I had a feeling that it was going to happen on December 5—the fifth day of the twelfth month.

Five-twelve. There it was again.

I even mentioned my feeling about the date to Maura that night on the phone. "Oh, my God …" she said. And to Vickie a couple evenings later, when I was checking in on Mike, who was now undergoing some serious chemotherapy. "Wow," she marveled in her Carolina accent.

I found myself praying hard—although I'd been praying hard for so long by this time that I was seriously wondering if God had just taken a vacation and altogether forgotten us. For the longest time my prayers had been that Mom would just get better and regain some sense of normalcy. But when that wasn't happening and her suffering knew no bounds—as I literally watched the life of the most life-loving, rabble-rousing, troublemaking person I'd ever known slowly, painfully, dreadfully vanish—I began begging

God to spare her any more of this. *Have mercy on her!* I pleaded with Merrick to help as well. I'd get so mad! *Why won't this end?! Come on!! Enough already!! I'm so tired.* Then I'd think, *Oh, my God. This isn't right. I love my mom. I'm so tired … What am I asking for?* Tears would usually roll silently from my eyes onto the pillow, and I'd doze off dreading that this would be the night that I'd be awoken by that horrible ringing of the phone.

Yes, the paradigm had shifted. But no one ever said that any of this—love, life, death—was easy.

It was the alarm clock—not the phone call I fully expected—that awoke me on Thursday, December 5, 2002. Whew. She made it through another night. Like every morning for months now, those were my first thoughts. Into the shower I went, where my prayers from the night before continued as the hot water beat down on me.

It was a cold, gray, and sad day—despite being the season to be jolly. After dropping Alex off at kindergarten, I went to work as usual—pretending, of course, that all was fine. Michele's morning e-mail update, which we had all grown so accustomed to in recent days, was a bit more upbeat than the past few days—despite the news of Mom's ever-worsening condition:

> *Good Morning to All.*
> *This morning's news: They gave Mom Lasix, since she is quite wet. Of course, Mom does not like to be suctioned but they have suctioned her through the night as well as last night. Lauren, her nurse, seems very, very caring. She said, "Her night was rough but your mom is such a sweetie." I asked her how she felt and Mom said, 'Not very well,' but in that manner we all know has been very innocent. She gave her morphine about 5:00 p.m. No vomiting and last night they were going to give her phenergan about 9:00 p.m. Last night's visit was a little better but still quiet.*
> *My brain has been up to some work again—could we add Chapter Two to Mom's journal??????? How about some Momisms,*

traits or famous quotes we find ourselves saying or doing? Let's make it light and I know what a wonderful night it was last Christmas reading her "Journal"... There are no set numbers that you must have but does that sound like a possibility? I would appreciate your input and hopefully everyone (grandkids too!) should be able to contribute a couple.

Good luck to Greg this morning with another interview ... put his guardian angel in his pocket, Maura ... Mike—we have been thinking of you and wondering how yesterday went. Over and out for now, Michele

I remember thinking to myself, *But what if she's not here on Christmas?* and then laughing as Maggie replied with some seemingly instantaneous Pegisms:

Let me begin the contribution to Chapter Two of Pegisms...

"Oh, stink ."

"Oh, shiiiiiiittttt."

"Did you get to Mass???"

"Did the kids get to Mass????"

"Tell your (boss, teacher, coach, husband) to hang it in his ear!!"

"... and God Bless Bobby Anderson..."

"He's a good egg."

"That's just a big marketing gimmick."

"Margaret, I wish you would enroll those kids in St. Bernard's."

"You must have inherited your talent from Grandma Parmeter."

"I miss Merrick so much."

"My Maura ."

"I hate good-byes."

"Thank you."

Over and out. Have a good day, all.

Love,
Maggie

The morning progressed. At 11:45 a.m., my e-mail beeped again—this time from Maura. Simply titled "Mom," I figured it was more Pegisms.

I was wrong.

> ——-Original Message——-
> From: Maura
> Sent: Thursday, December 05, 2002 11:45 AM
> To: Mcopeland; Michele Bednar
> Cc: Vickie Bednar; Jack & Beth; Eileen Bednar;
> Joni S; Joni Z; Martial & Barb Bednar; Bednar,
> Martial; Mark & Debbie Bednar; Mitch Bednar;
> Mollie; Mark Bednar; Shelly Bednar; Michael
> Bednar (E-mail)
> Subject: Mom
>
> *11:35a.m. Thursday 12/5/02*
> *Gang—*
> *Maggie just called b/c she is headed back to the*

308 *Nine Ms and a Mother Like No Other*

hospital. They called b/c there's been a change in Mom's status and Dr. Kellogg wanted the nurses to let the family know.

Mom's kidney functions do not look good, and she may be headed back to kidney failure. She's also very "wet" on the lungs—even though they've continued to suction her ... Not good news, I'm very sorry to report.

Maggie is headed to the hospital; that's all I have for now. Will update you as soon as I hear anything else.

Say some prayers ...

Love,
Maura

Seated at my office desk, I put my head into my hands, closed my eyes, and said an urgent, silent Hail Mary. My heart began racing. I closed my eyes, breathed slowly for a few moments, and fought back the tears that so desperately wanted to flow.

I began wondering with each passing minute what was going on in Room 343 at the Bradford Hospital. No news is good news, I told myself.

At 1:00 p.m., I headed half-heartedly into a meeting that I was to lead—again, acting as if nothing was wrong, pretending to be more interested than I actually was, given everything that was going on. Unbeknownst to me at the time, two more e-mails were beckoning me back in my office:

——-Original Message——
From: Maura
Sent: Thursday, December 05, 2002 1:22 PM
To: 'mcopeland'; 'MBednar'
Cc: 'Vickie Bednar'; 'Jack & Beth'; 'Eileen Bednar'; Joni S; Joni Z; 'Martial & Barb Bednar'; Bednar, Martial; 'Mark & Debbie Bednar'; 'Mitch Bednar'; 'Mollie'; 'Mark Bednar';

‘Shelly Bednar’; ‘Michael Bednar (E-mail)’
Subject: RE: Mom
1:20 p.m. … Maggie called. Mollie & Michele just got to the hospital.

Mom is continuing to weaken. Things are not looking good.

Please continue your prayers.
Maura

Followed by this simple but urgent one:

From: Maura
Sent: Thursday, December 05, 2002 1:24 PM
To: Bednar, Martial; Michael Bednar (E-mail)
Subject: Are you there?
Importance: High
Call me at 978-555-3149 when you get this.

At about 1:50 p.m., one of the office secretaries interrupted my meeting and handed me a little white piece of paper with a note. Oh, God help me, I instantly thought. It read:

URGENT!
Martial, pls call family conf. call.
1-800-555-8686
conference ID is 789-1234
call from Maggie
(sister)

I literally felt my blood rush from my face through my entire body at warp speed, as if a massive gusher had erupted and burst at my feet. "I'm sorry," I said. "I have to excuse myself …"

I raced down the hallway, closed the door to my office, and

dialed the numbers on the note frantically. Suddenly I became part of an amazing conference call.

To heaven.

Chapter 101

"... Oh, wait, it sounds like someone just came on the line," I heard Maggie say after two simple beeps.

"It's me, Mag," I said nervously as my heart beat a mile a minute. "What's going on?"

"Marsh ..." she began, in control but obviously in tears. "I've got just about everyone on the line. I'm here in Mom's room with Michele and Mollie. There's a nurse here, too, hon ..."

As the world around me started to spin, I heard a chorus of serious "hi's" and "heys" from my brothers and sisters and aunt and uncle in various parts of the country. Since we couldn't all be there as things were looking grimmer and grimmer, Maggie—in her infinite ingenuity—had used her business conference call line and the wonders of technology to bring us all to room 343 with our dying mother.

"Mom's really struggling," Maggie briefed me. "Her vitals have dropped ... Mom, Martial's on the line. Talk to Mom, Marsh."

"Hi, Mom," I instantly said, fighting back the tears. "I love you, Mom. Everything's going to be OK ..."

"Let's say the 'Our Father,' Maggie instructed. "I'll hold the phone up to her ..."

"Our Father, who art in heaven. Hallowed be thy name ..." we all began—an amazing flashback to the times as kids when Mom use make us get down on our knees around her bed and say the rosary.

"Thy kingdom come. Thy will be done, on earth as it is in heaven. Give us this day our daily bread and forgive us our trespasses, and we forgive those who trespass against us. And lead us not into temptation, but deliver us from evil. Amen."

"What's happening?" Those of us on the line needed a play-by-play.

"Let's keep going," Maggie instructed. "How 'bout the 'Hail Mary'..."

"Hail, Mary, full of grace. The Lord is with thee. Blessed art thou among women, and blessed is the fruit of thy womb, Jesus—"

"You guys! She just mouthed 'Jesus'!" Maggie exclaimed in amazement. I could hear Mollie and Michele marveling at the same thing in the background.

"... Holy Mary, mother of God, pray for us sinners, now and at the hour of our death. Amen."

A chorus of heartfelt "I love you's" underscored by tears engulfed the phone.

"Mom, it's OK," I cried. Then, as I had done in my prayers for weeks, I pleaded aloud: "Merrick! Please help us ..."

"Oh, my God!" Maggie exclaimed. "Martial ... what did you just say?"

"I said, 'Merrick ...Please help us."

"Mom just mumbled 'Merrick'!' And a big smile just came over her face," Maggie cried in astonishment.

Then there was an ominous silence from my three sisters in room 343.

"What's going on?" someone asked among the sniffles and broken voices.

Moments later, Maggie choked back the tears.

"She's gone," she said simply, quietly. The clock on my computer showed 2:05 p.m.

"She's blue ... the nurse tells us her breathing has stopped. She has no vitals."

"Oh, Mom ..." we all seemed to weep in unison.

And then someone suggested that we say the "Hail Mary" again. It was the most heartfelt prayer I think I've ever uttered. It gives me goose bumps just thinking about it.

"Hail, Mary, full of grace, the Lord is with thee. Blessed art thou among women, and blessed is the fruit of thy womb, Jesus.

Holy Mary, mother of God. Pray for us sinners, now and at the hour of our death."

Amen.

Chapter 102

It didn't matter that she had been deathly sick for sixteen months. Or that she had suffered so much.

It didn't matter that we all knew it would only be a matter of time. Or that she was seventy-three years old.

She was my mom—and as far as I'm concerned, you're never prepared to lose her, no matter what the circumstances. Plus, it's true: The higher you climb, the harder you fall—even with the death of a loved one. And there were so many of us who struggled with Peg for oh so long. Sixteen months. We fell hard. Very, very hard.

At only thirty-six years old, I was way too young for all this. To lose a brother, and now a mother—both like no other—was simply too much. The two bigger-than-life characters in this family, the two most high maintenance members of this clan who, for years, for better or for worse, commanded and demanded our utmost attention. The two who brought us together—and kept us together—in good times and bad. Gone. At least from this life.

I still sometimes have trouble believing it.

But what a joyous reunion in heaven it must have been for mother and son! While my heart breaks over our tremendous loss, it is warmed by the thought of Mom reunited with Merrick—I'm sure it was the tightest, happiest, greatest hug ever—and both of them whole again in body, mind, and spirit. I can't think of two people who deserve it more.

Thank you, Mom, for the amazing gift of faith.

Chapter 103

Why is it that at so many of the absolute lowest points of my life I find myself in the middle of a damned snowstorm?

Within hours after losing Mom, there I was in the middle of nowhere—Route Eighty-six, New York's Southern Tier Expressway, which I have traveled seemingly thousands of times, en route on the two-and-a-half-hour drive from Rochester to Bradford—driving through a blizzard that seemingly came out of nowhere. Of course it was pitch black (being December, it was dark by 4:30 p.m.), the snow was heavy, wet, and mean-spirited, and naturally, there was no plow anywhere in sight. Just me, creeping along in my Honda CRV, bawling my eyes out as I played Mom's favorite song—her theme song, as she had called it for years, "What I Did for Love"—over and over on the CD player, thinking of Mom, hoping to somehow get to Maggie's house in one piece. Thank God for my cell phone, which allowed this glutton for punishment to talk to Barb, who stayed back with Alex until the next morning, and keep myself from completely freaking out until I finally got as far as Olean. There I picked up Mollie's husband John, who greeted me with a sorrow-filled hug, and offered to drive the rest of the way to Maggie's.

From those earliest moments, the hours and days surrounding Mom's death remain surreal. Even to this day, it feels like it was a movie—a very sad, tragic, vivid movie—with me in the thick of it, yet simultaneously watching from afar. It was the exact same feeling I had throughout Merrick's death. In fact, I started grieving Merrick all over again. Didn't we just go through this? Mom's death obviously tore open the scab that had formed around that wound.

One of the most exceptional aspects of my family is how well we come together at times of true crisis—the time when most families, regardless of their size, usually come apart at the

315

seams. It's probably just because we've had so much experience. Mom's death was no exception. Despite our tremendous grief, we somehow automatically worked together at this very emotional time and agreed on the plans with relative ease. Then we put our talents and abilities to work—and began planning an incredible celebration of life for the ultimate party girl.

Mom's only requests—mentioned half-heartedly in happier, healthier times—were simple: She wanted two Franciscan priest pals from St. Bonaventure University to say her funeral Mass. She wanted the Mass at the University chapel where she used to play the piano on occasion at midnight Mass on Christmas. And she wanted her favorite local musician to play her favorite song. That was it. No other guidance from the woman whose only talk about death was her joke that the only difference between a wedding and a funeral is that you can smell the flowers at a wedding.

The rest was up to us.

It had been a hell of a journey. We certainly weren't going to let her down now.

Chapter 104

"You mean I'm never going to see Grammy Peg again?! Ever?!!"

Those were the angry words that my beautiful son Alex screamed at me in tears as I clutched him in my arms, trying to explain as gently as possible to our precious six year old that his dear Grammy Peg had died.

How do you tell an innocent child that someone he loves so dearly is gone forever? How do you help him understand death when you can't even understand it yourself? Barb and I had been dreading this moment for months. It will go down as one of our most painful and difficult moments of parenthood. Thank you, Mom, for the gift of faith, once again.

"Honey, I know you're upset, I am, too," I began, trying to maintain some sense of composure.

"Daddy, please don't cry! Please don't cry!" Alex pleaded in tears. The caring boy with the tender heart hated to see anyone cry—especially his father.

"Honey, it's OK to cry, it's sad, but Grammy's been sick for such a long time, and she went to a wonderful place called Heaven where she feels better, and can walk again, and she doesn't even need a wheelchair, " we tried to explain.

Barb and I held Alex tight. "… and Grammy still loves us, she'll always love us, and she can see us, it's like she's an angel," we offered. "Heaven is a wonderful place. She's with Jesus."

"Well, how do you get to heaven?" Alex finally demanded, after we tried our best to explain the biggest mystery of life to him. And then with such innocence, the literal and loving little boy tried to answer his own question in the only way that made any possible sense to him:

"Do you drive?"

Such a beautiful, albeit bittersweet, moment that I'll cherish in my heart forever.

I'm sure from her place in heaven that Mom does, too.

Chapter 105

I sustain myself with the love of family.

Those were the simple words on a card I had purchased and had been meaning to mail my mom right after seeing her the last time in the hospital. But I had been so busy, I never got around to writing it out.

So on the morning of her wake, I felt compelled to write one final note to my mother. I brought it with me to the funeral home.

Upon seeing my mom in her coffin for the first time, I literally collapsed to my knees.

"Oh, Mom," I sobbed, with Barb at my side. After regaining my composure, I placed the card, face up, in her casket, where it remained permanently. Somehow, that simple message—*I sustain myself with the love of family*—spoke volumes. Even more now than when I first bought it.

"I hate wakes," my mother would always say whenever she had to attend one. "Lord, why do I want people standing around me saying 'She looks great!'?"

And yet, that's exactly what I did—what we all did. But instead of "great," we used the word "beautiful." Because that's exactly how she looked. For sixteen long months, the one-time glamour gal looked anything but beautiful. In fact, it was like we had all forgotten how beautiful she was. So to see her transformed one last time from the sick and haggard nursing home patient back into the beautiful, glamorous woman we knew and loved was a gift beyond measure.

Through death, Mom was restored in body, mind, and spirit. Indeed, the greatest paradox of life.

Still, I didn't think I had the strength to make it through the wake. Hadn't we just gone through this with Merrick? But just like in Merrick's death, my entire family and I were uplifted and sustained by the love and support of so many.

It never ceases to amaze me how the worst of times brings out the very best in people.

Chapter 106

It's more than ironic that the funeral Mass of my mother—who always called us to not-so-subtly remind us on our answering machines to get to Mass on holy days—actually took place on a holy day: the Feast of the Immaculate Conception. A feast that honors, of all things, the Blessed Mother. It was as if Peg was, once and for all, giving us her final motherly reminder to get to Mass.

The sky was so uncharacteristically blue and the sun shone so brightly that freezing cold December morning that, if you didn't know better and were just looking up, you'd think you were in the sunny tropics instead of dreary Olean. But despite the brightness of that morning sun, our hearts were darkened by the veil of grief on December 9, 2002.

In the few short days from her death, we somehow managed to pull together Peg's Dream Mass—a personal, music-filled, and deeply moving liturgy that paid honor to a mother who truly loved going to church, and whose slow and dreadful death all but earned her (in our eyes, anyway) a triumphant entrance into heaven. After a magnificent prelude that included the always beautiful "Ave Maria" (which, ever since then, brings a lump to my throat and tears to my eyes every time I hear it), the Mass opened with the melancholy blare of a solo trumpet poignantly playing the refrain to "Lift High the Cross"—which, since Merrick's death, had somehow become the unofficial Bednar family anthem. As the organ joined in and the cantor (a friend of Peg's from years ago) began singing in his deep, rich tenor, Mom's three living siblings processed down the aisle, followed by her four beautiful daughters, and a total of nine priests who honored us—and Peg—with their presence.

My brother Mike—Peg's eldest son, now battling his own dreadful bone cancer and simply too weak to be a pallbearer—held the crucifix that had been in Mom's casket as high as he possibly could as Mark, Mitch, and I, along with the husbands of her daughters, wheeled her casket down the aisle of that simple chapel she loved so much. Yet another surreal moment of my life that I'll never forget.

It's still hard to believe that the two Franciscan priests that Mom had hoped would someday say her funeral Mass—Fr. Richard and Fr. Dan, who had befriended and impacted her some twenty years earlier when she was a wild, stand-out-from-the-crowd, non-traditional grad student at Bona's—were actually available and willing to do so. While Fr. Richard presided and opened the Mass with some warm remarks, it was Fr. Dan who touched everyone there with the most poignant reading of the Sermon on the Mount from the Gospel of St. Matthew that I've ever heard. He read the powerful words with such heartfelt emotion and simple eloquence:

How blessed are the poor in spirit, the reign of God is theirs.

Blessed, too, are the sorrowing. They shall be consoled.

Blessed are the lowly. They shall inherit the land.

And blessed are they who hunger and thirst for holiness. They shall have their fill.

Blessed are they who show mercy. Mercy shall be theirs.

Blessed are the single-hearted, for they shall see God.

And blessed, too, are the peacemakers, for they shall be called sons and daughters of God.

Blessed are those persecuted for holiness' sake. The reign of God is theirs.

And blessed are you when they insult you and persecute you, and utter every kind of slander against you.

Be glad and rejoice. Your gift will be great in heaven.

Initially, we weren't quite sure if the Beatitudes were even appropriate as a funeral Gospel, so we asked Father Dan as we were finalizing the details of the Mass.

"Is there a particular reason you want that Gospel?" he asked.

"Yeah …" I began, fighting to hold back my tears. "When Mom was so sick and we'd be visiting with her in the hospital, we'd cut out to go to four o'clock Mass. When we'd get back, she'd always ask what the Gospel was—or one of us would read it to her. Just a few weeks ago when I was visiting, this happened to be that week's Gospel. When I got back from Mass, she was so weak she didn't even ask about it. So I told her, 'The Gospel was the Beatitudes. I love that one.' And she just looked at me and blinked to say she did, too."

It's a moment etched in my memory forever.

"It's absolutely perfect," Father Dan assured us.

After the powerful reading, Fr. Dan then gave perhaps the most heartfelt homily I've ever heard—not unlike what Fr. Jim had done at Merrick's funeral some five years before. He had known Peg so well and for so long—and had known Merrick, and all the rest of us for many, many years—that his words seem to come from his heart directly to the hearts of all those present. They were laced with humor, and filled with stories of Peg the mother, Peg the student, Peg the party girl. He spoke of her hopes, her fears, her mistakes, her faith, and her love, of strangers, of friends, of merriment, of music, but most of all, of her family. His most poignant remark still resounds in my ears:

"… and yet," he said, "for all the beautiful music in the world that she loved, there was no sound sweeter to her than the sounds of your names." Fr. Dan's voice cracked and he fought to hold back his own tears as he faced us, Peg's kids. Peg's legacy.

I don't know how I did it, but somehow after Communion and a beautiful song of meditation that was one of Mom's personal favorites, I managed to do something that I was so mad at myself for not having the strength to pull off at Merrick's funeral: Get up and deliver the eulogy. It was my way of honoring my dear mother—and in a way, Merrick, too—and all I wanted to do was not be a maudlin mess.

As Maura had joked in between her tears just twenty-four hours before to a mournful cousin who didn't want to cry: "Oh, we've all been crying. We're going to get T-shirts that say 'We're the Bednars. We love to cry.'"

Inspired by Michele's very appropriate advice to me to overcome my nerves—pray "My Mother, My Confidence," as we had learned in high school—I was not only *not* a maudlin mess, I miraculously held it together and gave hands-down the best, and certainly the most personal and heartfelt public address of my life. Oh, the power and mystery of the Cross: To be stronger than you ever thought possible at your lowest moments in life. My remarks were followed by the melancholy sounds of the piano playing the instrumental version of Mom's favorite song, "What I Did for Love," just as she wanted.

And my message? That while Peg herself would be the first to admit that she did a lot of things wrong, she did a lot of things right. For that, we're eternally grateful.

God bless you, my beautiful mother.

Chapter 107

And then came the part that I despise the most: The burial at the cemetery. Is there anything more heart-wrenching and painful in life than that? If so, I don't want to know.

"I hate good-byes," Mom would always say. On this day, I couldn't agree more.

Even after the deeply moving and uplifting liturgy we had just celebrated, we drove in silence the mere mile up the hill to our little corner of St. Bonaventure Cemetery—to the exact same location that we had laid Merrick to rest seemingly just yesterday. The fresh snow from the night before gleamed in the bright sunshine and crunched loudly under our feet as we carried the casket from the hearse to the tent.

"Lord, I hate funerals!" I could practically hear Mom uttering yet another one of her classic Pegisms.

I do, too, Mom. I do, too.

Fr. Richard led the crowd of fifty or so that trekked up to the cemetery in some very simple prayers, and then blessed the casket one final time. As the group prepared solemnly to leave, I announced, "Wait a second, you guys … we've got one final thing to do." Then I gave the cue to our dear friends Teri and Mark, who had been secretly instructed to bring a big battery-powered boom box to the cemetery with them. Everyone was a bit confused at first, as you might imagine, until they heard Mom's favorite song blaring from the box:

Kiss today goodbye …
The sweetness and the sorrow
Wish me luck, the same to you
But I can't regret
What I did for love
What I did for love …

But then they got it.

As the song continued, the undertaker opened the back door of his black SUV to reveal a wonderful surprise that only a few of us there knew anything about: five dozen (five-twelve) helium-filled white balloons. Coupled with the music, this surprise temporarily transformed our overwhelming sadness into nearly giddy joy.

There was sheer wonder and delight at the sight of the sixty balloons—the perfect symbol to capture the true essence of Peg, that spirit-filled free-spirit who deplored funerals but absolutely loved parties and balloons. For a few brief moments, we all seemed to forget that we were at a burial. It looked—and felt—like we were at a big, festive party. And that's exactly what my party-girl mother would have liked! My balloon idea turned out to be more perfect than I had ever imagined. It turned Mom's death, if only for that moment, into a true celebration of her life.

There we were—priests, family, friends—in the middle of a cemetery on a freezing cold December day, each holding a simple white balloon. As "Mom's song" neared its end, we all began singing along, ultimately belting out the final chorus:

Kiss today goodbye
And point me toward tomorrow
We did what we had to do
Won't forget
Can't regret
What I did for love …
What I did for love …
What I did for love!

And up, up, and away went the balloons—higher and higher into the magnificent blue sky. We all stood there, gazing upward, transfixed, caught up in the incredible moment, marveling at just how miraculously high those balloons kept going.

Then, because our friend Mark was obviously caught up in the moment, too, he never thought to turn off the "Chorus Line" CD. So the song that follows began playing:

One
Singular sensation
Every little step she takes …

How appropriate! And leave it to my mom's siblings—my wacky but wonderful Aunt Pat and our party-loving Uncle Jack—to literally start jitterbugging at the cemetery in honor of their sister who loved to dance.

The only thing we could all do was grin from ear to ear and applaud heartily.

Only in the Bednar family. Indeed, only in the Bednar family.

Mark eventually had to turn off the music, of course, and that suddenly catapulted us back into the terrible reality that we were, in fact, burying our mother. But then someone looked up and saw that there was one stubborn balloon that had gotten stuck in the nearby tree and had not floated away to the heavens with all the others.

Someone shouted—I think it was Aunt Pat—"Peg! You *have* to go!!"

We all roared.

The undertaker then stepped on the back bumper of his SUV to reach the tree branches, which he shook until that lone balloon finally headed upward. But, believe it or not, this one headed in the exact opposite direction of all the others! It gave us all one final, wonderful—and wonder-filled—laugh.

And with that, an amazing life that began *under* a tree all those years ago ended, remarkably, *in* a tree on that indelible

December day. How classically Peg! In death—just as in life—she continued to march to the beat of her own drum.

After delaying the inevitable for as long as possible, the time had truly come for that final, awful farewell. The grief and despair had suddenly returned, as did the tears.

"Would you like us to take it from here?" the undertaker asked.

"No," my brothers and I replied. "We'll do it ..."

Defying tradition once again, we reverently carried Mom's casket from the tent to her final resting spot on this earth—a rectangular grave that had been prepared just a stone's throw away from her beloved son Merrick's and just rows away from her own mother and sisters. Everyone—all fifty or so of us—remained and watched as the graveyard workers lowered the casket with a winch into the ground.

My heart broke yet again. But for a woman whose biggest fear in life was being alone, my mom was surrounded by family and other loved ones to the bitter end. I am mighty proud of that—and I know she is, too.

"Our Father, who art in heaven, hallowed be thy name ..." someone began. We all joined in. "Thy kingdom come, thy will be done, on Earth as it is in heaven ..."

When the Lord's Prayer ended, my brokenhearted brother Mike bent down and snapped a single rose—Mom's favorite flower—off one of the arrangements that the undertaker had brought to the cemetery. He threw it on top of the casket, now lowered into the concrete encasement in the ground.

"I love you, Mama," her eldest son said.

"Love you, Mom," we all seemed to say as we began walking silently back to our cars, wiping away the tears and clutching whoever was closest. And at that exact moment, like a sign from heaven, the bells from Mom's dear University chapel began tolling twelve noon.

It was so perfect—and so Peg—that in the end, Mom's final

moments on this earth turned out to be just as memorable as her first. In fact, Peg's death, in so many ways, mirrored her life: big, dramatic, complicated, offbeat, chaotic, a bit messy, laced with humor—but ultimately, incredibly well done. Indeed, through her death and helium-filled ascension, Mom's life had literally come full circle.

* * *

Looking at the big picture, there's absolutely no denying that this entire circle of life has been one heck of a journey—of family and faith, heartache and joy, humor and hope, lessons and love—for this incredible but exhausting family of mine. And while there's so much about this grand adventure called life that I'll never even begin to understand, I am absolutely certain of this much: There are nine Ms and a mother like no other who traveled a remarkable journey from messed to blessed. And despite the numerous potholes we've encountered along the road, and the many bumps yet to come, we are eternally grateful just to be along for the ride.

Love …
Love is never gone
As we travel on
Love's what we'll remember …

* * *

Acknowledgements

I am, without a doubt, a blessed man.

I don't really know when I realized just how blessed I truly am. I mean, I didn't just wake up one morning and figure it all out. I know I never really thought I was as a kid, and there have been plenty of times even as an adult when "blessed" would be the last adjective I—or anyone—would have used to describe my life, or that of my family's. But throughout the ten years I spent writing this book (amazingly, a quarter of my life, and indeed its ten most intense years!), and in the years since its completion, I have come to see the countless blessings—both in plain sight and in disguise—that have colored my life and made me the person I am today.

Being blessed, I've learned firsthand, does not mean (unfortunately!) that I'm destined to win the lottery or will escape life's disappointments, heartache, or suffering. It does mean that I know faith, hope, and love in abundance, and have learned the importance of living with an "attitude of gratitude"—that is, the incredible gift of appreciating the good things in my life in real time. The result is a very grateful heart, and knowing that the Spirit of the Lord is always at work in my life, usually in ways I'll never fully understand.

Indeed, the Spirit was at work throughout my journey of writing this book. Those who know me well already know that this entire thing began on a lark. (I never even had an outline for the first five years!) That lark eventually became a promise (shared in these pages), and that promise eventually became a mission— a very personal mission—to honor, celebrate, and remember the people who mean the most to me, and to document an amazing family story that, despite living it, I still sometimes find hard to believe!

And so it is with a very grateful heart that I rightly thank the many people in my life who have inspired, supported, and/ or encouraged me—certainly throughout the writing of this book, but also throughout my life. I'll begin with my mom, Peg. As these pages reveal, she truly was a mother like no other, and showed me what unconditional—and unconventional!—love is all about. Ironically, I never set out to write a story about her life per se, yet she rightly became the person around whom this entire story is built. And proud though she was of her kids and my efforts, she was uncharacteristically apprehensive about her life being captured in print. I can still hear her ask in her sarcastic manner: *"Lord, why do I want the whole world to know what a lousy mother I've been?"*

Mom: I pray I've done you justice and shown the world just how wrong your self-assessment really was. I love you for what you taught me and for what you did for love. And while I miss you so very much, I've learned firsthand that as we travel on, love is indeed what we remember.

There's no doubt that I have been blessed with the most amazing siblings anyone could ever ask for: my extraordinary sisters Michele, Maggie, Mollie, and Maura, and my incredible brothers Mike, Mark, Mitch, and Merrick. Together, we obviously are the nine M's of which this book speaks. I love and thank each of them—and their spouses and kids—from the bottom of my heart. For if it weren't for their collective and steadfast love, support, and enthusiasm for my efforts, this book never would have been written. Indeed, this is not *my* story, but *our* story. So I thank you for allowing me to share our amazing journey from my perspective. I also thank you for the special relationship I am privileged to share with each of you. I am such a better person because of Michele's gentle and loving ways, Mark's enthusiasm for life, Mitch's guidance and wisdom, Maggie's "nothing is impossible" attitude, Mollie's fun and infectious spirit, and Maura's unparalleled support and generosity. She even bought me my first computer in 1995 so I would begin writing this book! It took me 14 years, but I finally made good on the deal!

Of course, the bonds I share with my brothers Merrick and Mike are so deep and profound that they transcend the ordinary. You can't give your bone marrow to anyone—let alone *two* of your brothers (Mike received my marrow in 2003, after the story you've just read ends and another begins!)—and not be forever connected in ways that go beyond words. Merrick, you will forever be my hero and the role model for our entire family; and Mike, you will always hold a special place in my heart for the incredible "bro" and man that you became. I—and so many others—miss and love you both more than words can ever express. But rest assured that "The Torch" definitely keeps on burning...

There are so many others I would love to personally thank here—beloved relatives, dear friends, gifted colleagues, special acquaintances, and even former English teachers!—for the amazing inspiration, influence, and/or support they have given me. Unfortunately, I simply don't have the space to do so, nor do I want to leave anyone out accidentally. But please be assured that I can and do thank each of you in prayer for the blessing you are in my life.

That said, as a first-time author on a very long road to "published author," I would be remiss if I did not acknowledge a few trusted friends and advisers who helped me with the mechanics of this book in ways bigger than they realize, giving generously of their time and talents: Kathy Lindsley, whose editorial expertise and way with the written word I respect greatly—and whose reaction to this story for the first time motivated me tremendously; Steve Boerner, whose Photoshop expertise ensured the inclusion of several old but important snapshots in this book; Kurt Brownell, whose photography and support have been a tremendous gift; and my longtime friend (turned lawyer) MaryAnne McCormick, whose periodic and trusted advice—not to mention initial praise—helped cement my desire to proceed on my own.

Finally, I must thank Teresa H., an incredible literary agent (and fellow Naz grad!) who believed in my story from the moment she first read it and who taught me so much about the crazy world of publishing—including when to take matters into my own hands. I truly value the guidance and wisdom you've shared with me in the past year.

Last, but certainly not least, are my two biggest fans—and hands down the two greatest blessings of my life: my extraordinary wife, Barb, and my equally amazing son, Alex. Not only do they both put up with me day in and day out (no small feat, I assure you!), they listen to my long stories, laugh at my corny jokes, cope with my off-key singing, and—when it comes to this book—never once stopped believing in me. That's why this book is not just *my* accomplishment; it's *our* accomplishment. I thank you both for inspiring me, nourishing me, sustaining me, laughing with me, crying with me, praying with me, dreaming with me, celebrating with me, and loving me just as much as I love you. No book will ever compare to my biggest accomplishment in life: our little family. You both are my life, and I can honestly say that no husband or father has ever been so blessed.

Someone far wiser than I once wrote—and I firmly believe—that all good gifts are sent from Heaven above. So I'll close with my simple but profound thanks and praise to the Good Lord for the many good gifts and abundant blessings he has bestowed upon me and the entire Bednar family. As these pages have revealed, my ordinary family's life story truly has been an extraordinary journey from messed to blessed. How grateful I am to know it, live it, and celebrate it!

Ignite Nine!

Now that you've read my story and understand the meaning of "The Torch" and the significance of the number nine in my life, you'll easily understand why I call my promotional efforts associated with this book "Ignite Nine!"

If you liked what you've read and have been inspired or illuminated in any way by this story or my words (which I hope you have), I ask you to simply "Ignite Nine." That is, please encourage nine (or more) people you know to purchase and read this book—and help me take the light and pass it on. Visit martial-bednar.com for more information.

With a humble and grateful heart, I thank you.

Martial

Breinigsville, PA USA
26 August 2009
223030BV00002B/12/P